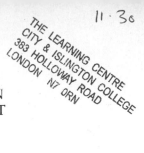
HANSARD SOCIETY SERIES IN POLITICS AND GOVERNMENT

Edited by
F. F. Ridley

HANSARD SOCIETY SERIES IN POLITICS AND GOVERNMENT

Edited by
F. F. Ridley

1. THE QUANGO DEBATE, edited with David Wilson

2. BRITISH GOVERNMENT AND POLITICS SINCE 1945: CHANGES IN PERSPECTIVES, edited with Michael Rush

3. SLEAZE: POLITICS, PRIVATE INTERESTS AND PUBLIC REACTION, edited with Alan Doig

3. WOMEN IN POLITICS, edited with Joni Lovenduski and Pippa Norris

The Hansard Society Series in Politics and Government brings to the wider public the debates and analyses of important issues first discussed in the pages of its journal, *Parliamentary Affairs*

Sleaze:
Politicians, Private Interests
and Public Reaction

Edited by
F. F. Ridley and Alan Doig

OXFORD UNIVERSITY PRESS
in association with
THE HANSARD SOCIETY FOR
PARLIAMENTARY GOVERNMENT

Oxford University Press, Walton Street, Oxford OX2 6DP
Oxford New York
Athens Auckland Bangkok Bombay
Calcutta Cape Town Dar es Salaam Delhi
Florence Hong Kong Istanbul Karachi
Kuala Lumpur Madras Madrid Melbourne
Mexico City Nairobi Paris Singapore
Taipei Tokyo Toronto
and associated companies in
Berlin Ibadan

Oxford is a trade mark of Oxford University Press

Published in the United States
by Oxford University Press Inc., New York

© Oxford University Press, 1995

First published in Parliamentary Affairs, 1995
New as paperback, 1995

A catalogue for this book is available from the British Library

Library of Congress Cataloging in Publication Data
(Data available)

ISBN 0-19-922273-8

Printed in Great Britain
by Headley Brothers Limited, The Invicta Press,
Ashford, Kent and London

CONTENTS

CONTRIBUTORS TO THIS VOLUME

Jørgen G. Christensen is Professor in the Department of Political Science, Aarhus University

Neil Collins is Professor of Public Policy and Management, MacGee College, University of Ulster

Alan Doig is Professor of Public Services Management, Liverpool Business School, Liverpool John Moores University

Patrick Dunleavy is Professor of Government, London School of Economics and Political Science

Christophe Fay is doing research at the Institut d'Etudes Politiques, Université Lumière, Lyon 2

Simon Green is doing research at the Institute of German Studies, University of Birmingham

Paul Heywood is Professor of Politics, University of Nottingham

Christopher Hood is Professor and Head of the Department of Government, London School of Economics and Political Science

Charlie Jeffery is a Senior Research Fellow at the Institute of German Studies, University of Birmingham

Kl. S. Koutsoukis is an Associate Professor and Director of the Hellenic Centre for Political Research, Panteois University, Athens

Roger Mortimore is a political analyst with MORI and editor of the British Public Opinion Newsletter

Dawn Oliver is Professor of Constitutional Law and Dean of the Faculty of Laws, University College, London

Hilary Partridge is a Lecturer in the Department of Government, University of Manchester

Colm O Raghallaigh is an executive with De La Rue Smurfit, Bray, County Wicklow

F. F. Ridley is Emeritus Professor of Politics and Senior Fellow at the Liverpool Institute of Public Administration and Management, University of Liverpool

Trevor Smith is Vice-Chancellor of the University of Ulster at Coleraine and Chairman of the Joseph Rowntree Reform Trust

Stuart Weir is a Senior Research Fellow in the Human Rights Centre, University of Essex and Director of the Democratic Audit of the UK

Robert Williams is Principal of St Aidan's College and Senior Lecturer in the Department of Politics, University of Durham

John Wilson is Chair of the Executive, Liverpool Business School, Liverpool John Moores University

Preface

The focus of the Hansard Society series is on current issues in government and politics. Sleaze is such an issue. Not so long ago one would have worried about using 'sleaze' as a keyword in the title of a serious book published by a university press of the highest repute. Would academic readers connect the word to government and politics? That hurdle passed, would the publisher shrink at too colloquial a title, more suitable for Soho bookshops? None of this is a problem now, which shows how familiar the word has become because the phenomena it describes have become all too familiar.

From conflict of interest to corruption, from the debatably inappropriate to the unquestionably illegal, the behaviour of politicians disturbs the public around the democratic world. Of course, it is only some ministers and elected representatives who are responsible for this state of affairs; and the behaviour of many of those is within standards of behaviour hitherto accepted by the systems in which they operate. Such distinctions are too fine for the public, however, and politicians as a class end unfairly tarred with the same brush.

Opinion polls show levels of distrust of politicans, or lack of respect for them, varying from country to country—but worrying almost everywhere. Though pollsters ask about politicans as a class, compared to other groups in society, popular judgement here is about personal qualities. Unfortunately, it comes at the same time as high levels of dissatisfaction with the ability of politicans to deliver what the public expects of government. To be fair, the public often expects too much and governments are far less able to fix the world than people think, but that does not change public opinion.

The decline in confidence in democratic politics, for whatever reason, is cause for worry. It is in this context that the study of sleaze is important as part of the study of government and politics—however entertaining scandalous stories relating to money or sex may be in their own right as well.

Politicians everywhere are aware of the problems they face as public opinion, fed by the media, becomes ever more critical. Many parliaments are considering what should be done to regulate the private interests of elected representatives and appointed officials. The questions raised often relate to governmental institutions and to law as well as to party politics and electoral behaviour.

This volume draws on a variety of contributors to build up an overview of sleaze and its problems in western democracies. Some of the names will be familiar, especially those writing about Britain. There is also a fine group of country specialists. We are fortunate to have been able to draw on them all, and I am especially grateful to Alan Doig for the role he played in this respect. Professor Doig is, of course, well known for this work on conflict of interest and scandal in politics more generally (*Westminster Babylon* is the title of one of his books).

Producing books on current issues is a challenge. We catch the tide, but the tide is always on the move. New scandals will be revealed, small ones almost weekly now in many countries, large ones rarer but certain to hit the headlines at intervals. And regulating standards of conduct is also on the agenda in many countries, with no obvious cut-off point.

The cases examined here will nevertheless remain the core of country overviews for a considerable time. The public reaction described through opinion poll data is unlikely to change soon either. It would be nice in both respects if this volume dated after a year or two: it could then be read as history of a period. Politics being what it is, that is unlikely, and a current issue sleaze will remain.

Because the media are interested in sleaze, any books has to compete with articles in the quality press. Good articles have appeared. A book can do much more, however, because of its size and wider range. After several chapters on Britain, there are chapters on eight other countries: America, Denmark, France, Germany, Greece, Italy, Ireland and Spain. Of course, the stories are different: the sort of misbehaviour that occurs and the sort of activities that scandalise the public vary with cultures and differ from one political system to another. Nevertheless, the reader will quickly see common trends, echoes in description and discussion, linking one chapter with another. If proposed solutions to common problems sometimes differ, there are lessons in that too.

Authors should not blow their own trumpets, perhaps, but editors, like a conductor, can praise their orchestra. We have a really good book here, useful as an academic study for students of British and comparative politics; and useful as political commentary for others — politicians and citizens alike.

F. F. Ridley

Causes, Concerns and Cures

BY TREVOR SMITH

UNTIL recently, the term 'sleaze', or more often 'sleazy' (which dates back to the seventeenth century) usually referred to disorderly houses, illicit liquor or drugs dens, low dives, questionable night clubs and other disreputable premises. Nowadays, it is invariably applied to the conduct of contemporary politics. That is to say, the adjective 'sleazy' once denoted a certain type of real estate, whereas the noun 'sleaze' is now commonly applied to the estates of the realm. The use of the word 'realm', however, should not be taken to suggest that the transmutation from adjective to noun, from property to politics, is an essentially British phenomenon, for this is clearly not the case. A quick scan of the recent and current behaviour of most western democracies reveals that sleaze is now widespread and endemic.

In Italy, continuing revelations show how close the relations were between the Christian Democrats — until recently the dominant party in all post-war governments — and the organised Mafia. To these exposures have been added criminal charges against senior executives in former Prime Minister Silvio Berlusconi's Finivest commercial empire and related questions about its undue political influence deriving from its near monopoly of the mass media. Criminal behaviour, however, has not been the exclusive preserve of the Right. The former Socialist Prime Minister Bettino Craxi fled into exile to Tunisia to avoid bribery charges, while his close associate and former Foreign Minister, Gianni de Michelis, has been sentenced to a four-year jail term for 'aggravated corruption' in accepting contributions to political funds from business-men lobbying to gain lucrative motorway construction contracts near his home town of Venice. He is under further investigation regarding Socialist Party funds lodged in Hong Kong banks. Even more worrying, however, have been the recent attempts by politicians to clip the wings of what they regard as over-zealous examining magistrates.

In France, numerous political scandals dogged the final years of François Mitterand's fourteen-year presidency. He sought to use the influence of his high office to shield friends and close political associates from adverse publicity and/or prosecution; these included Christian Prouteau, the head of the presidential police, who planted evidence in an attempt to frame three innocent people; the swindler and insider-dealer Roger-Patrice Pelat and Bernard Tapie, populist politician turned bankrupt. Alain Carignon, Communications Minister, was jailed for graft, while Gerard Longuet, Minister for Industry, was forced to resign when cited in financial irregularities. In the Balladur government four other ministers were accused of corruption, while in his last weeks in office Mitterrand appointed his old crony Roland Dumas as President of the Constitutional council for a nine-year term. As in Italy, corruption apparently has not been the monopoly of one wing of the political spectrum. Within two months of Jacques Chirac assuming the presidency, he was succeeded in his previous post as Mayor of Paris by his deputy, Jean Tiberi. During the long-serving Chirac mayoralty, allegations were made that Tiberi was responsible for administering some 1,300 municipally owned prestigious apartments in prime locations that were let out on a 'grace and favour' basis to prominent Gaullists at highly subsidised rents; tenants enjoying such largesse including Alain Juppé, appointed by Chirac to be his premier. Simultaneously, press reports revealed that judicial enquiries had been initiated into charges that Chirac's party, the RPR, had received bribes from companies in return for awarding building contracts to them.

In the Irish Republic a prolonged official enquiry into a beef scandal encompassed leading Fianna Fail politicians but skilfully avoided pin-pointing individual blame. Quickly following its report, however, accusations that the former Attorney-General had procrastinated in processing an extradition request regarding a paedophile priest, plus controversy over the circumstances of his subsequent elevation to high judicial office, led both to his resignation and the downfall of the Reynold's coalition government in late 1994.

The government of Felipe Gonzalez, that has been in power in Spain for the past twelve years, has been rocked by a series of scandals, culminating in the resignation of two ministers for authorising illegal phone taps on leading personalities, including King Juan Carlos. The government was able to retain its majority in the Cortes only because its Catalan partner was prepared to sustain it in office for six months during Spain's presidency of the European Union.

In the United States of America, where pork-barrel politics constitutes an essential and accepted element in government allocations, personal misconduct is much less tolerated. Thus, throughout the Clinton administration the Democratic Party has had to labour under the shadow of a variety of unfortunate incidents. These have included allegations regarding scandals of a financial and sexual kind relating to activities in Arkansas prior to the Clintons moving into the White House. Dan Roterkowski is under investigation for personal nest-feathering while chairman of the Ways and Means Committee of the House of Representatives. Furthermore, it took three presidential nominations before Janet Reno received Senate confirmation as Attorney-General, the previous two candidates having had to withdraw following disclosures that both had illegally employed non-registered immigrant child-minders.

Senior politicians in both Sweden and Belgium have been mentioned in connection with questionable arms-dealing, involving payments to party funds in return for approval for contracts. Sleaze, then, is not just a British disease.

Liberal democratic constitutions are intended to prevent, or at least minimise, corruption, patronage and other such malpractices, while simultaneously encouraging integrity among elected or appointed public officials: both aims have been central elements in the framing of democratic constitutions. The theory, if not always the practice, espoused in classical Greece and ancient Rome, placed the vocation of politics on a very high pedestal. The experience of government in the medieval and early modern ages fell far short of the ideals of antiquity, and it was only with the American and French Revolutions and after that constitutionalism became, once again, both a self-conscious pre-occupation and a civic aspiration. The revolutions of 1848 and the settlements that followed in their wake were, perhaps, the high water-mark of such activity. In the event, of course, no amount of ingenuity could stop political skulduggery breaking out from time to time. In more recent times the nefarious antics of Tammany Hall in New York or the sale of honours by Lloyd George and similar practices in those countries and elsewhere illustrate the ultimate inability of any set of regulations, whether written or otherwise, to prevent gross violations which periodically bring politics into disrepute. Somehow or other, politics usually manage to recover relatively unscathed. In the United States, according to Samuel P. Huntington,[1] periods of growing corruption are remedied every sixty years or so by reformist heart-searching and determined endeavour to put things right by means of appropriate amendments to the Constitution, Supreme Court decisions and popular movements.

In Britain such recourses are less formally available and recovery stems not so much from the fact that the electorate is naturally forgiving as that it has a notoriously short memory, one bonus for political transgressors being that wrongdoing is quickly forgotten. Coupled to this short-term collective memory loss is, perhaps, the rather healthy fact that few entertain very high expectations about those who occupy major public positions, especially elected ones. A further twist to such scepticism is that the public appears to be less disturbed by unsavoury stories about local government than those involving national political figures. It may, of course, be simply a matter of level. Local scandals such as those in the 1970s involving T. Dan Smith and the Poulson affair in the North-East, Liverpool in the 1980s, Westminster City Council in the 1990s and, most recently, the allegations of sectarian bias made against councillors in the Monklands constituency formerly represented by the late Labour leader John Smith, seem to occasion less outrage amongst the public than that registered in the case of national scandals. Nevertheless, a series of national scandals in recent years has led to a growing demand for new and higher standards to be observed in public life. Little comfort comes from the realisation that scandals are as extensive, or as bad, or worse elsewhere in the western world.

This reaction reflects the perception that sleaze in British politics now appears to be more widespread than previously. As a generic term, sleaze covers a variety of identifiably discrete, but by no means mutually exclusive, wrongful acts on the part of public office holders. These may be conveniently classified according to the distinguished judges who have been appointed to investigate them. First, there are the types of behaviour that Lord Nolan and his colleagues are currently examining which cover: conflict of interest between public duty and private interests, the misuse of inside knowledge and the concomitant issue of relations between Westminster and Whitehall on the one hand and outside lobbies on the other; and the exercise of inappropriate patronage, particularly when it borders on or tips over into nepotism or excessive partisanship. Secondly, there are the procedural malpractices of the kind Lord Justice Scott has been investigating with regard to the Matrix Churchill affair, where there have been allegations of interdepartmental communications failures and subsequent ministerial attempts at a 'cover up' by issuing Public Interest Immunity Certificates that prevented the law courts from considering evidence which otherwise would have established the innocence of the three businessmen accused of illegally selling arms to Iraq. Thirdly, there are sexual indiscretions that may well lead to the downfall of a minister, though often only temporarily, but which are occasionally the subject of an official investigation as when Lord Denning was asked to probe the implications of the Profumo affair; it has recently been revealed he was also asked by the Prime Minister, Harold Macmillan, to provide him with a confidential briefing on the sexual proclivities of other cabinet ministers who might be security risks.[2]

The pressures that led the government to appoint the Scott inquiry in November 1992, and fifteen months later the Nolan Committee to review the standards required of public service on a more or less continuing basis, were irresistible and were evidence enough of the need to respond positively to mounting public disquiet. Public opinion was becoming increasingly concerned with standards in public life. The Joseph Rowntree Reform Trust had commissioned MORI to survey popular views in *A State of the Nation* poll in 1991;[3] It repeated the exercise again in 1995; the results are analysed in detail by Patrick Dunleavy and Stuart Weir and comparisons made with the earlier survey. It is sufficient here to emphasise two significant shifts in electors' opinions. First, a sharp decline is recorded in how they view the governing of the country. Whereas in 1991, 23% felt that a great deal of improvement was needed, four years later this had increased to 35%, and correspondingly the proportion saying that the system works well had fallen from a third (33%) to a fifth (22%) over the same period; an earlier MORI poll in 1973 found that almost a half of the electorate (48%) thought that the system of governing the country was working well, so that the satisfaction rating has plummeted over the past 22 years. Secondly, while 59% of respondents agreed that Parliament as an institution performed well in 1991, this figure had also fallen sharply to 43% in 1995, with an even greater movement in the number saying it performs badly, increasing from 16% to 30%.

The polling data starkly reveal the extent to which public disaffection has risen over the past four years and few, if any, commentators would dispute the fact. There is less consensus, however, as to the causes or the significance of growing popular disillusion with politics and the political class, though most would accept that sleaze in all its manifestations has been a major contributing factor.

Contemporary conditions make the art of government immeasurably more difficult than in the past, both in Britain and elsewhere. Globalisation is perhaps the most important single cause, depriving domestic governments of much of their operational sovereignty and independence, for which intergovernmental collaboration, however expedient, is too often reluctantly pursued and in any event is a less than totally effective remedy for controlling the forces unleashed in the new international context. To the problems of controlling the environment and the activities of multinational enterprises are added the sheer scale of information and the near-instantaneous speed of its universal dissemination which renders considered policy reactions very difficult. Across and within national boundaries the nature of the modern mass media, both written but particularly visual, has had a deleterious effect on governing: the mass media have created the mass society in which the distance between the rulers and the ruled has been dramatically foreshortened but at the same time has widened equally dramatically, the gulf between the two. The televising of Parliament's proceedings and remorseless interviewing to the point of personal abusiveness (that has prompted even TV chiefs to utter cautionary warnings[4]) reveal politicians warts and all, thereby eliminating the social distance that previously obtained; while CNN and similar neteworks report the major issues facing politicians as events unfold further compounding their difficulties.

The importunities of the new technologies and the incursions of a new breed of intrusive and investigative journalists or broadcasters has simultaneously led to new kinds of press and public relations experts, spin doctors polishing the soundbite or limiting the damage, in ever more frenetic and competing attempts to gain control of the public agenda. In such circumstances it is little wonder that corners are cut, circuits are shorted and 'reliable' people are slotted into crucial posts: sleaze, in other words, almost inevitably becomes one of the necessary techniques of modern government. It is as though the double-dealing, dissembling and other black arts that once were generally accepted when occasions demanded in the world of international diplomacy, have now been imported into the world of domestic politics, almost without a blush to the cheek.

Indeed, shamelessness may well have contributed to the rash of Denning-type sexual scandals that were to be seen in the Thatcher government but which gathered momentum during the Major administration, involving both Cabinet and junior ministers and, with one exception, led eventually to loss of office. Initially, John Major viewed them as private issues and offered his support, but relentless press coverage and the frequency of revelations forced a change in policy so that resignations were automatically expected at the first whiff of trouble. With the ending of the Cold War such misdemeanours no longer carried implications for national security as had the Vassall and Profumo affairs of the early 1960s. However, they did have two adverse consequences for the government of the day; first, they added a further dimension to the sleaze afflicting the conduct of public affairs, and secondly, after 1993, when the government had sought to project itself as the champion of family values as part of its 'back to basics campaign, ministers were seen to be somewhat compromised, hypocritical and, not least, unfortunate in their timing. The smell of fin de siècle 'decline and fall' suggested that the worst features of Imperial Rome were being imitated.

By the summer of 1995 John Major's position was coming under intense pressure from two sources. First, he had to contend with the perpetual sniping and public disdain emanating from the Eurosceptics within his own party. Secondly, there was the continuing and growing sleaze factor. Nolan had issued its first report; there were leaks from the Scott enquiry's draft conclusions that could have serious implications for a number of Cabinet ministers. The Commons' Select Committee on Privileges censured two Conservative MPs who had accepted payment for asking Parliamentary Questions. Furthermore, two former ministers' conduct also attracted adverse comment: Sir Jerry Wiggin was adminished by the Speaker for putting down amendments to a bill, on behalf of a lobby to which he was a paid consultant, in the name, without permission, of his colleague Sebastian Coe MP while Sir Nicholas Scott was arrested for leaving the scene of an accident in which the car he was driving hit a small child. In the light of these twin pressures the Prime Minister took the bold decision to resign as leader of the Conservative party and submit himself for re-election calling for a vote of confidence. During the brief campaign, John Redwood, his opponent who had quit the Cabinet as Welsh Secretary in order to contest the election, took it upon himself to link his Eurosceptic criticisms of John Major's position with the need to tackle the problem of sleaze, or at least one aspect of it, namely sexual proclivities. He stated that he would personally quiz potential ministerial appointees to any government he might form about their personal lives, on the grounds that 'if a man is prepared to betray his wife, he is equally likely to betray his country'. That the logic is highly questionable and that many otherwise successful statesmen, both British and foreign, would have failed any such vetting are beside the point; what is relevant is that Mr Redwood chose to highlight the need to stamp on sleaze as an important plank in his campaign, though he ignored the more serious manifestations such as patronage and other corrupt practices.

Prior to the Prime Minister's dramatic gesture, the atmosphere was such that some Tory grandees felt obliged to address the difficulties that were besetting the government. Sir Peregrine Worsthorne excused ministers lying to Parliament on the following grounds:

'To give the truth, the whole truth and nothing but the truth has always been difficult, but today it is well nigh impossible, if only because the truth so often amounts to an undignified confession of impotence. And the problem is going to get worse. For while NATO affects only matters of defence, foreign policy and trade embargoes, the European Union affects pretty well everything ... Telling the truth about the reasons for Britain's fishing policy, for example, would almost certainly involve telling Parliament a murky story which any self-respecting minister would rather not tell; and, if told, would cause one hell of a stink ... In short, the myth of parliamentary soverignty would not long survive if ministers always told the truth. So perhaps it is a mercy that even the best of them do not do so.' (*Sunday Telegraph*, 11 June 1995)

Having exonerated ministers in such terms, he went on to castigate the excessive pay and perks awarded to the directors of recently privatised public utilities, which was yet another element of sleaze adding to the problems of a government that had initiated privatisation and many of whose ex-ministers now sat on the boards of such companies. Here Sir Peregrine recognised the problem but could not bring himself to condone the conduct; he is a Tory of the old school who could never quite accept completely the notion of 'red in tooth and claw' capitalism, and who harbours a disdain for those in trade: all he could do was to plead for an 'inspirational style of leadership' where outright greed would be tempered by discretion and prudence, especially at times of large-scale redundancies among the workforce of the former nationalised industries.

In a similar vein, but in reverse order, another eminent Tory journalist made comparisons between the apparent shortcomings of politicians and businessmen. Lord Rees-Mogg examined the fate of three previous corporate pillars of the Establishment, merchant banks experiencing severe difficulties (Morgan Grenfell, Barings and Warburg), and compared them to the troubles besetting his three friends on the Conservative benches (William Waldergrave, Sir Nicholas Scott and Sir Jerry Wiggin). He lauded the erstwhile qualities of the merchant bankers and excused their ultimate failure: 'There was not enough good banking business to go round, so each bank took on what turned out to be unsound business of one sort or another. High costs and uncertain profits undermined banks which had relatively little capital in international terms. Under these pressures even good managers make bad mistakes.' Turning to the three prominent politicians he wrote:

'When I read about some of the earlier Conservative casualties, whom I have never met, I assumed, as I think that most people do, that what had happened to them was the natural consequences of defects in their character. When one finds three of one's friends in trouble at the same time, one rather quickly stops talking about 'sleazy Tory MPs' and starts to examine the environment which has led to their problems, or their vulnerability. Plainly, as with the banks, something systemic and not merely personal has been going wrong . . . Men who feel themselves to be in some sort of trap are capable of behaving rashly, sometimes merely unwisely, sometimes inexcusably. In Parliament there has been a virtually complete takeover of the men, and the women, by the machine. The whips decide whose career has come to an end, and enforce their discipline on parliamentary voting . . . . . . Each generation has seen the whips increase their control of the House of Commons. The Members of Parliament, like the merchant banks, have lost their independence, and along with their independence they lose their self-respect. This is not just a problem for Conservatives; the Labour Party machine is just as formidable. Yet when people lose their sense of independence, tragedies, personal and public, will inevitably follow. (*The Times*, 8 June 1995)

Again, it is not the illogicalities deployed in the argument, nor the strange causes identified, that merit attention, so much as the fact that Lord Rees-Mogg felt impelled to contrive such an excruciating plea in mitigation on behalf of his friends. His motivation is significant evidence of the extent to which sleaze had become a major item on the public agenda.

In the same week as the Worsthorne and Rees-Mogg articles appeared, a leader in *The Spectator* (10 June 1995) took a more robust line in criticising the shortfalls in ministerial behaviour. Referring to leaks from the Scott inquiry, it condemned ministers for hiding behind the excuse that in signing Public Interest Immunity Certificates and in making subsequent but inaccurate statements to the Commons about the Matrix Churchill affair they were merely following the advice of their civil servants. In a touchingly quaint fashion, the editorial called for a reaffirmation of 'the doctrine of ministerial responsibility: civil servants advise, but ministers decide. And when things go wrong, it is the decision makers, not the civil servants, who must shoulder the blame.

The following month Bernard Levin published the most severe onslaught on the government. Writing about what he called 'the overpowering stench of Tory sleaze that is at this moment wafting heavenward', he condemns a catalogue of further ministerial transgressions, including issuing ' *new* (his italics) "gagging orders" which have no purpose other than to cover up more sleaze'. Echoing Lord Acton, he identified the cause as 'the greed for power', a power that is ultimately illusory. (*The Times*, 4th July 1995)

Such journalistic comments all appeared in what was to become the crisis month that culminated in John Major's re-election as leader of the Conservative party. They are of significance for two reasons. Firstly, as has already been remarked, they illustrate how sleaze had come to the fore of the political agenda. Furthermore, as in Italy and France, it was not just confined to governing circles but extended to industry and commerce in a series of scams and failures. These included the Barlow Clowes case, the Lloyds insurance underwriting debacle, the allegations of insider dealing surrounding Lord Archer and Anglia Television, the doubts regarding the sources of Mark Thatcher's fortune and the claims being made against him by former associates, employees and the US Internal Revenue Service, the Barings Bank crash and, most spectacularly, the gigantic Maxwell pensions swindle. There was also the continuing saga of excessive remuneration packages, including share option schemes, being awarded to the directors of privatised companies, especially the water companies and British Gas. To these were added the dramatic volatility in the share prices of both electricity generators and suppliers following leaks regarding new policy intentions on the part of the industry's regular, Professor Littlechild.

Secondly, the articles are significant for the way in which they can be juxtaposed: two are written in sorrow, and two in anger. These, of course, correspond to the age-old conundrum regarding determinism and free will. To what extent, that is to say, are systemic constraints as opposed to blameworthy individuals the cause of the latest sleaze epidemic? There is, therefore, an inherent clash between realism and idealism, and equally any plausible explanation is bound to involve a weighing up of both. It should be emphasised that any answer to the question, however definitive, would not necessarily or easily point to effective remedial action.

The point has already been conceded that globalisation and related factors, together with new societal cleavages based on gender, age, ethnicity and region, have rendered the roles of politicians and the art of governing very much more difficult than was previously the case: the nation-state is now a much more porous entity. Accordingly, general elections lead to a change of government but do not usher in much other change, either for good in the form of better policies in line with the electorate's expectations, or for ill in the form of continuing sleaze: all of this makes for further popular disillusion and disaffection.

Politicians throughout the western world are acutely aware of the alienation that exists between themselves and their constituents. They have endeavoured to respond to and re-engage with the voters in two main ways which, however, have the disadvantage, in practice if not in principle, of being antipathetic to each other. In the first instance, they have tried somewhat atavistically to return to old nostrums by means of conviction politics and fundamentalist renewal. This was the secret of success, in rhetoric rather more than in substance, of Margaret Thatcher and Ronald Reagan which their successors have tried vainly to emulate. The problem with this approach is that contemporary problems do not yield easily to simplistic remedies; and furthermore, as we have noted, the pursuit of a set of corporate puritanical goals on the part of a government means that any transgressions on the part of individual politicians are the more greatly resented. Secondly, such political strategies are prone to degenerate into an anti-intellectual authoritarianism which is inimical to pluralist democracy and alternative programmes are thereby almost outlawed. At the height of Thatcherism what, it might be wondered, would the Iron Lady and her acolytes have offered by way of a theory of loyal opposition had the idea ever occurred to them? Indeed, they explicitly articulated the policy of TINA ('there is no alternative'). When, inevitably, there is policy failure, civil war breaks out within the ruling party, with accusations of treachery and loss of faith in the fundamentalist paradigm; while beyond party there is a growing lack of toleration generally and a deepening cynicism about politics. Conviction politics is played in too high and heady an octave to be sustainable.

Secondly, as the gap between society and government widens, so politicians are driven by way of compensation to narrow the gap between themselves and the state. In far too narrow and specific a way, this is what William Rees-Mogg was hinting at when he accused the party machine and the whips of seizing too much power. The broader case was put much better by a Dutch political scientist when he said: 'it's still possible for the political class to realise that they have turned their back on civil society and they could do something at least to re-establish their ties with civil society and break the financial links and the patronage links with the state.'[5] He succeeds in placing the problem of sleaze in a wider and more appropriate context: it is a consequence of the fact that as politicians have found themselves increasingly cut adrift from civil society, so they have clung with an ever tighter grip on to the institutions of the state by means of patronage and highly questionable financial or commercial linkages. All of this has made them more open to accusations that they are failing by the stringent yardsticks they have set for others, and presumably themselves, in the tenets espoused in their fundamentalist, 'back to basics' ideology, and contractarian techniques, of which the Citizen's Charter and Contract with America are variants.

Nor should too much be expected of ad hoc codes of practice tailored to deal with specific scandals. The Nolan Committee's first set of recommendations regarding standards of parliamentary behaviour fell short of what the public wants, as the Joseph Rowntree Reform Trust/

MORI survey shows; voters want MPs to be subject to the full rigour of the law. Nolan's recommendations, in any case, are already in danger of being diluted and their implementation delayed in the course of committee deliberations in Parliament. Furthermore, in an attempt to lessen the fall-out from his final report, a pre-emptive campaign is well under way to undermine the findings of Lord Justice Scott and any recommendations he may make by bad-mouthing him as being politically naïve and procedurally flawed. Nobbling judicial investigators, by one means or another, it seems is not confined to Italian politicians.

The reality is that sleaze is symptomatic of a wider malaise which makes it highly unlikely that, left to its own devices, Parliament is capable of acting effectively. In other words, the political class will not by itself seek successfully to re-establish itself with civil society and thus the onus will be placed on civil society to facilitate a restoration of the linkages between the two. For that to happen, further outbreaks of hooliganism in high places — so much more corrosive of the body politic than the hooliganism of the mob — will have to erupt before effective remedial action is initiated.[6] One-off sets of protocols will not stop the rot. The problem is less that of individual misconduct so much as systemic crisis which is ultimately unacceptable. A purposive constitutionalism — in the 1995 survey, 79% of the electorate favoured a written constitution — that comprehensively and coherently reviews our formal institutional arrangements and procedures, with proposals for a new and codified settlement, would engender a civic ethos which, internalised by those in public office, would be a better antidote to sleaze than any amount of Nolan-type tinkering or attempts at a relaunch of conviction politics.

1   S. P. Huntington, *The Promise of Disharmony*, 1981.
2   cf R. Lamb, *The Macmillan Years 1957–1963: The Emerging Truth*, 1995.
3   Results reported in T. Smith, 'Citizenship and the Constitution', *Parliamentary Affairs*, October 1991.
4   cf John Birt, *For Good or Ill? The Role of the Modern Media*, Independent Newspapers Third Annual Lecture, Dublin, 1995.
5   Rudy Andeweg, *Analysis*, BBC Radio 4, 9 June 1994.
6   cf T. Smith, *British Politics in the Post-Keynesian Era*, 1985, for an early reference to emerging sleaze.

Untangling the Threads

BY ALAN DOIG AND JOHN WILSON

IN its introduction, the Nolan Committee Report[1] talked of the common threads—codes of conduct, independent scrutiny, and guidance and education—that would be necessary to underpin those principles it felt essential for ensuring standards in public life: selflessness, integrity, objectivity, accountability, openness, honesty and leadership. Any proposals for change, however, should be informed by the circumstances that led to the establishment of the Committee. The shorthand for these has been 'sleaze'—but what is sleaze? Is sleaze the consequence, as the Committee mentioned, of increased media interest in sexual misconduct, or of moral vagueness among politicians, or of the consequences of public sector change? Why should there be, as it claimed, 'no real precedent in this century for so many allegations of wrongdoing, on so many different subjects, in so short a period of time?' Is it true that the examples of sleaze are not, as it noted in a very thin survey of the background to its work, 'in the same league' as some past cases but do they, when taken together, 'create a pervasive atmosphere . . ., in which sexual, financial and governmental misconduct were indifferently linked'?

The Nolan Committee argued that there was a public anxiety, reflected in nearly 2000 letters and various opinion surveys, to be allayed quickly if it was not to give way to 'disillusion and growing cynicism'. The concern was based, however, on 'perceptions and beliefs . . . not supported by the facts'. Such a distinction is crucial. Is it true, as Lord Nolan said in his letter to the Prime Minister, that 'changes which have occurred over the years in the roles and working environment of politicians and other public servants have led to confusion over what is and what is not acceptable behaviour' or is it true that it is the 'widespread suspicion that much more occurs than is revealed to the public gaze'? Is the problem of the image of politicians and public officials, involving perceptions rather than proof of wrongdoing, or are there fundamental changes in the attitudes and conduct of those in public life? If the former, the answer may be to tighten up existing rules; if the latter then the Nolan Committee may be sitting in judgement on some of the consequences of sixteen years of Conservative government.

To answer such questions, the Committee could therefore have usefully spent much more time than it did on untangling the threads of sleaze. These can be grouped into six general areas: disillusionment and elective dictatorship—how far the public feels dissatisfied with the political and public sector changes since 1979; the semi-detached state, private gain and public loss—how far has the sense of public service been eroded and the public feels that others, rather than they, have benefited from the changes; a failure of regulation and Members' financial interests—are MPs exploiting their parliamentary position in furtherance of their financial interests; the tradition of the upright politician—the extent to which the public see the traditional expectations of politicians being replaced by self-gratification and self-interest; public concern or media power—how far the media focus on sleaze has been self-generated or is it more a reflection of wider public concern about the conduct of those in public life; reviving public confidence or re-inventing the wheel—is public concern new but is the political response invariably to placate that concern rather than seek to introduce effective reforms; finally, does tying the threads lead to the conclusion that the Nolan Committee is currently attending to the consequences rather than the causes of sleaze?

Disillusionment and elective dictatorship

Social commentators have increasingly reported the economic and social disparities that have opened up as a consequence of the Thatcher governments' approach to the economy—the promotion of entrepreneurial activity, the removal of controls from commercial, economic and financial sectors, and the encouragement of financial gain as a reward for and an indicator of worth, status and hard work—between those who have benefited and those who have not. The latter group is no longer limited to the growing untrained and long-term unemployed underclass which has suffered from the decline in public housing and the collapse of industrial jobs; it also includes those bearing the brunt of the apparent failure of government to deliver the rewards for political support, from the promises of green shoots of economic recovery and the emergence of the classless society, to the more immediate effects of the shedding of white collar jobs, of negative equity or static prices in the owner-occupier housing market, and a feeling of rising lawlessness.

While many commentators gave due credit to Mrs Thatcher's enthusiasm for economic realism, self-discipline and the promotion of the enterprise culture, their concern has been over the impact of self-centred materialism, the juxtaposition of private wealth and public squalor and, reflecting her proclamation that 'there is no such thing as society', the decline of its key elements: 'the preservation of such qualities as tolerance, mutual respect, the championing of reason over right, the concern for the less fortunate and the observance of the law that have made Britain a country worth living in'.[2]

At the same time, the Thatcherite approach to government has been predicated on depoliticising politics, where the ritual of elections and the theatre of politics, combined with the privatisation, deregulation and the promotion of consumer choice, has produced a society which has confined 'politics to a television spectacle and made the nation into an audience ... Thatcherism has promoted freedom as the right not to be bothered with public affairs ... Politics is not where you invest your hopes. Life is elsewhere. Politics is a nuisance. The less of it, the better'.[3] While political participation for the majority of the population may be no more than the occasional vote at elections, the overt assertion of conviction politics has rested uneasily with the traditional willingness to leave decision-making to the discretion of the government of the day so long as it generally accords with public expectations and avoids the appearance of acting like an elected dictatorship. The enthusiasm for radical reform, however, took the Thatcher governments into areas where some commentators felt unease about the use of the political system not just as a vehicle of continuing and comprehensive change, but also a means to overcome objections to that change, particularly where the concentration of power in the hands of the government has allowed it to exercise increasing control over the distribution, allocation and expenditure of public funds as well as over who should be involved in that process.

Persuading the public, however, that there is little left within the responsibility of government that should now concern them after the privatisation of public utilities, the devolved responsibility for the health and education services, as well as the restraints put on the expenditure of local government, and that they would do better, with the advent of choice, Citizens Charters and performance indicators, to concentrate on their rights as consumers rather than as voters, has raised the question of the democratic deficit: who determines the range and levels of public services, how the public interest is represented in that provision, who is accountable for the quality and availability, and who would benefit from that provision? This concern is underlined by issues over the political bias of those appointed by ministers to manage public services, whether in NHS Trusts or Non-Departmental Public Bodies (colloquially termed 'quangos'), over the financial rewards available to those who have taken what were once seen as publicly-owned utilities into the private sector, and over the uncertainty as to where the public interest is represented at governmental, parliamentary and agency levels. The public and media reactions to the increasing use of quangos and the rise in ministerial patronage, the pay awards and other perks of directors of the privatised utilities, the movement of former ministers to privatised companies or those companies now involved in the delivery of public services, as well as the substantial number of Conservative MPs paid by financial interests which have benefited substantially from government policies, may be seen as the actions of 'an unaccountable and self-perpetuating oligarchy. The result in the nineties of the neo-liberal economic policy of the eighties has been a regime of private poverty and public sleaze. This is the real import of the current debate about sleaze — that it taps a profound public suspicion that, over the past fifteen years, the institutions of the British state have been so deformed that no clear or reliable distinction can any longer be made between those that are meant to be politically impartial servants of the public interest and those which serve the interests of the Conservative Party and members of the Conservative government'. (*Guardian*, 7 November 1994) To the public, therefore, the benefits of change seem to be steered toward a handful of individuals or interests rather than society as a whole: '. . . what is happening in British life is both a sharp decline in standards of general behaviour among those in power and . . . a breakdown in the traditional rules that kept such behaviour within acceptable limits. Lady Thatcher has much to answer for in her glorification of personal gain and her persistent denigration of public service. So has a general culture driven by consumerism, aided and abetted by deregulation, which has greatly increased the opportunity for individuals to enrich themselves improperly as well as properly.' (*Observer*, 30 October 1994)

The semi-detached state, private gain and public loss?

Unease that the weaknesses of the political system are being exploited for political advantage by successive Conservative governments has been particularly noticeable in relation to the treatment of public services. The short reference in the 1979 Conservative manifesto that the reduction of waste, bureaucracy and over-government would yield substantial savings has been elevated to a blueprint for reform while, unlike the 1968 Fulton Report which proposed reform within a public service framework, the Thatcher and Major governments were concerned primarily with the process of change within an unbending belief that private sector values, procedures and practices provided the best framework for the delivery of public services either by the private or public sectors.

The means to drive down costs and introduce managerialism into the public sector, from the Rayner scrutinies to the Financial Management Initiative, were perceived as ineffective and slow. After the 1987 general election, a range of legislative and organisational reforms, including market-testing, internal markets, Next Steps Agencies, compulsory competitive tendering, devolved budgetary and management responsibility, were introduced to create the context for comprehensive change in public services. On the other hand, the cultural and organisational shift from administration to managerialism, from policy to delivery and from process to output increasingly required officials, often without much training, to take on new roles and to be judged by new criteria, within fragmented structures and with the increasing involvement of the private sector. Not only has there been uncertainty and confusion over the purpose and end result of the process of change—'it is not unusual, I guess', said Sir Robin Butler, Head of the Civil Service, 'for an organisation in the process of evolution not to know what its final state will be'[4] — but that process may have led to a 'misunderstanding among public servants about the quasi-private sector environment . . . (and) . . . inaccurate perceptions of private sector values and practices'.[5] In the eyes of the public the conflict of interest between personal benefit and public service, as well as the inadequacy of the means of accountability and oversight, must thus also be seen within the wider context of concern over the range, level and quality of the services now being delivered. The promises of Citizens Charters and consumer choice are often perceived as secondary to the development of a much reduced and managerial public sector where the ability to pay and the intentions of the deliverers will radically alter the provision of public services: 'the voters are now facing up to the downside of the politics of self-gratification that they bought so eagerly in the eighties. And they don't like it with its manifold insecurities and privations, its destruction of public service, its determination to know the price of everything and the value of nothing . . .' (*Observer*, 7 May 1995)

In addition to the sometimes conflicting objectives of speed of delivery, cost-cutting and performance by results against those of availability, due process, procedure and precedent there have been a number of well-publicised cases where the effects of dysfunctional change were noted. These have included: worries over job security, the potential conflict of interest over privatisation and public position, poor management control, misinterpretation of performance rewards, over-ambitious projects, mismanagement or misappropriation of public funds, and the failure to enforce or police regulations and procedures. It is hardly surprising that such a background should affect existing standards in public life. In December 1993 the Audit Commission's survey of fraud and corruption in local government warned that maintaining probity had been 'rendered more demanding and complex by recent changes to the nature and operation of local government services. Many of these changes, such as the delegation of financial and management responsibilities, while contributing to improved quality of service, have increased the risks of fraud and corruption occurring'.[6] In January 1994 the Committee of Public Accounts was even clearer: 'there have recently been fundamental changes in the way in which government departments and public bodies . . . carry out their work . . . In recent years we have seen and reported on a number of serious failures in administrative and financial systems and controls within departments and other public bodies . . . these failings represent a departure from the standards of public conduct which have mainly been established during the past 140 years'.[7]

A failure of regulation and Members' financial interests

The one group which has seemed synonymous with personal gain from sixteen years of change in public life have been Members of Parliament. Parliament has never come to terms with whether being an MP is or is not a full-time occupation, while retaining the tradition that allows MPs the independence and freedom to order their lives as they think fit. Despite the view of some, for example Richard Crossman, who believed that MPs were powerless ciphers, MPs do have privileged access to confidential information, to draft legislation and to the wider decision-making processes. The value of that access has increased substantially since 1979 to interest groups and lobbyists with a legislative programme driven by reforming Conservative governments rather than emerging from lengthy Whitehall-led consultative processes.

Lobbying has now become a highly organised industry which has gone beyond wining, dining and briefing sympathetic MPs. The impact of the government's legislative programme on company fortunes and the number of MPs involved in lobbying and consultancies has reached the point when even Parliament's ineffectual regulator, the Select Committee on Members Interests, admits that 'the business of the House and the duties of Member of Parliament are so all-embracing in their scope that inevitably there are occasions when a Member's private pecuniary interests are pulling in a different direction from the policy of his party, or his wider responsibilities as an elected legislator.'[8]

Concern over lack of transparency and potential for conflict of interests in relations between MPs and outside financial interests is not new; they were the subject of two parliamentary inquiries in 1969 and 1974. The first Select Committee on Members Interests inquiry sought to disentangle advocacy—MPs promoting specific issues solely for payment—from interest-representation where an MP may be paid but would be speaking from the basis of prior involvement or knowledge. It proposed banning the former, and regulating the latter through a code of conduct and a more comprehensive declaration. It looked to the Committee of Privileges to take on the responsibility for policing what it thought would be the very occasional lapse because it assumed that MPs' innate sense of honour rather than a register of financial interests and a supervisory committee would be the most effective safeguard against abuse.

Within five years Parliament, driven by the need to counteract public concern over the involvement of MPs in the Poulson affair, was ill-temperedly panicked into acting. It avoided the distinction between advocacy and interest-representation by trying to regulate both by implementing the code, the declaration, the register, together with a Select Committee on Members Interests to oversee the completion and publication of the register. Caught by the limitations of its primary role of overseeing the register, as well as the continuing belief that MPs were entitled to privacy in terms of disclosing the purpose or details of their financial interests, and that the responsibility for deciding the relevance of a financial interest, in terms of disclosure and registration, rested on the judgement of the individual MP, the committee has failed to stamp its authority on the Commons.

It has been unable, in a number of recent reports, to impress upon MPs the importance of avoiding, and being seen to avoid, any conflict between their financial interests and their parliamentary duties. It has failed to clarify the rules on the dislosure of the financial interests by MPs and Ministers and been highly reluctant to take a proactive role in dealing with media allegations that Members are selling access or failing to declare their interests. The Committee itself has recently admitted that neither the register nor the requirements of dislosure deters those MPs who wish to disregard them. Both it and Parliament have continued to place excessive faith in compliance with both the spirit as well as the letter of the rules on the judgement of MPs, as well as on a collective consensus on acceptable behaviour within the House, when both have become increasingly elastic in the past decade. Research in the early 1980s suggested that a substantial number of MPs were aware of the problems caused by a conflict of interest but the 'aura of collegiality that envelopes the House' protected it from further reform and ensured toleration of colleagues' activities until they were likely to bring the House as an institution into public disrepute. More recent research suggests that is in part what has happened; the failure of the House to respond to concern about the behaviour of some MPs and the lack of clearly defined standards of conduct has led 'to a progressive legitimization of behaviour that is more and more removed from the original boundaries of probity ... (where) once exceptional and questionable practices ... become routine and unremarkable'.[9]

While MPs may consider that any behaviour that does not offend against the existing rules is acceptable and that, in any case, their private financial interests are of no concern to the public so long as they do not conflict with their parliamentary duties, the public may think otherwise. Thus on the one hand a poll reported in the *Independent* in May 1995 showed that 57% of all MPs believed that 'an individual's private behaviour does not affect their fitness for public office' while, on the other, a poll in *The Sunday Times* two months earlier had the public put MPs at the top of their list of those who did not uphold high standards (journalists were next in the list) which, despite politicians's protestations to the contrary, would suggest that the public views an MP's private behaviour as affecting their fitness for office, a perception that very much reflects a tradition that all aspects of a politician's life is seen, publicly at least, to be above reproach.

The tradition of the upright politician

The tradition of high standards of personal morality and probity has been evident since the mid-nineteenth century as the steady expansion of the electorate exposed those in public life to the more rigid codes of respectability and responsibility of the middle and lower-middle classes.[10] While David Mellor could claim that an adulterous affair 'was not a reason in this day and age for a Cabinet minister to resign', the tradition has been periodically reinforced by the departure from office of those whose conduct has been adjudged—by official inquiry, adverse media comment, court appearance, or at the suggestion of the Whips—to be unacceptable, or, more importantly, politically indefensible by ones colleagues in the face of public or media criticism. It thus still has a resonance in public life which, given the unpredictability of public reaction, is an area of moral high ground that no political party would willingly concede to their opponents.

If, however, a party seeks to make a political virtue of that tradition, and the values that it implies, then they must be prepared, individually and collectively, for the consequences if the apparently private conduct of its MPs is held up to judgement against the party's public stance. This was particularly evident following the controversial attempt by the Conservative Government at the 1993 Conservative Party Conference in Blackpool to regain electoral support by announcing a campaign to get the country 'Back to Basics'. The underlying theme was that fundamental Conservative values—ranging from free trade to respect for law and order, from sound money policies to the sanctity of the family, from self-discipline to respect for the church and the monarchy—were at one with the core values of the nation. Inevitably it was also, despite later Conservative protests to the contrary, seen as a moral campaign, particularly when assessed in the context of other speeches which were made around that time by Cabinet ministers on, for example, single parents or social responsibilities.

The campaign proved disastrous for the Conservatives in general and the Prime Minister in particular. Almost immediately there unfolded a series of events which reinforced the initial scepticism of many that the Conservatives were singularly badly positioned to launch such a campaign, exposing the Government to allegations of political expediency, double standards and the apparent failure to live by the values that the government was calling for, from others. Following the highly publicised resignations of David Mellor in September 1992 and of Michael Mates, Northern Ireland Minister, in June 1993 after revelations concerning the fugitive businessman Asil Nadir, there were in the twelve months following the Back to Basics speech, a number of well-publicised allegations and incidents involving Tory figures, including the bizarre death of Stephen Milligan, the PPS to Defence Minister Jonathan Aitken in February 1994, Allan Clarke's tangled relations with the wife and daughters of a South African judge in May 1994, the allegations involving share dealing and Lord Archer in July 1994 and the dispute in October 1994 over who paid the Paris hotel bill of Joanathan Aitken, then Chief Secretary to the Treasury. More significant for the government, however, were the number of resignations from government posts during the same period, including: Tim Yeo, Countryside Minister, who resigned in January 1994 after disclosures about an extra-marital affair; Lord Caithness, Transport Minister, who resigned in the same month after the suicide of his wife and whose resignation was followed by newspaper speculation about his private life; David Ashby, a PPS, who also resigned in January 1994 after admitting sharing a bed with a male friend to save costs during a holiday in France; Hartley Booth, who resigned March 1994 after newspaper disclosures of his friendship with a female Commons researcher; and Michael Brown, Party Whip, resigned May 1994 after allegations of a homosexual relationship with a student. At the same time there were also ministerial departures in relation to money: Alan Duncan, another PPS, resigned January 1994 after it emerged he had lent money to a neighbour to buy a house from Westminster City Council at a discount and that Mr Duncan had then bought the house from him. Graham Riddick and David Tredinnick were suspended as PPSs in July 1994 pending an inquiry into *The Sunday Times'* allegations that they were prepared to accept cash to table parliamentary questions. Neil Hamilton and Tim Smith, respectively Corporate Affairs and Northern Ireland Ministers left office after it was alleged in October 1994 that they received financial and other benefits as backbenchers in connection with Mohamed Al-Fayed, the owner of Harrods. The continuing revelations, particularly allegations involving payments to politicians, led in October 1994 to the Prime Minister's decision to establish the Nolan Committee.

Public concern or media power?

The decision to set up the Committee raises the issue of whether there was genuine and growing public concern or whether the government was stampeded into reaction to a vociferous and unrelenting media campaign. Nolan itself was aware of the 'growth in media activity' and 'periods when instances of real or alleged malpractice seem to be reported in the newspaper every few weeks' while MPs' views on other professions revealed in a poll in the *Independent* in May 1995 that 77% of them listed journalism as the profession with the lowest honesty and ethical standards, lower than foreign exchange dealers, advertising executives, lobbyists and building contractors. Shortly before the Nolan Committee, Jonathan Aitken, subject of continuing media interest in his financial interests, publicly talked of using the 'sword of truth' to deal with the cancer of twisted and bent journalism when he announced his intention to sue his accusers (he subsequently resigned to pursue this course of action).

The self-proclaimed role of watchdog journalism has long attracted the hostility of politicians. Harold Macmillan complained of Parliament and the public being 'continually stimulated into a sense almost of hysteria' during the Vassall affair, Lord Denning blamed the atmosphere of the Profumo affair on press 'trafficking in scandal for reward' rather than 'a decline in the integrity of public life' while the late Harold Wilson bitterly accused 'cohorts of distinguished journalists' of combing the country for information with which to damage the Labour Party.

Nevertheless the growth of the media's investigative capability has been significant in uncovering misconduct by politicians and public officials; an addendum in the 1976 Royal Commission on Standards of Conduct in Public Life stated that 'almost all the investigations that have led to prosecution have been sparked off either by "*Private Eye*" or by commercial television or by other branches of the media or by other unofficial bodies or individuals. They have not been initiated from any official source . . .' Nearly twenty years later Labour MP Tony Wright was to suggest that, during the current controversy over sleaze, 'not one resignation has been forced by information uncovered by MPs. The Commons has become a mere echo chamber for noises off'.

The growth of investigative journalism during the 1960s and 1970s, however, did not substantially increase sales or profits. As inflation began to spiral so did costs and wages, largely driven by a number of print unions whose organisational strength and control over the various stages of production led to competitive wage demands and disruption of publication that was a source of bitter but privately expressed concern among managers and editors as well as a reason for existing owners to be prepared to sell. The arrival of a Conservative Government committed to curbing union power and deregulating media ownership coincided with the purchase of a number of newspapers by commercially-minded owners who saw the profits that could accrue from properly managed production that also took full advantage of new technology. Strong editorial support for the government, allied with aggressive competition between rival newspapers, ushered in an era of competitions and sensationalism colloquially termed 'bonk journalism'. The popular press has enthusiastically pursued the private indiscretions of figures in the public eye intended, from the editors' view, to find a story 'more dramatic than the last' but seen by others as the arrival of a new 'dark age' with 'sewer-oriented journals' competing 'to entertain their readers with titillating stories . . . told with a reckless regard for the need to check the truth or accuracy . . .' The voracious pursuit of such stories, as well as the techniques and the payment used to obtain them, did prompt the government to set up the Calcutt inquiry to consider means to impose a degree of restraint and responsibility on the press. Its recommendation for improved self-regulation was accepted by the government as the final opportunity before the imposition of any statutory policing, described by the government minister with responsibility for the press, David Mellor, as 'drinking in the last chance saloon'.

Mellor's subsequent departure from office, in part because of an affair with an actress revealed by the *People* and in part because of a libel case brought by the daughter of a leading PLO figure against the *People* over a story alleging Mellor accepted free flights and a holiday from her, however, had the unexpected consequence of revealing the double-edged value of an unregulated press. The editor of the *Sun* alleged that the Government itself was prepared to feed information to damage the reputation of political opponents. His stance was sustained by support from other newspapers. *The Sunday Times* (26 July 1992) argued that it was less a question of standards than the existence of double standards where politicians publicly pontificated about the behaviour of others while their 'private peccadilloes are left unreported', and the 'rank hypocrisy' of politicians who maintained their lives were their own while not being 'above dishing the dirt on a fellow politician if it suits their own political or personal purposes'. The publication of stories about politicians' private lives was 'a legitimate matter to bring into the public domain, especially in an age when politicians are eager to promote their "happy family" image to curry favour with voters'.

Such sentiments, following the departure of Mrs Thatcher and, subsequently, some of her more abrasive colleagues, from office meant that the Back to Basics campaign was tailor-made for unfettered market-place journalism's predeliction for sex-and-politics stories at the same time as the relationship between the government and the popular press was no longer so mutually beneficial. Similarly, the departure of those responsible for the relentless pressures exerted on television saw the somewhat muted levels of investigative journalism begin to revive during the early 1990s, helped by the revelations over the Supergun, Matrix Churchill and Pergau dam affairs as well as those concerning MPs' financial interests, the highly publicised District Audit inquiry into the affairs of Westminster City Council (the Conservative local government 'flagship') and the numerous reports from the National Audit Office and the Committee of Public Accounts about public sector waste and mismanagement.

Such stories are not media inventions, nor are they coming from or reported by a single source. At the same time, given their acute antennae concerning what concerns their readers, the popular press is, as a July 1995 poll noted in *The Sunday Times*, very much aware that the public does not, as much as the government says otherwise, think that better times have arrived for them. Much of their 'feel-bad' factor is therefore directed at those for whom better times have arrived — and invariably they have been party to or part of the changes wrought by Conservative governments in the past sixteen years. There is very much a cumulative sense among the public of a collective flouting of expected or acceptable standards by public figures as they indulged in bed-hopping, self-enrichment, influence-peddling and rule-bending while those in power exploit their public position for themselves and their friends in a way that the public found both hypocritical and unacceptable. That sense of self-interest and double standards — for which 'sleaze' has become the catch-all phrase — has also become all-embracing in terms of its belief not only that standards were declining but that politics and political activity were about personal benefit instead of public interest, encompassing well-paid chairs of privatised utilities as well as MPs who took cash for questions, partisan quango appointments and peerages for party funding, unaccountable decisionmaking as well as unregulated one-way traffic to well-paid seats in City boardrooms.

Reviving public confidence or re-inventing the wheel?

To the public, therefore, sleaze is not about 'moral vagueness' and 'grey areas'. These are invariably phrases advanced by those whose conduct has been called into question by the public or the media. When challenged they claim that there were no rules and no guidance to warn them that they might be straying into areas where their motives and conduct may be questioned. Sleaze is more about a belief among the public that those in public life are pursuing personal gratification, advancement or enrichment against a background of an official facade of respectability, rectitude and probity and, usually, economic, social and other circumstances that deny similar possibilities, opportunities or incentives to the rest of society.

On the other hand, such concerns are not new, and neither is the use of an official inquiry to respond to them. The Lynskey Tribunal, seen as 'a reaffirmation of integrity of the British Civil Service and of the political morality of the members of Parliament',[12] was the first major sleaze inquiry this century.[13] It was established when Labour Prime Minister Clement Atlee had to contend with increasing public suspicion of standards in public life against a background of post-war petty restrictions and regulations, shortages and straitened economic circumstances, blackmarketeering and fiddling which permeated all levels of society. After the departure of Garry Allighan, a Labour MP whose news agency sold confidential stories on politics, and Hugh Dalton, the Chancellor of the Exchequer, whose sin was the inadvertent leaking of budget information, persistent rumours of an influence-peddler asking for money to pay bribes to a junior Labour minister to circumvent trade restrictions prompted Atlee to set up a public inquiry through a quasi-judicial Tribunal: 'the investigation captured a mood of restless frustration after three post-war years of rationing, unobtainable luxuries, buraucracy everywhere, and no end in sight. Controls and shortages were justified by the Government on grounds of fairness. The suggestion that rules were being bent to ease the lives of politicians and officials who were responsible for enforcing them stirred the embers of popular resentment.'[14] Though at the outset the government may have been privately concerned to balance the level of ministerial involvement in the inquiry while trying not to 'unduly magnify the importance of the allegations', the aggressiveness of the hearings in eliciting the details behind the allegations, the findings of the Tribunal, the prompt resignation of the minister most deeply implicated in the allegations, and the unanimity of all parties to support the whole process did much to end the rumours and innuendoes.

The second major 'sleaze' case concerned Conservative Minister John Profumo whose persistent refusal to admit to rumours of a short-lived relationship with Christine Keeler came at a time of problems with the economy and major changes in society's values and attitudes. A number of Conservative figures had been the subject of allegations concerning their private conduct while the government had had a confrontation with the press over what turned out to be unfounded allegations about the relations between a senior minister and a homosexual civil servant working as a spy for the Russians. This background gave the Profumo affair its context and elevated a minor sexual escapade (which also involved a Russian official and provided the tenuous security angle that both the press and the Labour Opposition used to keep the story alive) into a major issue of ministerial deceit and, more generally, a sense of sleaze. There were persistent and widespread rumours of sexual immorality among those in public life, prompting those concerned about the apparent decline of standards in public life and of the example set by those in public office to complain, as did the Bishop of Southwark, of the smell of corruption in high places and 'a repudiation of the simple decencies and the basic values' or to call, as did Selwyn Lloyd, the former Chancellor of the Exchequer, for 'courageous and confident leadership, not based on expediency but upon obedience to high moral standards and irreproachable behaviour'. The belated admission of the affair by Profumo, immediately followed by his resignation, appeared to burst the dam of speculation that was then dissipated by the trial and suicide of one of the principal figures in the affair, by the publication of the Denning report which swept aside allegations of widespread political misconduct and coverup (the subsequent resignation of another Conservative MP following attempted sexual blackmail by the Russian was a muted affair) and, some months later, by the election of a Labour Government.

The last period of sleaze in politics occurred during the 1970s and was responsible for a number of inquiries into standards of conduct in public life. In 1974, twenty years before the Nolan Committee was set up, another Prime Minister's committee chaired by another peer (Ted Heath and Lord Redcliffe-Maud) was reporting on local government rules of conduct. Within months of its assertion that, 'despite widespread current disquiet', local government was 'essentially honest' another Prime Minister (Harold Wilson) chose yet another peer (Lord Salmon) to chair a Royal Commission on standards of conduct in public life which also argued that public life was generally honest, even if a 'significant minority' did not measure up to acceptable standards, but warned that 'our evidence convinces us that the safeguards against malpractice in the public sector are in need of review'.

Although both inquiries were primarily prompted by the bibery-and-contracts network run by the architect John Poulson, the suspicion of enrichment by politicians, at local and national levels, and the blurring of public duties and private interests built up over a long period. Beginning with concern over politicians' involvement with lobbyists which was largely responsible for the first Commons inquiry into MPs financial interests in 1960, it continued through the revelations of Poulson's relations with MPs which triggered off hasty reforms in 1974 primarily intended, as Tory MP Jim Prior said of himself and his colleagues, to show 'we are not crooks and we want it to be seen that we are not crooks'. It ended in the latter half of the decade with the activities of Harold Wilson's office staff in land reclamation (or speculation) deals, the trials of senior politicians such as John Stonehouse and Jeremy Thorpe, the row over Harold Wilson's Resignation Honours list, the continued concern over MP-consultants, extensive cases of fraud and corruption across the public sector and, following a strong press campaign in the face of government attempts to avoid it, a select committee inquiry into the three MPs alleged to have received payments from John Poulson.

In terms of the capacity to deal with specific areas of misconduct and the wider sense of public disquiet, the Lynskey Tribunal may have dealt decisively with specific allegations but it also left a residue of suspicion about politicians' motives in the mind of the public: 'for every reader who pondered on the true significance — and triviality — of the affair, there must have been ten who snatched from the headlines a hazy impression of politicians living it up in Mayfair orgies . . .'[16] Additionally, the subsequent select committee inquiry into whether traditional lobbying was generally shading into influence-peddling appeared to assume that professional lobbyists could not secure 'a knowledge of the workings of the system' by themselves. Yet, within a decade, MPs were increasingly involved in lobbying as the means. Labour MP Francis Noel-Baker warned in 1961 of the grey zone of MPs' involvement in public relations and pressure group work that was leaving the door open 'for a new form of political corruption'.[17] The Denning Report on Profumo was not particularly critical of sexual misconduct; the seriousness depended on the potential for blackmail and the ministerial appointment of the person concerned. It also did not look beyond the activities of a handful of individuals to understand what the scandal said about the informal codes that governed political and personal relationships within the political world, about the failure to deal with the problems at the outset and about the exercise in damage-limitation that followed, thus avoiding 'a wholesale condemnation of certain structures of loyalty and complicity which are hard for anyone to see and understand, and especially hard for those who, like judges, live and work at the heart of the establishment which sustains those structures'.[18]

The Redcliffe-Maud and Salmon Reports, despite failing to conduct any research into the cases to understand the extent of corruption, why the cases happened and why they were, in the words of the DPP, able to continue for so long undetected, produced a long list of eminently sensible if mundane recommendations. These included proposals on the declaration and registration of interests in the public sector, MPs' financial interests, public relations consultants, codes of conduct, gifts and hospitality, post-retirement employment of public officials, external scrutiny and means of investigation, and revisions to the law which included bringing MPs within the criminal law. Few of the recommendations from either report were implemented; neither was debated by the House of Commons which was also reluctant to support the committee report on the three MPs and failed to take any action when the new Select Committee on Members' Interests failed to publish any report for a number of years because some MPs refused to complete their entry in the register. The expectations of official inquiries, therefore, are very much that they seek to deal with the specific issues, often as firefighting exercises, usually while reaffirming the general integrity of those in public life, but rarely attempting to quantify the actual incidence or patterns of misconduct, nor look at the wider organisational or cultural circumstances that gave rise to them. Effective reform, or effective policing of existing standards, has not generally resulted from their deliberations, very much reflecting their establishment as a consequence of external rather than internal pressure. Consequently, failure to own the process of inquiry extends to the ownership of the recommendations which, in any case, lose their urgency if public attention dissipates or turns to other matters.

Conclusion: Tying the threads together

The Nolan report would suggest that it may have fallen into this pattern, given the parliamentary response so far, and, if by focussing on specific and immediate issues largely surrounding politicians, the committee cannot achieve effective reform then there is little likelihood of any substantial progress in those areas—civil servant, quangos and NHS bodies—where little attention has been given to its recommendations. By seeking to enforce more rigorous standards in Parliament the Committee may be hoping to secure public confidence in the visible core of the political system and send a message to the rest of the public sector and to the public. Nevertheless, although the Nolan Committee may help allay public concern, it has not addressed the wider issues that would have been achieved by pulling together the threads of sleaze, then undertaking a more fundamental analysis and evaluation of the circumstances from which they have developed.

It can be contended that the UK continues to suffer from the corrosive effects of the Thatcher experiment and its continuation by the current government. It may be argued that the public feel dissatisfied with the political and public sector changes since 1979, a feeling reflected in rather than caused by the media. There is a sense that the provision of public services, and the sense of public service that underpinned them, have been eroded while individuals, rather than the public at large, have been seen as the first to benefit from the changes. Those they expect to guard the public interest, as well as practise the values and conduct to which governments regularly refer as important for society, are seen to have feet of clay. Pulling together the threads would suggest that the Nolan Committee is currently attending to the consequences rather than the causes of sleaze and that sleaze has less to do with MPs financial interests than the general deterioration of public standards, and public confidence in politicians and the political processes, during the past sixteen years.

If that is the case then the current purpose and effectiveness of the Nolan Committee must be in doubt. The maintenance of public service values and standards are essential in principle irrespective of the party in power but, within the prevailing Conservative political philosophy, the government remains opposed to any prioritising in favour of public services and collective provision. The most effective safeguard against declining standards is a reaffirmation of the merits of public service and public service provision, as well as a rejection of the simplistic and destructive idolisation of market forces and individualism. Such an unbalanced philosophy brings with it not only concomitant Galbraithian problems of private affluence and public squalor but also creates an environment in which questions of morality and social implications of individual action are, at best, of secondary importance. The continuing mismatch between Conservative and public opinion is more disturbing given that the former will continue to seek a reduction in public expenditure as a proportion of Gross Domestic Product and remains ideologically committed to reducing taxation rather than increasing public expenditure. The transition from Thatcher to Major may not have been seamless but nor is it clearly demarcated. The strategic ideological imperatives of reducing public expenditure, the role of the state and the size of the public sector and enhancing wherever possible the role of the market combined with reductions in taxation remain. This has been the prevailing orthodoxy since 1979 and, because of its inherent nature, has led inexorably to the excesses which have led to the Nolan Committee's establishment but raise serious questions about the committee's capacity and commitment to look beyond the consequences to the causes and, in so doing, secure a change in the political environment and a jettisoning of the dogma of the last 16 years.

1   First Report of the Committee on Standards of Conduct in Public Life, *Standards in Public Life*, Cm 2850–I, HMSO, 1995.
2   R. Chesshyre, *The Return of a Native Reporter* (Penguin, 1988), p. 332.
3   Professor Z. Baumann in *New Statesman*, 29 July 1988.
4   Quoted in M. Dynes and D. Walker, *The New British State* (Times Books, 1995), p. 99.
5   J. Harrow and R. Gillett, 'The Proper Conduct of Public Business', *Public Money and Management*, 1994/2, p. 4-n5.
6   Audit Commission, *Protecting the Public Purse* (HMSO, 1993), p. 2.
7   Committee of Public Accounts, *Eighth Report: The Proper Conduct of Public Business* (HMSO, 1994), p.v.
8   First Report, *Select Committee on Members Interests* (HMSO, 1991–92), HCP 326, para 87. See A.

Doig, 'Full Circle or Dead End? The Future of the Select Committee on Members' Interests', *Parliamentary Affairs*, 1994/3.

9   S. Williams, *Conflict of Interests* (Gower, 1985) and M. Mancuso, 'Ethical Attitudes of British MPs', *Parliamentary Affairs*, 1993/2, pp. 186–7.

10   A. Doig, *Westminster Babylon* (Allison and Busby, 1990).

11   See B. McNair, *News and Journalism in the UK* (Routledge, 1994), p. 146, and A. Doig, *Westminster Babylon*, p. 305.

12   M. R. Robinton, 'The British Method of Dealing with Political Corruption', in A. J. Heidenheimer et al (eds), *Political Corruption*, (Holt Rinehart and Winston, 1970), p. 258.

13   The earlier Marconi scandal concerned a different type of scandal, of more concern to politicians and their supporters than the public at large, overlayered with political partisanship, anti-semitism and, ultimately, government expediency over protecting the reputation of Lloyd George, its leading vote-winner.

14   B. Pimlott, *Hugh Dalton* (Jonathan Cape, 1985), p. 557.

15   See the Prime Ministers Committee on Local Government Rules of Conduct, *Report*, Cmnd 5636, 1974 and the Royal Commission on Standards of Conduct in Public Life, Cmnd 6524, 1976.

16   M. Sissons and P. French (eds), *Age of Austerity* (Greenwood Press, 1963), pp. 274–5.

17   F. Noel-Baker, 'The Grey Zone: The Problem of Business Affiliations of Members of Parliament', *Parliamentary Affairs*, 1961–2. p. 91.

18   W. Young, *The Profumo Affair: Aspects of Conservatism*, (Penguin Books, 1963), p. 111.

Politics and Public Perceptions

BY ROGER MORTIMORE

THE British demand high standards from those they elect to serve them in public life. Yet that does not imply that they are confident that those standards will be met. Recent 'sleaze' allegations and other scandals have made public confidence in politicians and political institutions a topical issue, and made clear that the public hold their leaders in very low regard. But it does not follow that the low regard stems from the allegations—indeed, rather the contrary. It seems likely that an existing general disdain and distrust of politicians has made the public consciousness a fertile ground for sowing more specific suspicions. Nevertheless, the appearance being created by the press coverage since the 1992 election that low standards are rife—an impression partly the result of what has seemed, at times, a deliberate blurring by some sections of the media of the distinctions between sleaze proper (that is, corruption or misuse of office) and other more venial misdeneamours (especially of a sexual nature)—seems to have deepened public mistrust. It seems to have contributed to an alarming fall in public confidence in the state of Britain's democracy and democratic institutions.

The belief in sleaze

Public perceptions of politicians and opinions on issues connected with sleaze have been extensively measured by opinion polls over the last decade or so. Earlier evidence is more sparse, in itself an indication of a subtle shift in the climate of opinion—absence of opinion poll data on a question frequently points to its not having occurred to anybody that it was worth asking. If no polls were carried out to determine whether the public thought MPs were corrupt, one reason may well have been that few people were suggesting that they were.[1] The public have long held the view that corruption in public life is an unusually heinous evil. In 1980 more people (73% of British adults) considered 'politicians accepting gifts for services rendered' to be 'morally wrong' than thought the same of the use of cannabis (70%), racial discrimination (61%), adultery (60%), bloodsports (59%) or pornography in the cinema (55%) (MORI, Jan. 1980). And today, they take a strict view of what is acceptable: 89% say MPs should never accept money or gifts in connection with the performance of their parliamentary duties, and majorities agreed that not only is it wrong to accept free holidays abroad, a weekend with the wife at the Ritz or payment for asking a parliamentary question, but even free tickets to sporting events; and almost half would condemn accepting even free lunch at a restaurant or bottles of wine or whisky at Christmas (Gallup, Oct. 94). Furthermore, they are happy to admit they demand a higher standard of behaviour from politicians than from others: 70% said in January 1994 that 'we, the public, are right . . . to expect MPs to behave according to a higher standard of moral behaviour and financial honesty than ordinary people' (MORI).

Unfortunately, the public are also quite convinced that British politicians today are not living up to those expectations. In October 1994, a horrifying 64% agreed that 'most members of Parliament make a lot of money by using public office improperly' (Gallup). There is also a widespread belief that corruption extends to government abuse of powers of patronage: 63% believe the government prefers known Conservative supporters and people who have donated funds to the party when making appointments to 'bodies like regional health authorities', only 17% thinking such appointments are made strictly on merit; and 47% have the impression that the government is 'packing' quangos with Conservative supporters, only 11% disagreeing (Gallup, Oct.). Almost a third (29%) believed 'from what you know of the Scott Inquiry and the arms-and-aid deal with Malaysia' that the government 'is corrupt and/or abuses its power' (ICM, March 94). Naturally, in specific cases of alleged sleaze fewer of the public are prepared to express an opinion, but the majority of those that do believe in MPs' guilt: in the case of Neil Hamilton, for example, 28% thought that 'Mr Major was . . . justified in accepting Mr Neil Hamilton's denial of any wrongdoing in connection with his dealings with Mr Mohammed Al-Fayed', but 38% thought he was not (Gallup, Oct. 94).

Opposition politicians may be tempted to feel that while a cloud of scandal seems to have engulfed the Conservatives, their own hands have been seen to be clean. Some of the media coverage has clearly sought to make the distinction. In particular, one might note the controversial investigation by the *Sunday Times*, when a number of both Conservatives and Opposition MPs were offered £1,000 to table a Parliamentary Question by undercover reporters posing as businessmen—the fact that both of those who accepted the offer were Conservatives was fully reported. In fact, however, the public does not seem to discriminate, and politicians are apparently all being tarred with the same brush. As far as the public is concerned, the opposition's probity is just as much in question. When asked in October 1994 'From what you know, do you think Conservative MPs are more likely to behave in this way [accepting money and gifts when they should not have done] than Labour and other Opposition MPs or not?', 49% thought Tories were no worse than any other MPs (Gallup). In other words, Tony Blair cannot sweep into Downing Street on a tide of disgust at Tory sleaze: 47% agreed that 'The Conservatives are no worse than most. My vote at the next general election won't be affected by all the current talk of sleaze', the same proportion who disagreed and thought that they were 'less inclined to vote for [the Conservatives] than I was before' (Gallup, Oct. 94). At a period when Tory support in the polls was a record low, and people seemed prepared to compare them unfavourably with Labour on almost any criterion, their unwillingness to do so on this issue is particularly interesting. On the other hand, when the parties are considered collectively, the Tories come off worse. At the start of December 1994, 73% agreed that 'The Conservatives these days give the impression of being very sleazy and disreputable', while only 21% thought the same was true of Labour (Gallup). However, the proportion considering Labour's impression was sleazy had more than doubled in under six months (from 10% in July), the 11-point increase being almost as sharp as that suffered by the Conservatives (up 13 points from 60% over the same period).

An international comparison emphasises the depth of the problem. There is a stereotype of 'middle England' as being full of jingoistic Colonel Blimps who, however much they may grumble nostalgically about declining standards, are still convinced that the British system is the best in the world and that corruption begins at Calais. Not so. In fact only 29% now think that the ethical and moral standards of political leaders in Britain are higher than those of other countries and 19% think they are lower (Gallup, Oct. 94). Most of the British public draw no distinction in type between Messrs Major, Blair and their colleagues on the one side and their foreign counterparts on the other. In the light of the stories about foreign government being reported in the British media in 1994, this implies that at least 19% have a very low opinion indeed of ethical standards at Westminster. Finally, there is little respect for politicians' motives. When asked 'Whose interest do you think MPs put first—their own, their constituents', their party's or their country's?', 52% think MPs put their own interests first and a further 26% their party's (MORI, Jan. 94).

Investigating and preventing sleaze

As might be expected, the public also strongly support attempts to regulate the behaviour of MPs. A survey in October 1992 — well before the Nolan Commission had been conceived—found 83% support for setting up 'a commission, independent of Parliament and the government ... to examine complaints made about the way MPs perform their duties as MPs' (MORI). More recently, 41% believed that an independent committee headed by a judge should regulate MPs' declarations in the Register of Members' Interests and 38% that it should be done by the courts, with only 8% supporting the status quo of regulation by a committee of MPs (ICM, Nov. 94). In the 1995 State of the Nation survey for the Joseph Rowntree Reform Trust, only 26% felt they could trust MPs to enforce 'the rules which govern their conduct in Parliament', while 38% thought the rules should be given force of law and administered by an independent commission and the civil courts. 29% felt breaches of the rules should be criminal offences to be investigated by the police. Even higher proportions were in favour of external investigation of allegations against government ministers (MORI, Apr.–May 95).

For the most part, they are also supportive of the role of the media in investigating and revealing suspected cases of abuse of office. They are certainly more tolerant of press investigation of politicians than of other public figures. However, the public is much more ambivalent if the subject matter of a story involves merely personal rather than public misdemeanours. This complicates matters considerably, as the media coverage of political events in the last couple of years, especially in the popular press, has tended to blur the distinction between abuse of office and sex scandals. A number of high profile cases, resulting in resignation from government posts after media pressure, have involved only sexual indiscretions but are persistently catalogued as demonstrating a government in deepening crisis and frequently referred to under the catch-all term of sleaze. The media has contrived to create a climate of all-encompassing suspicion surrounding politicians—especially but not exclusively Conservatives—which smears indiscriminately; it seems unlikely that the general public mood now draws fine distinctions in its impressions between abuse of office and more generally immoral behaviour, unless it is specifically prompted to do so.

The mood was set in the case of the first Cabinet casualty after the 1992 general election, David Mellor; the press campaign for his dismissal began with sexual revelations (on the 'public interest' justification that his affair was making him too tired to perform his government duties properly), then moved swiftly on to ridicule (alleging—in the public interest—that he had sex wearing a Chelsea football shirt). Later, having kept his place in the Cabinet through this storm, more serious allegations emerged of having accepted free hospitality from a friend with PLO connections which raised questions of conflict of interest and seemed to throw possible doubt on the integrity with which he made decisions. These allegations forced his resignation. The *Sun* headline which announced the news, however, referred back to the sex scandal and seemed to imply that it was this that had forced the Prime Minister's hand.

The British media has kept up an almost constant barrage of scandal stories since the autumn of 1992. A few of the allegations fall clearly within strict definitions of sleaze or corruption, but many equally clearly do not. A political sex scandal, of course, sells more newspapers than a political corruption story. Furthermore, there has been some justification for viewing sexual misdemeanours by Tory MPs as being politically relevant in the light of Conservative campaigns on the importance of the family, on the damage done to the social fabric of the nation by single parenthood, and in particular the 'Back to Basics' campaign.

Launched at the 1993 party conference, it argued that 'old-fashioned' standards of behaviour and morality were a necessary ingredient of national regeneration—consequently any Conservative MP who endorsed the policy, even implicitly by silence, could be accused of hypocrisy if he was less than pure himself and was therefore fair game. This has given the popular press a licence to muddy the waters.

However, the public seems to regard this link as specious. There is high support for proper investigative journalism of matters of real public interest: 78% agree press intrusion is justified in the interests of national security, 68% where the blackmail of public figures is concerned, and even higher proportions 'to expose the conduct of someone like Robert Maxwell' (84%) and 'to right an injustice such as wrongful imprisonment due to police corruption' (81%) (Gallup, Jan. 94). Only 49% thought the newspapers were right to publish the story of David Mellor's affair, 39% to publish the five year old story of Paddy Ashdown's affair, and 26% to publish the story that Health Secretary Virginia Bottomley had been (many years before) an unmarried mother (MORI, Aug. 92). And when the Deputy Governor of the Bank of England, Rupert Pennant-Rea, resigned after his former mistress took her story to the press, 68% thought that he should not have resigned and 57% that newspapers were wrong to report the matter (MORI March 95). Nor is this new: in the Profumo affair in the 1960s, despite its obviously grave implications, 51% thought the newspapers were giving it too much publicity (Gallup). Nevertheless, sympathy for the role of the press seems to be slowly increasing. Tolerance of the invasion of privacy of every single group included in MORI's survey rose between November 1989 and August 1992, but was highest in the case of politicians.

1: Q. For which of these groups of people, if any, do you think it is justifiable for the press to invade their privacy in pursuit of a story? (MORI)

	November 1989	August 1992	Change 1989–92
	%	%	±%
Politicians	32	40	+8
Magistrates and judges	29	39	+10
Police officers	29	36	+7
Royalty	16	33	+17
Clergymen	19	28	+9
Lawyers	20	26	+6
TV and showbusiness personalities	19	26	+8
Journalists	19	25	+6
Civil servants	18	25	+7
Businessmen	15	23	+8
Teachers	15	22	+7
Sports personalities	15	21	+6
None of these	46	33	−13

The public's attitudes to press coverage are mirrored by the seriousness with which they regard the substance of the allegations. The view of the majority that politicians' private lives are irrelevant to their public duties seems long established. At the time of the Lambton-Jellicoe affair in 1973, 53% agreed that 'Cabinet ministers should be able to lead their private lives as they wish', while only 42% took the contrary view that 'their private lives should be above reproach'. Ten years earlier, in the aftermath of the Profumo affair, only 35% took the tolerant view and 57% thought they should be above reproach, but this change may have owed as much to the different nature of the cases and the different gravity of their political impact as to any liberalisation of public attitudes on sexual matters.

Twenty years later, with a very different question tackling the same issue, almost identical results to those at the time of the Lambton and Jellicoe scandal were found: in January 1994, at the height of the 'Back to Basics' furore, when the cases of Tim Yeo and Alan Duncan were fresh in the public's mind, 41% agreed that 'if it is discovered a minister has committed a serious moral or financial indiscretion in their private life, they should resign', and 53% that 'if these matters are entirely private and not illegal, that as long as they perform their job well as ministers, they should not be required to resign'. Even so, 75% agreed the press is right 'to expose ministers or MPs who say one thing in public but behave in a sharply different way in their private lives; (MORI, Jan. 94). These two, almost contradictory, findings in the same survey seem to suggest that the blurring of the issue has had its effect in confusing the public. The reporting continues and the public, though it may disapprove of the messenger, seems still to be absorbing the message.

While almost two-thirds (62%) may think a minister's marital infidelity 'is not a matter of proper concern for the press' (Gallup, Jan. 94), there are nevertheless clear signs that the public is becoming less tolerant. One in five (19%) think that it should be held against an MP if he is cited in a divorce case, compared with 8% in 1977; a third (32%) would hold it against him that he had an illegitimate child (16% in 1977) or that he had had sex outside marriage (19% in 1977). Even on an issue where general public attitudes have liberalised over the period, homosexuality, there has been a slight increase in intolerance — 38% would hold a homosexual relationship against an MP compared to 34% in 1977. But even so, the intolerant remain a minority (Gallup, Jan. 94). After the death of Conservative MP Stephen Milligan in bizarre sexual circumstances, 69% said that they regarded the incident as 'an essentially private personal tragedy', and only 23% 'as putting in doubt the integrity of the Conservative Party and the government' (Gallup, Feb. 94). By contrast, 73% say that they would hold it against an MP that he or she had taken drugs (Gallup, Jan. 94).

Putting the belief in sleaze into context

The public's low regard for politicians is, for the most part, a generalised impression and not based on particular personal experiences or knowledge. Only half the public can name their own MP, and almost as many think he or she personally is doing a good job;[2] probably few would accuse of serious wrongdoing any individuals of whom they had specific knowledge. However, mud sticks. What is worse, all the mud is the same colour: with a general bad opinion of MPs firmly stuck in their minds, the public seem to take a cynical view on any specific question they might be asked. They think MPs are overpaid (even when it is specifically pointed out to them that their salaries are much lower than those in comparable jobs in industry). They think MPs do not work hard. They think MPs have a low standard of morality. They think MPs can not be trusted to tell the truth. And almost inevitably, on the same reasoning, they are quite ready to believe that MPs are fundamentally corrupt. While they may not believe it of their own MP, the public seem to think sleaze is widespread among all the rest.

The public standing of politicians can be compared with that of other professions. Pollsters carry out such exercises relatively regularly, using a variety of criteria for comparison: which group is most respected, most trusted to tell the truth, has the highest moral or ethical standards, performs its role in society best, and so on. It is an almost unvarying result of such tests that politicians (or MPs or government ministers, however the question is framed) score worse than almost every other group. Their only competitors for last place tend to be estate agents and — much more relevantly — journalists.

There are two commonly employed means by which pollsters can compare public perceptions of different groups or institutions, each of which has its own advantages and its own limitations. One is to show respondents a list of, for example, professions and ask them to pick out any of which they consider a particular statement is true or which in their opinion have a particular attribute; they may then be shown the list again, and asked about a contrasting statement or about those professions which do not have the attribute. For example, MORI showed a list of eleven groups and asked 'Which of these groups of people do you think uphold high moral standards?' and then 'Which do not?' This form of question will tend to elicit a limited number of answers: for those categories about which the public does not have strong opinions either way, many respondents will not select them from the list in answer to either question. Consequently, it measures not only the direction of opinion about a particular group but also the salience of those opinions. Sometimes, if this is of particular relevance, the number of answers may be deliberately restricted to accentuate this effect, for example by starting the question 'Which two or three on this list ... ?' It is noticeable that in Britain, negative opinions about politicians have been very salient indeed — not only is the public hostile to them, but it is very much a top-of-the-mind issue and MPs tend to reap high negative scores. Only 6% in March 1995 named MPs as upholding high moral standards, a low score but better than journalists

(3%) and business executives (4%); but MPs had a clear lead among the groups named as not upholding standards, picked by 46%. Journalists were clear in second place (38%), and the rest nowhere.

A drawback of this technique, of course, is that it does not reveal much about public opinion of the groups which are not 'top-of-the-mind' and makes direct comparison difficult. The alternative is for pollsters to work systematically through their list, asking for an opinion on each group. Unless the question is very obscure, this will elicit only a small number of 'don't know' answers and the remainder of respondents will give a positive or negative rating to each group in the test. This was the approach of MORI's 'veracity' polls in 1983 and 1993, asking for each group 'whether you generally trust them to tell the truth or not'. Overall, the level of trust rose slightly over the ten year period, but at the bottom of the league it fell: the proportion trusting 'politicians generally' to tell the truth went down from 18% to 14%, government ministers from 16% to 11%; but dislodging ministers from the bottom place they held in 1983, trust in journalists fell from 19% to just 10%. (Five times as many people, incidentally, said they trusted pollsters to tell the truth.) By this method, of course, it is not so clear which groups they feel most strongly about and on which their opinion is only marginal.

2. Q. Now I will read out a list of different types of people. For each, would you tell me whether you generally trust them to tell the truth or not? (MORI)

	Tell Truth		Not Tell Truth		Net Improvement
	1983	1993	1983	1993	1983–93
	%	%	%	%	±%
Teachers	79	84	14	9	±10
Doctors	82	84	14	11	+5
Clergymen/priests	85	80	11	13	−7
Television news readers	63	72	25	18	+16
Professors	n/a	70	n/a	12	n/a
Judges	77	68	18	21	−12
Ordinary man/woman in the street	57	64	27	21	+13
The Police	61	63	32	26	+8
Pollsters	n/a	52	n/a	28	n/a
Civil servants	25	37	63	50	+25
Trade union officials	18	32	71	54	+31
Business leaders	25	32	65	57	+15
Politicians generally	18	14	75	79	−8
Government ministers	16	11	74	81	−12
Journalists	19	10	73	84	−20

Perhaps veracity is an unfair test for politicians, however; there may be to some extent a resigned acceptance that not telling the strict truth is part of a politician's job. The more general question of 'respect' illustrates both MPs' low standing and the fact that this is not of recent manufacture. For it would be wrong to attribute the present low public regard for politicians to the scandals of the last couple of years or for that matter to recent political events: the opinion is long established and although the public view in the mid-1990s has deteriorated since the 1980s, it is only a marginal fall and the standing of politicians has been low for a long time. In February 1980, just 17% rated the 'honesty and ethical standards' of MPs as high and 25% as 'low', with local councillors scoring marginally worse; only trade union leaders were viewed more unfavourably. To put the figures in context, 73% thought the standards of doctors and 51% those of police officers were high. Similarly, in 1979 when the public were asked which two or three groups respondents had most respect for, MPs came last of ten with just 4%. Even earlier—as early as 1973—a poll found 58% agreeing that 'MPs are there for their own gain or ambition' (ORC), and the previous year a survey of the middle class and skilled working class found that only estate agents were viewed more unfavourably than MPs, though the figures were much less damaging, 40% having a favourable impression of MPs and 18% an unfavourable one (MORI, Oct. 72).

3 Q. Which two or three of the groups of people on this list do you yourself have most respect for?
(MORI)

	1979	1986	1987	April 1989	August 1989	Average
	%	%	%	%	%	%
Nurses	–	–	75	–	–	75
Doctors	80	76	70	65	77	74
Policemen	54	51	50	42	55	50
The Royal Family	–	–	–	–	31	31
Teachers	24	30	20	23	30	25
Social workers	25	19	14	14	19	18
Scientists	24	17	12	11	–	16
Company directors	6	10	3	4	5	6
Trade union leaders	5	6	3	3	5	4
Civil servants	5	6	3	2	4	4
Local councillors	–	–	–	–	4	4
Architects	–	–	–	–	4	4
Members of Parliament	4	3	4	3	5	4
Journalists	5	2	1	1	3	2
Estate agents	–	–	–	–	1	1
None of these	3	3	1	–	4	
Don't know	2	1	1	–	3	

This is not to suggest that two years' obsession with sleaze has had no effect. What seems to have happened is that the scope of the public's contempt for politicians has been widened. In October 1994, 78% believed that 'To win elections, most candidates for Parliament make promises they have no intention of fulfilling'; this was not a substantial increase from 72% in 1985. Similarly, 82% thought 'Most politicians care more about keeping power than they do about the best interests of the nation' (up from 75%) and 87% that 'Most Members of Parliament will tell lies if they feel the truth will hurt them politically' (up from 75%). But the deterioration of MPs' image on morality and sleaze has been far sharper. The number believing 'Most Members of Parliament have a personal moral code' fell from 42% to 26%; and the number thinking that 'Most Members of Parliament make a lot of money by using public office improperly' rose from 46% to 64%. (Gallup).

It is interesting to compare public attitudes to MPs with their attitudes to the police who, over the past decade have also suffered from a series of extremely damaging revelations, including a number of high-profile cases which raised a clear suspicion that officers had been economical with the truth to obtain convictions. Yet the public standing of the police seems on some evidence to be as high as ever—more people in 1993 said they generally trusted the police to tell the truth than in 1983—and although some other measures have found a noticeable fall in confidence in the police over the same period, overall levels of satisfaction remain very high.[3] This appears to suggest that falling public satisfaction with politicians is not simply part of a wider disillusionment with the whole establishment. Of course, the police have not over that period been subjected to a general campaign of vilification by sections of the national press.

Conclusion: the effects

Distrust of politicians naturally enough leads to distrust of political institutions. Whether or not sleaze is the cause, public confidence in Parliament has dropped precipitately in the last four years. In 1973, 54% thought that Parliament worked either very well or fairly well, and by 1991 the figure had climbed slightly to 59% (MORI). In January 1995, however, only 37% thought it worked well, and they were outnumbered by the 38% who thought it worked badly. At the same time, 60% agreed that 'Britain needs a Bill of Rights to protect the liberty of the individual', with only 8% disagreeing (MORI).[4] Gallup's regular monthly tracking since August 1992 on the question 'On the whole are you very satisfied, fairly satisfied, not very satisfied or not at all satisfied with the way democracy works in this country?' has also found a sharp decline of confidence, from 38% dissatisfied in August 1992 (and in January of that year), to depths of 56% dissatisfied in July 1993 and 55% in August 1994.

The potential danger that Parliament and its members being held in contempt by its electorate poses to the wellbeing of the political system is obvious. At the very least, there is the possibility that the unpopularity of the present Parliament and distrust of MPs could be harnessed to generate support for drastic constitutional change without proper debate and with unforeseeabele consequences. At the other extreme, and per-haps less obvious, is the extent to which reform might be hampered. There is considerable support, for example, for restricting the degree to which parties can be funded by company or trade union donations, but there is very little support for using public money to fill the vacuum—public funding of political parties was opposed by 53% in the 1991 State of the Nation poll (MORI) and by 79% in June 1993 (ICM). It may be as difficult to generate confidence in a reformed system as for the status quo if the political elite which must operate a reformed system continue to attract the present level of hostility. Furthermore, rebuilding public confidence in politicians is unlikely to be a quick or easy process.

A second possibility is raised by the fact that public hostility towards the media seems as high as that towards politicians. Protection of privacy legislation in general would be likely to receive broad public support as a means of punishing the media's behaviour. There is a risk that the blurring of the line between real public interest issues and sex scandals could prove a two-edged sword, being exploited by aggrieved politicians to generate public support for draconian measures which would reduce the ability of the media to investigate real sleaze cases.[5] Already, it is possible to find surprisingly sizeable sectors of the population which would be happy with further restrictions on the press. (In June 1987, for example, 25% thought party political broadcasts on TV and radio during election campaigns should be banned, 22% would have banned *all* coverage of an election on TV and radio and 16% would have banned all coverage in the newspapers! — MORI.)

Opinion polls measure perceptions, not facts. They give no evidence whether sleaze is really prevalent, only whether the public thinks it is. Nevertheless, what the public thinks is also a fact, and a relevant one. Arguably, the present atmosphere of distrust is almost as damaging to democracy in Britain as the actual existence of unsuspected corruption would be. It is clear that this distrust has not simply been whipped up from nothing by a hostile press campaign but was built on the solid foundation of existing public cynicism. Rooting out the rotten apples from the barrel — even assuming that there are any to root out — is unlikely to go more than a very short way towards solving the deeper problem.

1   The MORI/NOP 'State of the Nation' survey, conducted for Granada TV in November 1973, examined in great depth a wide range of issues regarding public confidence in the political system and satisfaction with its operation, yet included not a single question on the possibility that MPs might be corrupt — this despite the fact that the revelation of the Poulson scandal was a very recent memory. Gallup's published record of its British polls over the same period (*The Gallup International Public Opinion Polls: Great Britain 1937–1975*, records no research on whether the public thought the Poulson case to be an isolated one.

2   51% were able to name correctly the MP for their constituency; 44% said they were satisfied with the way their own MP was doing his job (28% dissatisfied), whereas on the more general question, 32% were satisfied with 'the way MPs are doing their job' and 56% dissatisfied. This comparatively high level of satisfaction has remained unaffected by the fall in MPs' general standing since 1992, 43% saying they were satisfied (and 23% dissatisfied) with the job their local MP was doing (MORI, Apr.–May 95).

3   For example, in January 1994 found that 66% agreed 'I feel I can trust the police', although this represented a ten-point fall from the 76% who agreed with the same statement in 1989 (MORI).

4   The 'State of the Nation' survey in March–April 1995 put the same Bill of Rights questions towards the end of a long questionnaire drawing attention to many of the areas of concern which have fuelled support for such a bill, and found 79% in favour.

5   Indeed, the way in which Jonathan Aitken's attack in April 1995 on the TV and broadsheet newspaper allegations about his Arab connections and role in an arms trading deal was given momentum by a tabloid exposé of 'three in a bed' activities concerning another Tory MP suggests that the danger may already exist.

The Nolan Committee

BY DAWN OLIVER

THE Committee on Standards in Public Life under the chairmanship of Lord Nolan was appointed in October 1994 'to examine current concerns about standards of conduct of all holders of public office, including arrangements relating to financial and commercial activities, and make recommendations as to any changes in present arrangements which might be required to ensure the highest standards of propriety in public life.' For these purposes public life included ministers and Members of Parliament. The remit did not encompass the investigation of individual cases, but general concern about the financial interests of MPs had created a climate in which allegations of sleaze were repeatedly being made in the media. The Prime Minister had taken the view that this concern required an independent inquiry which would consider the standards of conduct across many areas of public life, not only those of MPs.

The Nolan Committee was appointed in the wake of 'cash for questions' issues, which the Committee of Privileges of the House of Commons was investigating at the time. Allegations had been made by the *Sunday Times* that two named MPs had each accepted £1,000 for tabling a Parliamentary Question, and a third had agreed to table a Question in return for £1,000 before telephoning back and requesting the cheque be made out to his favourite charity. In April 1995 the Committee of Privileges reported that in relation to one Member it did not 'consider that short-term consultancies which predominantly relate to participation in parliamentary proceedings on behalf of a client can possibly be proper'. It recommended a resolution to the House that the conduct of the Member fell below the standards which the House is entitled to expect of its members, and that he be reprimanded and suspended for ten sitting days with suspension of salary for that period. On the second case it found a serious error of judgement that also fell short of the standards to be expected; a reprimand and suspension for twenty sitting days with suspension of salary were recommended. In the third case it found that it must be wrong for a member to link payment to a charity or any other body however worthy with asking a Parliamentary Question or tabling a Motion or an Amendment or making a speech. Such conduct, the Committee argued, diminished the standing of Parliament and, if it became prevalent, could lead members of the public to believe that such a contribution would give them an advantage in dealing with their MP. Here, however, it did not consider it appropriate for the House to take any action. These recommendations were accepted by the House. The Privileges Committee also found that the *Sunday Times'* conduct of its enquiries (which had included the clandestine recording of meetings within the House) had fallen substantially below the standards to be expected of legitimate investigative journalism, but it recommended no action on that. (HC 351–I, 1994–5)

One reason for appointing an independent committee was the need for the public to be confident that there would be no whitewash, a charge that could be made if an inquiry were conducted by MPs or ministers. This point about independence raises the issue of what might be called 'political public choice', the difficulties placed by vested interests (in this context, the interests of MPs who supplement their incomes by various financial arrangements with outside bodies) in the way of open investigation, independent findings and, if necessary, change. It is significant, though not surprising, that public choice theory has been used by Conservative governments in the last fifteen years or so to justify breaking vested interests in local government, the civil service, trade unions and the professions, but not until now in relation to ministers or MPs. As we shall see, political vested interests were influential in the Commons debate on the Nolan Report, and this is likely to be a major issue in the implementation of certain of the recommendations.

The Nolan Committee was constituted as a standing body with its members appointed for three years. It decided to concentrate on issues relating to MPs (the focus here), ministers and civil servants, and executive Non-Departmental Public Bodies for its first report, which was published on 11 May 1995 (CM 2850, 1995). Further reports are to be made on, for instance, standards of conduct in the House of Lords.

The findings of the Nolan Committee in relation to the outside interests of MPs clearly reflected public concerns about their conduct. It believed that the activities of MPs, particularly in the fields of lobbying, advocacy and consultancy, had undermined respect for the House of Commons, its authority and the ability of MPs to discharge their functions, as they should, free from conflicts of interest, according to their own judgement and in the interests of their constituents and the general public. It was clear from the evidence that arrangements were being entered into by some MPs which seemed to negate the duties of MPs to put public interests first, and that the status of MPs was falling in public opinion.[1] Given the obvious fact that some dubious arrangements are entered into and that there is widespread public concern about standards, the Committee felt that there was no need to quantify the problem; to have sought to do so would have delayed proposals unnecessarily and undermined the momentum essential if any reforms were to be introduced. It did, however, go out of its way to record that 'the great majority of people in public life meet high standards'.

The root of the problem the Nolan Committee identified was that MPs were not aware what standards of conduct were expected of them. Somehow it was assumed that these were known. The absence of articulated principles was very obvious in the Cash for Questions affair where the Committee of Privileges frequently referred to 'the standards of conduct to be expected of MPs' but nowhere spelt any of them out. It is not easy for MPs or outsiders with whom they deal to know what is permissible and what is not.[2]

It seems that MPs have commonly assumed that, as long as an interest is registered under the rules relating to the Registration of Members' Interests and declared where required, it is acceptable for them to allow that interest to influence their discharge of their functions. This, the Nolan Committee pointed out, is clearly wrong. The registration requirements do not spell out the values that should inform the conduct of MPs or precise 'dos and don'ts' that they need to know; they deal only with pecuniary and material interests and not with allegiances and pressures of other kinds.

The Committee identified a climate of 'slackness' in parliamentary politics, about the causes of which one may speculate. They may include the fact that the rules about what is proper and what is not, drawn from resolutions of the House from time to time, are not collected together and available to MPs, or the fact that new MPs do not have any kind of induction programme which would inform them about their constitutional role and the standards of conduct expected of them. They may also include the fact that many MPs rely on the payments received from consultancies and the like to supplement their parliamentary income, which is modest and for many MPs, especially from the Conservative side of the House, represents a severe drop in income as compared to what they were earning before election.

The Nolan recommendations

The Committee concentrated on how standards relating to MPs may be affected by conflicts between their parliamentary duties and their outside interests. It tried to steer a middle course between forbidding all outside interests that might produce conflicts and the existing very liberal regime. Its recommendations may be summarised as follows. MPs should remain free to have paid employment unrelated to their role as MPs, but the House of Commons should restate the 1947 Resolution[3] barring MPs from entering into contracts which in any way restrict their freedom of action in Parliament. MPs should be prohibited from entering into agreements to provide services for organisations acting for multiple clients, and the House should set in hand its own inquiry into the merits of parliamentary consultancies. There should be fuller disclosures of agreements relating to parliamentary services given by MPs and fuller disclosure of interests. Guidance on avoiding conflicts of interest should be expanded, with attention to standing committees.[4]

A new Code of Conduct for Members should be introduced (the Report included a draft Code). A Parliamentary Commissioner for Standards should be appointed and a new procedure for investigating complaints about Members established. These proposals, the Committee felt, could be implemented either with a minimum of delay or within a year. Its promise to return to the issues in a year imposes some pressure on the House of Commons to take prompt action.

Two issues underlie the Report: what standards should MPs have, and how should those standards be enforced. The Committee sought to tackle both.

STANDARDS.   There is no single authoritative statement of what is and is not appropriate conduct for an MP. The Committee did not think it right that MPs should have to search through *Erskine May* (the large official tome on parliamentary procedure and practice) and other texts and therefore recommended that standards should be codified in some way. This it sought to do by formulating standards of conduct at a number of levels of generality and for different purposes. It produced Seven Principles of Public Life which should apply to all aspects of public life and are not targeted only at Members of Parliament; and they are worth setting out in full:

Selflessness. Holders of public office should take decisions solely in terms of the public interest. They should not do so in order to obtain financial or other material benefits for themselves, their family or their friends.

Integrity. Holders of public office should not place themselves under any financial or other obligation to outside individuals or organisations that might influence them in the performance of their official duties.

Objectivity. In carrying out public business, including making public appointments, awarding contracts or recommending individuals for rewards and benefits, holders of public office should make choices on merit.

Accountability. Holders of public office are accountable for their decisions and actions to the public and must submit themselves to whatever scrutiny is appropriate to their office.

Openness. Holders of public office should be as open as possible about all the decisions and actions that they take. They should give reasons for their decisions and restrict information only when the wider public interest clearly demands.

Honesty. Holders of public office have a duty to declare any private interests relating to their public duties and to take steps to resolve any conflicts arising in a way that protects the public interest.

Leadership. Holders of public office should promote and support these principles by leadership and example.

Having articulated these principles—which, it is hoped, are not controversial and should command general public support—the Committee went on to elaborate further principles, some of which are to apply to MPs (as a draft Code of Conduct), others to ministers, and others to civil servants. Indeed, it recommended the production of codes of conduct based on the Seven Principles across many areas of public life. It also proposed that more guidance for MPs, including induction sessions should be available. The device of a code is in line with the progressive 'normativization' of politics and government that has been taking place over the last decade, including codes of practice in local government, the new code promised for the civil service, the Citizen's Charter and the sectoral charters that followed, framework documents in executive agencies, and so on.

The Committee's draft Code of Conduct for MPs starts with a statement of general principles drawn from previous resolutions of the House and *Erskine May*, and which generally reflect the Burkean theory of representation. They do not mention party, they impose personal responsibility for their conduct on MPs, and give precedence to the interests of constituents and the public interest against other interests.

The text states: It is the personal responsibility of every Member of Parliament to maintain those standards of conduct which the House and the electorate are entitled to expect, to protect the good name of Parliament and to advance the public interest.

Members should observe those general principles of conduct which apply to all people in public life.

The primary duty of Members is to their country and their constituents. They should undertake no actions in parliament which conflict with that duty.

Because Members of Parliament enjoy certain privileges in law, which exist to enable them to fulfil their responsibilities to the citizens they represent, each Member has a particular personal responsibility to comply fully with all resolutions and conventions of the House relating to matters of conduct and when in doubt to seek advice.

A Member must not promote any matter in Parliament in return for payment.

A Member who has a financial interest, direct or indirect must declare that interest in the currently approved manner when speaking in the House or in Committee, or otherwise taking part in parliamentary proceedings, or approaching ministers, civil servants or public bodies on a matter connected with that interest.

Where, in the pursuit of a Member's parliamentary duties, the existence of a personal financial interest is likely to give rise to a conflict with the public interest, the Member has a personal responsibility to resolve that conflict either by disposing of the interest or by standing aside from the public business in question.

In any dealings with or on behalf of an organisation with whom a financial relationship exists, a Member must always bear in mind the overriding responsibility which exists to constituents and to the national interest. This is particularly important in respect of activities which may not be a matter of public record, such as informal meetings and functions.

In fulfilling the requirements on declaration and registration of interests and remuneration, and depositing of contracts, a Member must have regard to the purpose of those requirements and must comply fully with them, both in letter and spirit.

This draft Code, the Committee recomended, should be restated at the start of each new Parliament, thus giving the House 'ownership' of the standards.

This approach to normativization—formulating broad principles and then building on them to deal with particular situations—is in line with the approach to regulating the standards of conduct taken by a number of the liberal professions. The Code of Conduct of the Bar of England and Wales, for instance, sets out 'fundamental principles' and then goes on to make special provision for particular situations. The rules and principles governing solicitors, and the Securities and Investment Board rules adopt a similar approach. The technique can be an effective way of establishing professional standards without resorting to a high degree of legalism. If a non-statutory approach is to be adopted—and, arguably, it should in relation to Parliament—then a set of Principles and a Code built on precedents establishes a sound foundation and tackles the problem of ignorance which the Committee found. The mechanism for enforcement, however, is crucial to the success of the technique.

ENFORCEMENT. How and by whom the standards of conduct of MPs should be regulated raises sensitive questions of parliamentary privilege. It is a long established principle that the Houses of Parliament, and not the courts, take cognisance of their own procedures; the Bill of Rights of 1689 adds statutory force to this rule by providing that the freedom of speech and debates and proceedings in Parliament are not to be called in question in any court or place outside of Parliament. The two Houses have long asserted the exclusive privilege of dealing with breaches of privilege and contempt of Parliament. Any suggestion that there should be an independent element in the formulation and supervision of standards of conduct for members of either House appears at first sight to challenge this principle and is bound to meet resistance from traditionalists. Concern about this was a prominent theme in the first Commons debate on the Report (18 May 1995).

In considering how parliamentary conduct should be regulated principles underlying the 'privileges' of the two Houses should be borne in mind. They are, broadly, to protect the Houses collectively and their members individually against outside interference, so as to enable them to carry out their constitutional functions effectively. The two Houses justify the special rights, powers and immunities conferred by parliamentary privilege as being necessary for the welfare of the nation, and without which according to *Erskine* May, 'they could not discharge their functions'. The Committee of Privileges, in its report on the Cash for Questions affair, spelled out its own understanding of privileges: 'their purpose is not to protect individual Members of Parliament but to provide the necessary framework in which the House in its corporate capacity and its Members as individuals can fulfil their responsibilities to the citizens whom they represent.' The privileges of Parliament, therefore, are not to be exercised for the benefit of MPs but are to ensure that parliamentary functions are exercised for the general benefit.

It was clear from the fact that the Nolan Committee had been established that registration of interests was not broadly regarded as a sufficient guarantee of standards or conduct—public concerns about standards of conduct are not for the most part based simply on complaints about failure to register interests. The Register has weaknesses in that it does not give important information about the amount of payment and work undertaken by an MP (e.g. how much time is made available to the 'sponsor', what the MP will do in the way of lobbying or advocacy). Such information, the Committee felt, would enable the public to form a view about the independence of Members and should be disclosed.

There are complex reasons why the workings of the Committee of Privileges and the Select Committee on Members' Interests have not been sufficient to prevent the problems identified by the Nolan Committee. It is not just chance that problems have arisen: it seems that there is a genuine degree of 'ethical lassitude' among many MPs[5] and there is no reason to believe that behaviour will change solely as a result of widespread concern or scandals affecting particular MPs that attract media attention. Parliament may respond to public opinion from time to time and penalise MPs for breach of standards, but the Committee of Privileges took over a year to produce its report on the 'Cash for Questions' complaints, and encountered considerable divisions within its membership on e.g. whether it should sit in public (refusal to do so led Tony Benn to leave it) and the fairness of its proceedings (the accused MPs were not permitted to see or comment on the evidence against them).

The Nolan Committee was not satisfied that existing institutional arrangements—the jurisdiction of the Privileges Committee and the Select Committee on Members' Interests—were adequate. Nevertheless, how a Code for MPs should be enforced raises very delicate questions concerning the House's privilege to regulate itself. There would be difficulties in giving the courts enforcement powers over complaints about the conduct of MPs that falls short of criminal offences. It would also be inappropriate for all breaches of standards of conduct to be treated as unlawful (the professions do not regard all matters to do with professional ethics as deserving legal sanctions and, if MPs are in some respects members of a profession, there is no strong reason why

Parliament should be different on this matter). On the other hand, the Nolan Committee did recommend that the position in relation to the criminal liability of MPs for bribery should be clarified. The Select Committee on Standards in Public Life, appointed to consider the Nolan Report, agreed on this point and so did the House (19 July 1995). The Select Committee recommended that the Law Commission report on this issue.

Given the difficulties that would arise if jurisdiction over a code of conduct were invested in the courts, the Nolan Committee recommended a parliamentary mechanism, the appointment of 'a person of independent standing' with 'a degree of tenure' as a new Parliamentary Commissioner for Standards. The Report went into some detail about the functions, powers and procedures of such an officer. He or she would become responsible for the Register of Members' Interests, advise on the Code of Conduct, provide induction sessions for new MPs on matters of conduct and propriety. He or she should also receive complaints about MPs and investigate their conduct. The Commissioner should have the same ability to make findings and conclusions public as the Comptroller and Auditor General and the Parliamentary Commissioner for Administration.

An investigation by the Commissioner would be conducted in private, the Commissioner would have the discretion to dismiss a complaint, to find it proved and agree a remedy with the MP concerned, or find a case to answer and refer the complaint to a committee of the House. The Nolan Committee felt that the Commissioner should be able to demand the attendance of witnesses and the production of papers. It was, in part at least, because such a power could only be granted to an officer personally by statute (which the Nolan Committee did not believe to be appropriate) that it proposed that a parliamentary committee should work with the new Commissioner, having at its command the powers of such committees if standing orders give them to send for persons and papers. The Nolan Committee therefore proposed that a sub-committee of the Committee of Privileges, consisting of up to seven very senior Members, should take forward individual cases recommended by the Commissioner for further consideration. It should normally sit in public for hearings and MPs being investigated should be entitled to be accompanied by advisers. It should be able to recommend penalties when appropriate (to be voted by the House).

Given the improbability of the House of Commons consenting to the establishment of an extra-parliamentary body supervising its standards (and legislation would be required for this, else it would be in breach of the Bill of Rights and parliamentary privilege), the proposals for a Commissioner for Standards seem to be a realistic compromise. No suggestions were made in the Report about the procedure for appointing the Commissioner for Standards. This was a matter which was considered in some detail in the Report of the Select Committee on

Standards in Public Life appointed to consider the Nolan Report and in the ensuing House of Commons debate. The Commons and the Select Committee accepted in principle the proposal for such an appointment. A problem is that there is no direct analogy with other 'officers of the House'. The Comptroller and Auditor General is a statutory officer, appointed by the Crown by letters patent on recommendation of the Prime Minister after consultation with the Chairman of the Public Accounts Committee. The Parliamentary Commissioner for Administration is also a statutory officer, appointed by the Crown by letters patent. The Select Committee felt that it was not yet appropriate for the proposed new Parliamentary Commissioner to be a statutory officer, and that the method of appointmnent of the C and AG and the PCA would not be appropriate for the post. A new recruitment and appointment procedure would have to be devised. It recommended that the appointment be set in hand under arrangements to be made by Madam Speaker on the advice of the House of Commons Commission and in accordance with the recommendations of the Select Committee. The House passed a resolution to that effect in the debate on 19 July 1995. The Select Committee also recommended that the post should be advertised (as is the case with the House of Commons Director of Finance and Administration and the Director of Catering Services); and that the House should be involved in the appointment by ratifying the recommendation eventually made by the Speaker.

Recommendations were also made for the principal duties of the Commissioner, broadly in line with those proposed by Nolan. The Committee proposed an initial two or three year full-time 'contract', with the possibility of subsequent renewal on a part-time basis. But the Commissioner would, it envisaged, be an Officer of the House, not a servant of the proposed new Select Committee on Standards and Privileges. The Commissioner would be removable from office by a substantive resolution of the House of Commons.

It is not surprising that the Nolan Committee did not make more radical proposals involving extra-parliamentary mechanisms, but one may note that there are, at least in theory, other ways of policing the conduct of MPs. One would be the establishment by statute of an independent Commission outside parliament to investigate complaints about MPs' conduct, and that of their 'sponsors', reaching decisions about alleged breaches of standards. Such a Commission could be required to report to the Speaker, and a duty could be imposed on the House to accept the findings and record them in the Journals of the House. This model borrows from the example of the election court, thus maintaining the appearance of parliamentary decision. A variation would be the establishment of a permanent Commission on Standards of Conduct in Public Life charged with investigating complaints concerning a wide range of bodies, including the Houses of Parliament but extending also to quangos, civil servants, local government, non-departmental public bodies and other parts of the public sector, with different provisions for enforcement of findings according to the nature of the body concerned.

The House of Commons Response to the Nolan Report

The House of Commons first debate on the Report took place on 18 May 1995. The Nolan Committee's proposals in respect of a Commissioner for Standards met with a mixed response. Broadly, the Opposition supported most of the proposals and resistance came mostly from the Conservative backbenches. Many Conservative MPs had deep-rooted objections, as did Tony Benn MP, though his preference would have been for statutory regulations of the House. But the Opposition spokesperson, Ann Taylor MP, endorsed the recommendation for a Commissioner and indeed many of the Committee's proposals. On the Code (which attracted little attention in the debate) she proposed that the House should ask the Clerk of the House to draw up a Code based on points in *Erskine May* and her proposal was endorsed by the Select Committee. This 'do it yourself' approach to code-making may make the device more palatable than outright adoption of the Nolan draft.

The Commons resolved to appoint a Select Committee on Standards of Public Life, charged with considering the First Report of the Nolan Committee so far as it related to the rules and procedure of the House, to advise on how its recommendations might be clarified and implemented, and to recommend specific Resolutions for decision by the House. It was to report no later that 7th July and publishing its report on time, the Commons debated its recommendations on 19 July 1995. That debate was conducted in a far cooler and more consensual temper than the initial debate on 18 May. The Leader of the House, who had chaired the Select Committee, had achieved a high level of consensus in a non-partisan spirit, and there was very little objection by the time the matter returned to the House in July to proposals for a Commissioner for Standards, a Code of Conduct and the merger of the Privileges and Members Interests Committees into a new Committee on Standards and Privileges.

We have already noted that the Select Committee endorsed the proposal for a Parliamentary Commissioner for Standards, and this approach was accepted by the House in the July debate. As far as other recommendations of the Nolan Committee are concerned, the House endorsed the principle of a Code of Conduct and instructed the appropriate Select Committee to prepare a draft for approval as soon as possible; such a code should consist of broad and readily understood principles rather than a detailed set of rules, though it would need to be supported by more detailed rules on particular aspects of conduct as was the case with the registration of interests. The Select Committee felt that it should itself embark on the task of preparing the code pending the appointment of the new Select Committee on Standards and

Privileges and that the Clerk of the House should begin work during
the summer recess. The House agreed.

The Select Committee were comfortable with the Nolan recommendation that the terms of the 1947 resolution should be restated—this
resolution was read by Nolan as placing an absolute ban on Members
entering into contracts or agreements which in any way restrict their
freedom to act and speak as they wish, or which require them to act in
Parliament as representatives of outside bodies. Problems arose here
over the possible narrow interpretation of that resolution, and the
assumption which had developed since the creation of the Register of
Interests, that any activity declared is acceptable. The Select Committee
considered that the matter could best be dealt with by adding to the
proposed resolution in relation to the Code the words: 'and whilst
restating its commitment to the objectives of the 1947 Resolution,
accepts the need to review its wording in the context of the work to be
undertaken on the draft Code'. The House endorsed this view.

The greatest difficulties experienced by the Select Committee and the
House in consideration of the Nolan recommendations were in the field
of consultancies and disclosures in the Register—the subject where the
vested interests of Members are most directly affected. There were
clearly problems over the imprecision of the Nolan proposals, and the
Select Committee also felt that it would be unacceptable if new rules
were put in place which affected existing agreements entered into by
Members in good faith. The Committee was not ready to put forward
recommendations on these matters and offered instead to make a
further report to the House before the end of the current session as a
matter of urgency.

Conclusions

As might have been anticipated, there was initially considerable resistance on the government side of the House, especially among backbenchers, to the Nolan proposals. It was partly due to a sense of outrage over
the implication that MPs were, as one MP put it, 'a bunch of crooks',
and partly due to the financial self-interests of those who currently rely
on their earnings from consultancy arrangements to top up their
parliamentary salaries. In any proposal for the reform of Parliament
vested interests are bound to place impediments in the way of progress.
Here the influence of the Opposition and a wish for a bipartisan or non-
partisan approach can help to achieve a solution.

The consensus achieved on the Select Committee enabled the House
to approach the matter in a less obviously self-interested mood in the
July debate. It agreed to endorse the need for an examination of the
Nolan recommendations relating to consultancies and disclosures in the
Register of Members' interests and to instruct the Select Committee on
Standards in Public Life to seek to bring forward proposals on these
matters by the end of the session. This decision seems to have been

motivated largely by genuine concerns to make sure that any rules were clear and unambiguous. Some, though relatively few, Members expressed strong opposition in principle to more detailed disclosure or banning of certain kinds of advocacy arrangement. It may be that the self-interest that MPs have in enhancing their reputations and status have been recognised to outweigh the financial interests and interests in privacy that are at stake where matters of declaration or outlawing of interests are concerned.

Meanwhile, the Nolan Committee, having indicated which reforms it considers should be implemented immediately and which within a year, will keep up the pressure on Parliament to put its own Houses in order. Given the fact that there is in the United Kingdom no body superior to Parliament to compel reform of standard setting and enforcement procedures, the only available antidotes are publicity and public opinion — mobilised by an impeccably independent body.

1 Cf Ivor Crewe's evidence to the Committee, *First Report*, vol 2, pp. 106.
2 Some of the ancient resolutions of the House, for instance the resolution of 1695 against accepting bribes, do not seem to be taken seriously, perhaps because they are too general in terms and couched in picturesque but dated language.
3 Following the W. J. Brown case: HC Deb, 15 July 1947.
4 A significant point in the light of the row about Sir Jeremy Wiggin tabling an amendment to a bill in the name of Sebastian Coe MP which erupted within a few days of the publication of the Report.
5 To borrow the phrase of M. Mancuso in *Parliamentary Affairs*, April 1993.

Media, Opinion and the Constitution

BY PATRICK DUNLEAVY AND STUART WEIR

The unprecedented growth of public disquiet about sleaze in contemporary Britain can be interpreted in a number of different ways. Defenders of the status quo point to the relatively sudden and distinctive emergence of the sleaze issue as a concept in public debate, arguing that it is only (or primarily) a mass media creation, a spasm or temporary moral panic in which a small number of problems are overdramatized and ascribed implausible levels of significance. For this school of thought, sleaze is a minor issue or a non-issue for most of the public, and its sudden prominence has no lasting constitutional significance beyond perhaps triggering a few, incremental safeguards of the kind recommended in the first Nolan Committee report. By contrast, more critical voices suggest that the 'sleaze' furore is indicative of a substantial and recurring problem within the British polity, left unresolved by previous periods of reform, and now eliciting strong calls for fundamental constitutional change from the majority of citizens.

In the past, the difficulties in deciding between these two views have been considerable for a number of reasons. First, it was hard to say anything very objective about the media's behaviour. Second, the available survey information about public opinion on these issues was fragmentary and often seriously defective in terms of the questions asked or the methods used. Against a background where media influences and public attitudes could only be rather impressionistically described, it was much harder to determine the significance of problems with established institutional rules. Here we remedy these difficulties using two new data sources—information derived from a systematic analysis of mass media behaviour on the sleaze issue, discussed in our first section; and data from the comprehensive survey of public attitudes to constitutional reform questions contained in the Joseph Rowntree Reform Trust's *State of the Nation* surveys in 1991 and 1995, discussed in the second section. The conclusions show how these findings put the current sleaze furore into a different perspective. The media's impact in creating an integrated issue is acknowledged. But the public's response to the disparate concerns included in the overall issue reflects longer-term and fundamental problems in traditional constitutional arrangements and with the dominant 'self-regulation' ethos of Britain's governing elites.

The emergence of the sleaze issue

Sleaze is an odd concept to have sprung into prominence in the mid-1990s. In general usage the term is a loose one, denoting something slatternly or tawdry, and until recently it was not widely used. The Concise Oxford Dictionary unhelpfully defines its meaning only as 'sleaziness', the alternative noun form of the idea, while most short dictionaries have the adjectival form 'sleazy' but neither of the noun forms of the concept.

However, in contemporary British usage sleaze is a populist word standing in for corruption and semi-corruption, or near-corruption, in public life. Its closest synonym is the term 'malversation' (corrupt or unethical behaviour by someone in a position of trust), which Christopher Hood forecast several years ago would grow as a result of the rise of 'new public management' practices.[1] Specifically, the concept of sleaze which leapt to prominence in 1994–5 married together quite disparate areas of near-wrongdoing across several parts of public life which had previously been considered entirely separately. These were:

1. Alleged financial wrongdoing by ministers and MPs, involving shady deals, breaking or pushing at the previously accepted frontiers of rules of conduct in public life, and the misleading of others in public life about business or financial issues.

2. A perception that commercial and business lobbying of government and MPs had increased dramatically, and had become widespread and now involved serious intermediary players (such as professional lobbying companies) and very large numbers of MPs.

3. Alleged partisan 'packing' of appointments to quasi-governmental agencies (QGAs, misleadingly known as 'Quangos' in popular parlance) by ministers, with differential overrepresentation of Tory supporters and exclusion of other parties' supporters.

4. A 'jobs for the faithful' syndrome where Tory financial backers, or people from Tory-supporting companies, receive in return QGA ('quango') jobs and are also systematically advantaged in the honours lists.

5. Movements by former ministers (and also by former senior civil servants) into very well paid City or business directorships, or into senior jobs or well-paid consultancies, in companies with which they previously had dealings while in public office—notably banks and stockbrokers, firms which benefited greatly from organizing privatizations.

6. The alleged illegitimate or secret raising of large-scale finances for political parties, especially donations by private companies or private individuals (some of them foreigners) to the Conservative party.

7. The unconventional behaviour of ministers or even backbench MPs in terms of sexual mores, an aspect especially salient for individuals associated with a 'high' moral tone on 'family' issues. Where politicians

are found to practice a different thing in their private life from their public stance the media has been particularly concerned, stemming principally from John Major's failed 'Back to Basics' campaign.

8. Finally, the overall issue of political sleaze also includes a largely separate aspect sometimes linked with it and at other times handled separately (under shorthand headings such as 'fat cats'), namely the large-scale and unjustified increases in the incomes and share options of directors in formerly state-owned public utilities, now in the private sector.

These eight aspects of public life were never closely bound together by any other concept before sleaze came into widespread use to cover them all. Subsequently, the Prime Minister recodified the matter somewhat by giving terms of reference to the Nolan Committee which rigorously excluded point 8 above (because it related to private companies' behaviour) and point 7 (because sexual mores or peccadillos concern individuals). In addition, Major tried very contentiously to exclude point 6, using the officialese concept of 'standards of conduct in public life' to do so. These restrictive efforts met with varying degrees of success. The exclusion of sexual misconduct from the purview of sleaze was generally agreed by the 'quality' press and broadcasters, whereas the tabloid press continued to run the two together. The issue of public utility firms' behaviour continued to be closely linked with the sleaze concept, despite being excluded from Nolan's purview. And while Lord Nolan's efforts to broaden his inquiry to cover party funding was rejected by Major in May 1995, the dispute ensured that the media as a whole continued to include point 6 within the sleaze concept, despite Whitehall efforts to narrow it down.

This uniquely complicated bundle of issues was put together, and acquired such a heightened importance in media and public debates, because of a number of factors. Labour Party front-benchers and their researchers, together with left-wing units, had begun accumulating evidence of Conservative misuses of power from the late 1980s onwards. The growing constitutional reform movement lead by Charter 88, and the support of newspapers such as *The Independent* and *The Guardian*, broadened awareness of these concerns. Opposition to the growth of QGAs also began to mount in this period, together with documentation of who had actually obtained appointments on these bodies.[2] The erosion of local government powers by QGAs especially attracted cross-party criticism. The declining popularity of privatization in the 1990s added a further dimension, as evidence mounted of large-scale public utility profits and weak regulation arrangements. Huge increases in directors' remuneration focused consumers' discontents. And in the mid-1990s, after a lag of several years, it began to be apparent that within the House of Commons itself there were important malversation problems involving MPs taking cash for asking questions, briefing ministers on behalf of lobbyists and so on.

Modern methods of studying the mass media allow us to chart the rise of the sleaze issue, and some aspects of what it covered, with considerable precision. The 'Profile' text database includes the full text of most British newspapers, allowing us to search for all occurrences of the word sleaze and to ascertain which words are used in conjunction with it. Having a very distinctive search word like 'sleaze' creates the best possible conditions for an exercise of this kind. The first column of table 1 shows the raw number of articles mentioning 'sleaze' on Profile's UKNEWS file. However, since the number of newspaper included in the database increased consistently over this period, so the overall numbers of UK news items stored also greatly increased in later years. The second column of table 1 accordingly shows a score for mentions of sleaze which is adjusted to take account of the increase in the total number of items. The final column shows the percentage of total UK press coverage in each year which mentions sleaze.[3]

Table 1a shows that the adjusted scores for mentions of sleaze slowly increased from 1985–6 in each year through to 1992–3, consistent with a general popularization of the term. But from 1993 onwards the

1: The development of sleaze mentions in UK news coverage in the Profile press database, 1985–95

	Raw scores	Adjusted score	% of all items
(a) Annual data			
June 1985–May	21	50	.01
1986–87	26	45	.01
1987–88	63	98	.02
1988–89	151	201	.05
1989–90	100	118	.03
1990–91	164	182	.04
1991–92	197	175	.04
1992–93	271	204	.05
1993–94	735	452	.10
1994–95	3,479	1,955	.45
(b) Quarterly data			
Jun 1992–Aug 1992	75	96	.06
Sep 1992–Nov 1992	65	81	.05
Dec 1992–Feb 1993	52	63	.04
Mar 1993–May 1993	79	82	.05
Jun 1993–Aug 1993	137	136	.08
Sep 1993–Nov 1993	102	97	.06
Dec 1993–Feb 1994	294	296	.17
Mar 1994–May 1994	202	189	.11
Jun 1994–Aug 1994	170	163	.10
Sep 1994–Nov 1994	1,534	1,294	.76
Dec 1994–Feb 1995	758	698	.41
Mar 1994–May 1995	1,017	850	.50

(Notes. Annual data are in all cases for 1 June to 31 May. Adjusted annual data involve multiplying column 1 (the sleaze items in year x) by (total items in year x) divided by (the annual average for total items across the 1985–95 period). Quarterly data are adjusted by multiplying column 1 (the sleaze items in quarter y) by (total items in quarter y) divided by (the quarterly average for total items across the 1985–95 period). Percentage figures are obtained by dividing column 1 data by total items for the relevant period and multiplying by 100.

numbers of mentions mushroomed upwards, and in 1994–5 the term was used 40 times more frequently than a decade earlier (on the adjusted scores). In 1994–5 alone the term occurred more frequently than in the previous nine years put together.

Looking at the timing in a bit more detail, Table 1b shows the quarterly scores for the last three years. An earlier minor increase in sleaze mentions occured in the period December 1992 to February 1993. But the explosion of sleaze as an issue occurred in the autumn of 1994 the period of the 'cash for questions' furore, when mention increased dramatically. When the Nolan Committee was set up the issue receded a good deal, returning to the headlines again in May 1995 with the publication of the committee's report.

The Profile data also help shed light on the various different meanings and shadings of the complex sleaze concept outlined above. We searched the last three year's data for three other sets of keywords occurring in items mentioning sleaze: minister, ministers or Cabinet; MP, MPs, House of Commons or Parliament; quango or quangos. The frequency of associations between sleaze and these words provides a useful if rough-and-ready indication of the extent to which the problem is seen as associated with the executive, the legislature or quasi-governmental agencies. Table 2 shows the results. The rising political salience of the issue is born out by the tenfold increase in items linking sleaze to both ministers and Parliament or MPs, with steep increases also in associations between sleaze and ministers or the Cabinet alone. Associations between sleaze and MPs only (i.e. without mentioning ministers or the Cabinet) show a less dramatic increase, reflecting the fact that as the sleaze issue built up, ministers and the Cabinet could not stand aside from controversy about misconduct by MPs but were increasingly required to spell out official reactions. Finally, quangos and sleaze began to be associated in 1993–4. At the peak of the issue in 1994–5 nearly one in ten sleaze items mentioned quangos.

2: Associations between sleaze and the executive Parliament and 'Quangos'

	Total Items	Ministes and Parliament	Items mentioning: Ministers only	Parliament only	'Quangos'
1992–3	271	14	21	17	0
1993–4	735	211	132	61	49
1994–5	3,479	1,142	806	362	337

All the patterns discussed here fit an S-curve form, with its characteristic initially slow build-up, followed by a rapid rise to a peak. Downs suggested that this pattern marks the early phases of a regularly recurring 'issue attention cycle', with a period of 'alarmed discovery' of an issue followed by strong public consensus on the need for change.[4] Later stages of Downs' cycle, still not played out in the sleaze issue yet, are marked by a period of public disillusion as the problem proves more costly and intractable than at first appears. After that, the salience of the issue declines gradually as some solutions are institutionalized and others rejected as too costly. Eventually, coverage of the issue reaches a routinized base-level, although probably at a higher level than before. However, Downs' account is vague about the mechanisms by which 'alarmed discovery' of an issue takes place. He stresses the usual pluralist input politics processes (interest groups, political parties and electoral competition) and depicts the media as chiefly responding to such societal influences.

A significant reworking of the same ideas emphasizing the critical influence of the mass media in highlighting issues and creating alarmed discovery is provided by the German social theorist Nicholas Luhmann.[5] In his account: 'the political system, in so far as it rests on public opinion, is integrated not by rules governing decisions but by rules governing attention.' The mass media are a specialized part of the social system whose job is to orchestrate a never ceasing and intense competition between different issues for a necessarily short-lived period of public attention. This competition does not respond directly to the objective salience of issues. Instead, securing attention depends first on the ability of the social interests promoting an issue sufficiently to kick it into play with the media at a minor level. The next (take-off) stage depends on media professionals' conjuring up a 'word formula' which encapsulates elements of 'pseudo-novelty'. If this reworking succeeds, the issue may become the focus of intense media and hence public attention. Where such a 'word formula' cannot be found, an objectively important issue will nonetheless languish, squeezed out by more successful competitors. By contrast, a successful word-formula may allow an 'old' issue to be replayed as the focus for public debate in a refashioned guise for a time. It is an essential aspect of the mass media's operations that all attention is short-lived: 'after everything has been said about an issue, it is obsolete.'

The sleaze issue perfectly fits Luhmann's model. The component sub-issues listed above are all long-standing questions of middling importance, few of which would ever be discussed on their own outside short items in the home news pages or the occasional reflective piece by a columnist in one of the quality newspapers. However, the invention of the word-formula 'sleaze' packaging these disparate concerns together, and the association of sleaze with the fact that the Conservatives had been continuously in government since 1979, transformed the situation. The sleaze label allowed the otherwise discreet problems to be connected in an innovative but easily understandable way, in the process automatically making sleaze take on 'pseudo-crisis' features. Phenomena previously described under numerous different labels were now captured by the same word-formula, ensuring that sleaze should appear to increase. The word-formula alone also allowed the disparate bundle of issues to migrate from the inside pages of the qualities to the front pages of the tabloids and the headlines on TV news. This intense and repeated exposure was crucial to the formation of public opinion not just about sleaze as a whole but also about the component issues in the bundle.

Public attitudes to sleaze

The complexity and novelty of the sleaze concept which emerged in Britain in 1993–5 largely caught opinion pollsters unawares. In general, British government has carefully cultivated a self-image as a 'clean' country, without the problems of large-scale corruption which plague some other liberal democracies. It is part of the conventional wisdom that since 1945 there have been only isolated incidents of political misconduct or corruption — such as the Profumo affair under Macmillan or the Poulson and local government corruption scandals of the late 1960s and early 1970s. As a result, opinion polls rarely asked about the public's perceptions of corruption, concentrating instead on whether politicians and officials were seen as trustworthy, involved in public life for their own interests and so on (see Roger Mortimore, this volume). Very few of the questions asked attempted to place people's views in the context of their wider opinions about constitutional questions. And most poll questions were very general in their wording, implicitly assuming that the public would be largely ignorant of, or have no opinions about, detailed institutional arrangements. The wide scope of the 1990s sleaze issue and its unprecedented resonance with the public raise important questions about this assumption. However, the *State of the Nation II* poll allows us to give a much more authoritative snapshot of public attitudes towards sleaze in April and early May 1995.[6] Three series of questions explored attitudes towards standards of conduct for MPs, for ministers and civil servants, and for quasi-governmental agencies.

THE CONDUCT OF MPS emerged from the survey as an area of high public consensus. We started with a carefully neutral question, listing the external activities of MPs in a detailed but easily understandable way and asking which should be banned and which allowed (see table 3). Between two thirds and four fifths of voters had a view on these quite detailed issues, with the proportion of people answering 'don't know' or not expressing a view rising on the more contested and least consensual issues.

Table 3 shows that there were three sets of responses. The first were issues where a clear majority of respondents felt that some kind of external activity or outside interest should be banned. The extensive list here shows that the Nolan Committee's 'solutions' were badly out of touch with public opinion. Nolan suggested banning MPs from being 'cab rank' consultants for parliamentary lobbying firms — and an overwhelming majority of voters backed this idea. But there were equally large majorities for two key recommendations which Nolan rejected. Nearly four out of five voters wanted MPs to be bound by the same rules as local councillors and banned from speaking or voting on any issue where they have a financial interest. And 78% wanted MPs banned from receiving fees from any private company in return for lobbying on its behalf at Westminster. Nolan's view that this practice should continue to be allowed was backed by a negligible number of respondents.

Faced with these dramatic results, Tory backbenchers may be tempted to take refuge in the idea that they reflect a partisan or anti-business reaction by the current mass of Labour and the Liberal Democrat supporters in the polls. In fact, the hard core Conservative supporters in the Rowntree/MORI survey were almost equally insistent on banning questions for money (74%), MPs working for lobby firms (74%), any paid company links (72%), and speaking or voting on issues where MPs have a financial interest (68%).

On a second set of issues involving MPs' external links, there was a clear majority view but also a substantial dissenting voice amongst respondents. Labour's gleeful targeting of Tory sleaze and company entanglements in 1994–5 may be moderated by the finding that more than twice as many voters wanted trade union sponsorship of individual MPs banned as thought it should be allowed. (It should be noted that the proportion of people not expressing a view on this issue was greater than elsewhere). Even amongst Labour voters alone, 42% wanted sponsorship banned, compared with only 27% who thought it should

3: Voters' attitudes towards the external activities of MPs, April–May 1995 (%)

	Banned	Allowed	Majority for a ban	No view/ don't know
Consensus view				
Asking questions in Parliament for money	83	3	+80	14
Receiving fees from private companies in return for lobbying on their behalf at Westminster	78	3	+75	19
Speaking or voting on issues where they stand to gain financially	77	4	+73	19
Receiving fees from specialist lobbying companies to promote their clients' interests at Westminster	76	2	+74	22
Speaking or voting on issues which affect commercial interests or private companies from which they receive payment	73	4	+69	23
Majority view: no consensus				
Being sponsored by trade unions towards election and campaigning costs in their constituencies	48	21	+27	31
Having any paid job outside Parliament	48	28	+20	24
Being the paid representative of a non-commercial interest group (eg the Police Federation)	44	22	+22	34
No majority view				
Being paid to write articles for newspapers and magazines	43	35	+8	22
Carrying on a trade or profession (eg as a farmer, lawyer or dentist) while being an MP	33	45	−12	22

Note. The question asked was: 'Here is a list of things that some MPs do. Which, if any, do you think they should be allowed to do? And which, if any, do you think they should be banned from doing?')

be left to continue. Nearly half of respondents felt MPs should have no outside jobs at all, and slightly fewer wanted the practice of MPs acting as paid consultants for interest groups to be ended (although again don't know/no view responses were higher on this issue).

The third category of MPs' outside work elicited divided views among our respondents, with roughly as much public support as hostility. The activities involved were MPs writing paid articles for newspapers, and carrying on a trade or profession (such as a lawyer, farmer or dentist). Fully a fifth of all respondents wanted a ban on all forms of paid activity by MPs included in our question.

Asking who should make the rules governing MPs' conduct exposed an enormous gulf between rulers and ruled in Britain, and highlighted the inadequacy of the Nolan committee's suggestions (table 4). Only one in 16 respondents, and only one in eight Tory voters, agreed that the status quo should be maintained. The Nolan solution of tightening up the current rules but maintaining parliamentary self-regulation attracted less than one in five respondents. Most people supported exactly the changes which Nolan considered but left alone for fear of attracting MPs' wrath. A moderate option of embodying MPs' codes of conduct into law but staying clear of the criminal law attracted the greatest endorsement. But nearly three out of ten wanted a completely different system, agreeing that breaches of the rules should be seen as crimes. These results should shock MPs, whose post-Nolan select committee opted for a watered down set of recommendations. Appreciably more voters wanted conduct in the Commons to be regulated by the criminal law than supported either the status quo or minor rule changes. Overall, more than twice as many voters wanted Parliamentary rules written into law than supported the current unwritten codes and self-regulation.

4: Public attitudes towards Parliamentary self-regulation, April–May 1995 (%)

Question: 'At the moment, MPs as a whole make and enforce the rules which govern their conduct in Parliament. Which of these comes closest to your own view, from what you know or have heard?'

'The existing system of rules, with MPs making and enforcing them, works well and should not be changed'.	7
'The existing rules should be tightened up and enforced by MPs, without involving the police, courts or any outside body'.	19
'The rules should be made law, with an independent commission and civil courts overseeing MPs' conduct'.	38
'The rules should be made law, making breaches a crime investigated by the police and punishable by the criminal courts'.	29
Don't know/other	9

Note. Answers here and in table 6 come to more than 100% because some double responses were wrongly recorded.

THE CONDUCT OF MINISTERS AND SENIOR CIVIL SERVANTS also elicited near-consensus majorities for revising current rules, by which retiring ministers can easily and almost immediately take up directorships in companies with whom they have had dealings when in office. Senior civil servants making the same move must seek permission within a two year period, but the review committee supposed to police this arrangement almost invariably accedes to requests. By contrast, the *State of the Nation II* respondents wanted a flat ban by large majorities (table 5).

5: Public attitudes towards ministes and senior civil servants taking jobs with private companies (%)

Question: 'Do you think that MPs senior civil servants should or should not be allowed to take jobs in companies they have dealt with within two years of leaving office?'

Ministers		Civil servants	
Should not	77	Should not	70
Should	15	Should	19
Don't know	8	Don't know	11

Again, we asked a question to test whether ordinary citizens had confidence in the prevailing culture of self-regulation as it relates to accusations of wrong-doing affecting the executive (table 6). This issue was highlighted in late 1994 and early 1995 by allegations regarding whether Jonathan Aitken had accepted hospitality at the Paris Ritz while a minister and his conduct as director of an arms company prior to becoming a minister. The supposed 'investigation' of the Ritz issue by the Cabinet Secretary, Sir Robin Butler, also aroused public controversy — since it seemed to consist of accepting Aitken's own denial of any wrong-doing. We put to respondents two status quo options for handling such cases, namely investigation by the Prime Minister or by the Commons. Just over one in ten felt each of these to be the best method of investigating ministerial misconduct. The vast majority of people (78%) instead chose either investigation by an independent commission or a full-fledged police enquiry and court prosecution as their preferred solution.

6: Public attitudes towards executive self-regulation (%)

Question: 'How do you think allegations of serious professional misconduct by government ministers should be investigaged?'

'The Prime Minister should make enquiries, as now, into whether the allegations are true, and decide if the minister should resign'.	11
'The House of Commons should make enquiries and decide if the minister should resign'.	12
'An independent official commission should investigate and decide whether ministers should resign'.	47
'The police should investigate and decide whether or not ministers should face trial in court'.	31
Don't know/other	3

QUASI-GOVERNMENTAL AGENCIES were also covered in the first Nolan report, and again there was high level of public consensus about their arrangements. Our question ran: 'Many important services are now run by "quangos" — boards of people appointed by the government. I am going to read out a number of statements about how services might be run in future, and for each one could you tell me to what extent you agree or disagree.'

Table 7 shows the results, with large majorities agreeing that quango boards should meet in public and that legal rules to require balanced composition were needed. There was only fractionally less support for statements requiring parliamentary scrutiny and a general public say in appointments. However, the last question in table 7, expressing acceptance of unfettered ministerial appointments, showed more support for the status quo on partisan lines—with 42% of Conservative supporters agreeing, 28% of Liberal Democrats and 20% of those supporting Labour.

7: Public attitudes to how Quangos should be run (%)

	Agree	Disagree	Neither	Net agree
'Quangos should hold their board meetings in public and make all their board papers available to the public, subject to protection of commercial confidentiality and people's privacy'	81	3	17	+78
'There should be clear legal rules to ensure that all quango boards are balanced in their composition'	80	2	17	+78
'All appointments to quangos should be subject to scrutiny by parliamentary committees'	72	7	21	+65
'The general public should have a say in appointing some people to each quango'	71	10	20	+61
'Government ministers should have the right to appoint whoever they thnk is most suitable to run quangos'	26	50	25	−24

Conclusions: the significance of sleaze

So far we have convincingly established two apparently contradictory things. First, the sleaze label is quite clearly a very recent media confection, a particular word-formula which dramatizes and integrates under one concept what would otherwise be much less salient governance problems. Second, public opinion takes a robust, no-nonsense approach to sleaze, with a strong public consensus favouring more sweeping and principled reforms than the recommendations of the first Nolan report (much of which may not even be consistently implemented). In this final section we argue that nonetheless there are no grounds for thinking that the public reaction is simply 'whipped up' artificially by the media, or is any less genuine and salient than other aspects of 'public opinion'.

Although the British media have presented the issues examined here for mass consumption using the sleaze label, our survey questions did not. Thus the public reactions charted here are not simply a Pavlovian reaction to a particular verbal cue. Nor is there any reason to suppose that current public concerns about politicians' standards of conduct date only from the media's sleaze boom (see Roger Mortimer, this volume). Indeed, Luhmann's point is not that intervention by media professionals is necessary only in order to persuade the public to worry about non-issues (although pseudo-crises of course happen). Word formulas are equally essential if the media are to re-present salient but familiar issues to people in competition with other novel issues. Invented labels and concepts like sleaze are thus the structural device by which the mass media can cope with the many cyclical qualities of societal development.

There is ample evidence that the current public reaction to sleaze issues reflects a groundswell of discontents amongst British citizens about the constitutionally ungrounded character of the UK's political system in general—the extent to which it is based on unspoken understandings, conventional limits, the self-restraint of political elites, and a 'muddling through' revisionism as a way of coping with emerging problems. We can sum up this much longer-developing, and deeper-rooted public reaction as a rejection of an unfixed constitution, a demand for properly entrenched rights, and hostility to the 'club ethos' which has dominated British politics since the reforms which decisively modernized the state between 1870 and 1920. The scale (and limits) of the demands for constitutional reform on non-sleaze issues are sketched in table 8, which shows the public consensus behind freedom of information, a Bill of Rights and limited devolution of powers from Westminster.

8: Public attitudes towards constitutional reforms, 1991 and 1995 (%)

	respondents supporting reform	
Pro-Reform Consensus	May 1995	1991
Scottish devolution (in Scotland)	81	83
Freedom of Information Act	81	77
Britain needs a written constitution	79	–
Britain needs a Bill of Rights	79	79
Make political parties publish the identity of large donors	75	–
Welsh devolution (in Wales)	67	–
Scottish devolution (in Britain)	65	59
Reform majority, but no consensus		
Fixed term general elections	57	56
System of government out of date	50	45
Welsh devolution (in Britain)	49	42
Devolution to Northern Ireland	49	42
Change voting system to PR	46	50
Elected second chamber replacing House of Lords	43	40
UK rights less well protected than in the rest of EU	43	38
Reform case rejected		
Devolution to English regions	26	27

Four out of five voters agree that Britain needs a written constitution 'providing clear legal rules which government ministers and civil servants are forced to operate'. This consensus largely existed in 1991, and has only strengthened slightly further in the intervening years. Thus the attitudes we have charted above are consistent with a stable set of public values, not set apart or isolated from a broader consistitutional agenda.

Traditionally, the British constitution has survived virtually unchanged since the 1920s for two reasons. First, once in government neither Conservative nor Labour leaders were prepared to sacrifice any real power in pursuit of constitutional reform, no matter what they might say in opposition. Second, public opinion on constitutional issues has been seen as shallowly based, expressing mainly the fleeting discontents of current opposition voters. Elites of both parties simply sat out or sat on demands for change, confident that only the 'chattering classes' would remember them. Now, the furore over sleaze demonstrates that not only are the Labour and Tory leaderships unable to make the usual 'establishment' deal stick, but that the great mass of voters are insisting on change, and sticking to their guns.

The 'club ethos' of closed, self-regulation by political elites themselves has clearly broken down. Reform demands for open, external regulation of politicians and Whitehall are now supported by voters across all parties and all social classes. The diehard Tory backbench idea that the 'professional classes' share their interest in maintaining self-regulation is inaccurate: in fact, the demand for legal controls and rights is strongest amongst professionals and the upper middle class.

The sleaze controversy is an outrider of the constitutional changes which must now happen if support for the British political system is not to continue decaying at its current alarming rate. The pressures for change at elite level are strong—with the implementation of Nolan mark I, new topics in Nolan mark II, and the Scott report on the sale of arms to Iraq all due—and with a change of government or hung Parliament in prospect. Even the low-burn issue of electoral reform may revive powerfully as a general election approaches, if Labour's opinion poll ratings 'normalize' and the Conservative share of the vote returns to its historic minimum of 38% in general elections since 1900.

None of this is to imply that effective institutional changes will inevitably be introduced. But the likelihood must be that if they are not, then the declining legitimacy of Britain's political institutions will continue. Table 9a shows that the proportion of people expressing strong support for the system of government as a whole has declined appreciably. In 1973 people split half and half in thinking that the system of government worked well versus needing improvement. By 1991 almost twice as manay people urged improvements as believed things were working well. And by 1995 the proportions were three to one in favour of 'quite a lot' or 'a great deal' of improvement, rather than minor changes.

In the 1990s table 9b shows that the balance of public opinion swung even more sharply towards criticism of the House of Commons. In 1991 for every two people who felt Parliament worked badly, there were eight who felt it worked well. But today, for every two people who think Parliament works badly there are fewer than three people who think it works well. Asked how Parliament 'is doing its job these days' in another question, only 34% of the 1995 respondents were satisfied, 31% were dissatisfied, and the remainder were neutral or didn't know.

9: Public attitudes to the British system of government, and to Parliament 1973–95 (%)

(a) Which of these statements best describes your opinion on the present system of governing Britain?

	1995	1991	1973	Change 1991–5	Change 1973–95
Works extremely well and could not be improved	3	4	5	−1	−2
Could be improved in small ways but mainly works well	19	29	43	−10	−24
Could be improved quite a lot	41	40	35	+1	+6
Needs a great deal of improvement	35	23	14	+12	+21
Don't know	3	5	3		
Works well	22	33	48	−11	−26
Could be improved	76	63	49	+13	+27
Majority for works well	−54	−30	−1		

(b) Overall, how well or badly do you think Parliament works?

	1995	1991	1973	Change 1991–5
Very well	4	5	12	−1
Fairly well	39	54	42	−15
Neither well nor badly	22	21	–	+1
Fairly badly	19	12	34	+7
Very badly	11	4	5	+7
Don't know	6	4	5	
Very well or fairly well	43%	59%	54%	−16%
Very badly or fairly badly	30	16	39	+14

(Data for 1973 are drawn from the Report of the Royal Commission on the Constitution. In Table 9b the 1973 question options excluded 'Neither well nor badly' and so are not strictly comparable.)

This is the slenderest base of public support—to give a point of comparison, 49% of the same respondents were satisfied with their local council, and only 21% dissatisfied.

These results suggest that if the Commons and the government fail to implement convincing changes in the rules governing standards of conduct, public alienation and suspicion will grow apace. The conclusions of the first Nolan report represent a complex establishment fix-up, designed more to secure a unanimous report, Cabinet endorsement and acceptance by Tory backbenchers than to make an intellectually convincing attempt to combat sleaze. The likelihood must be that most voters will not understand or accept the Committee's patch-and-mend solution and are already convinced they are inadequate to tackle current problems.

1   C. Hood, 'Beyond the Public Bureaucracy State?', LSE Inaugural Lecture, 1990.
2   See S. Weir and W. Hall, *EGO Trip: Extra-Governmental Organization in the United Kingdom and Their Accountability* (Charter 88 Trust, 1994), also summarized in 'Questions of Democratic Accountability', Parliamentary Affairs, April 1995; and S. Weir and W. Hall, *Behind Closed Doors: Advisory Quangos in the Corridors of Power* (Channel 4 Television/Democratic Audit of the UK, 1995).
3   Given that there are hundreds of competing issues, the raw percentage scores are naturally low, a fraction of 1% in all years. What matters here is not the absolute level of coverage but the variation across years.
4   A. Downs, 'Up and down with ecology – the issue attention cycle', *Public Interest*, 28/1, 1972.
5   For a summary of Luhmann's ideas in English, see E. Noelle-Neumann, *The Spiral of Silence: Public Opinion – Our Social Skin* (Chicago University Press, 1993).

6   The poll was commissioned by the Joseph Rowntree Reform Trust. Most of the 1995 questions asked
     (including all the sleaze questions) were devised by Dunleavy and Weir for the LSE Public Policy
     Group, in consultation with the Bob Worcester and Simon Braunholtz of MORI, and Professor Trevor
     Smith. We also thank Helen Margetts (Birkbeck) and Jojo Iwasaki (LSE) for contributing to the
     question-setting. The survey was carried out by MORI, who interviewed a representative quota sample
     of 1,758 adults in 258 enumeration districts sampling points across Great Britain, with additional
     booster samples in Wales and Scotland. Interviews were conducted at home, face-to-face in April and
     May 1995. Data were weighted to match the profile of the population. Full survey details are available
     in the MORI tabulations, 'State of the Nation 1995', with highlights in its newsletter, *British Public
     Opinion*, June 1995.

Feet of Clay

BY F.F. RIDLEY

FAR from history having ended in the permanent triumph of liberal democracy and the market economy, spectres are still haunting Europe, if not those Marx and Engels thought to see 130 years ago. The discredit of politicians as a class, which risks spilling over into discredit of democratic politics, then democracy itself, is one of those spectres. In some countries new leaders, anti-system, are already centre-stage, promising to clear the stables—Berlusconi winning a battle if not yet the war in Italy, Le Pen applauded by a worrying minority in France. Elsewhere, actors remain in the wings so far, waiting their chance. In some countries, as in Britain, there are no political leaders to orchestrate an attack on the established system, and it is hard to imagine one. If proportional representation were introduced, however, a plausible actor would probably appear and we can not be sure that his vote would be less then Le Pen's on similar slogans: 'out the ins' as well as immigration or law and order.

In any case, the play does not stop simply because there is no plausable opponent of democracy in the cast. The cast itself may bring democratic politics into disrepute through its own behaviour. As in Greek tragedy, disaster requires no enemy: the leading characters destroy themselves. And there is little point in asking whether the play is a false representation of reality or whether the audience misunderstand, for it is audience reaction that matters; the reality that counts in the end is public opinion.

Democracy depends on many things. The ability of governments to deliver a reasonable part of what citizens have come to expect for example: If 'feel good' disappears over the horizon, in some countries under Conservative governments, in others under Socialist, problems arise. But democracy also depends on trust in those who govern, going beyond the government to cover the political establishment as a whole, government and opposition, leaders and backbenchers. The growing public mistrust of politicians which Britain and other countries face today is not just functional, related to their seemingly inevitable failure to assure economic growth and security of employment or law and order at home and peace abroad; it is also personal. Without personal respect for its political establishment, democracy is undermined. Everyone sees some enemies in the political establishment; that is proper so long as personal respect remains. Mrs Thatcher is a good example (concerns about her as a too fond mother of a son with questionable interests notwithstanding).

It may take a Lenin to make a revolution or a Hitler to build a dictatorship, but collapse of democracy can occur from within if faith in those who represent it withers away. All societies have their idols, showbiz stars, sporting heroes, even a beautiful princess. Political leaders are idols of a sort as well, even in a democracy, and it can be argued that something of the sort is necessary: trust in leaders is required if a political system is to work, and this involves an element of faith in societies inevitably less than wholly rational.

It would be an over-simplification, no doubt, to equate trust and respect. The latter can take different forms. Political systems counted as western democracies have long featured politicians who are honoured as a result of the office they hold or the power they wield, respected in that sense (respectful means showing deference according to the Concise Oxford Dictionary): in deferential cultures office may suffice, the man inside the uniform irrelevant, perhaps hardly known. Britain's deferential political culture lies in the past however. When politicians are stripped of their finery (or finery becomes a joke, as when officers of Parliament with titles like Black Rod and fancy dress to match are seen on television), when they lose their titles (or titles only impress when reserving a table in a popular restaurant), then respect must be earned in a way that earlier politicians did not have to. Interestingly, respecT-worthiness seems to depend less on ability to deliver the goods than on good character; and that, as media searchlights roam, now includes conduct in private life.

Of course, idols have always had feet of clay. Politicians were not better in the past than today. Sex and money have always been a driving force, probably a stronger instinct, save in the exceptional man, than service of King and Country or nation and national interest. And politics for all but a few was probably never so much a path to the power political scientists tend to focus on (as distinct from social anthropologists) than a pursuit of personal wealth or rank in society — though all are linked. A seventeenth century aristocrat told an aspiring politician that MPs had no better lottery than the Commons in which to push their fortunes, and Samuel Johnson famously described politics as nothing more than a means of rising in the world.

Those were freebooting days, perhaps, and some may argue that the nineteenth century brought greater respectability to politics, but soberly dressed Victorian gentlemen had no fewer vices than their more elegant predecessors in Parliament. The secret gardens of their sex lives have been explored and their business dealings were as hard-hearted as those of the great landowners in the House of Lords who earlier cleared the Highlands. The difference was that in the later nineteenth and earlier twentieth centuries much remained hidden under cloaks of high morality and altruistic public service which the upper classes before would hardly have felt obliged to wear.

What changed as the present century progressed is the distance between politicians and public. Mistresses were as common in earlier times as now but the aristocracy made no secret of it; they were an accepted fact of life in the circles that mattered—and the opinion of those outside the ruling circle did not matter. The common people knew it was not their place to judge their betters; if they had opinions, their distance from power made them irrelevant anyway. And if affairs were to be kept quiet, in bourgeois society that was not too difficult either. A valet would know what his gentleman was up to, but who else?

The peacock feathers of the quality have gone. Even in grey Victorian times one could distinguish MPs, proper gentlemen, from Mr Pooter and other would-be gentlemen by their complexion and the cloth of their suits. Such indicators have declined (how long since novice MP Julian Critchley was told off for wearing suede shoes? Kenneth Clarke now wears hush-puppies). Titles are still bestowed by politicians on each other: Rt. Hon. for those who climb the greasy pole, Sir for long service at its base, MPs all honourable, ex-soldiers gallant and lawyers learned in addition. Such labels carry no weight with the public. Most MPs, of course, present themselves as like the rest of us, or their voters at least, when they mingle. But meeting to discuss their own affairs, the privileges of the House for example in the Palace (signficant word) of Westminster, they see themselves as privileged, parts of a sovereign assembly rather than representatives of the people.

To recognise politicians' feet of clay, the public must get close enough to see them properly. If ordinary people have no entry to the temples the idols inhabit, are not on visiting terms with the political elite in other words, then the way one gets close now is through the media. Few of our fathers knew Lloyd George: they learnt of the sale of honours scandal through the press; revelations of the old goat's other scandals waited longer. Investigative journalism (a favourable term) or through-the-keyhole exposures (less favourable) bring private lives into the open. Paradoxically, such information may bring one 'closer' to the persons involved than acquaintance in Westminster or the City. Acquaintances see a face warts and all but may see little more, especially in club-like situations where colleagues are assumed to be decent fellows (increasingly discovered a costly mistake in other spheres of activity as well as politics).

There are really two points here. The first is the media revolution: the press, and public demand for a certain type of press, no long allow the private family lives and business dealings of politicians to remain the gossip of insiders. The country mice are now almost as well informed as the town mice who frequent Westminster and Whitehall, though often later and sometimes only when a scandal crisis breaks. That is the media revolution, but also the customer-driven market economy encouraged by the Conservative Party and enshrined in the Citizen's Charter: the customer is king (or queen). Idle to ask whether the press responds to what the public wants or moulds public demand if an impersonal market is the measure of things. If one result of Conservative ideology is the discomfort of Conservative politicians, some of the blame is their own.

Few really knew Lloyd George and few King George V. Everyone knows about John Major and his ministers, just as they know a good deal about the Queen and her extended family. Neither group has fared well: on balance, stories have been critical, if only because good news is no news while scandals, like bad news, sell papers. Sex stories sell best as far as the tabloids are concerned—for reasons that need not be discussed here but also because they are easier to understand; other misconduct stories are effective only if simple headlines suffice to tell the tale. The quality press can devote half a page several times to the complexities of financial misdealing; and even that simplifies what can take months of presentation in court and leave a jury mystfied at the end. Barbara Cartland is easier to follow than Le Carré's convoluted plots.

The second point is the social revolution: the shortening of the distance between political elite and public mentioned earlier. The political establishment now looks too much like ordinary people, sometimes richer but no less ordinary for that. Ideology is a factor too. Conservative populism has played its role (to stay with the party in power in Britain; the same could be said about Socialists in government elsewhere). Whether equality is the doctrine or just equality of opportunity, the result is the same. If John Major can become Prime Minister then Jack will be inclined to say he is good as his master—and entitled to criticise the behaviour of those who rule him. He may or may not be better himself, he may also have sexual adventures outside marriage or engage in grey financial transactions. Calling the kettle black may be a favourite pastime of the pot, but if pot-citizens want better behaviour than their own from their representatives, customer-populism encourages them to think it their right. In many cases, of course, rank and file party members may have higher (or more 'conservative') moral standards than their more sophisticated MPs: one thinks of Conservative county ladies or old fashioned trade-unionists, straight-laced both in their different ways.

Public opinion about politicians, MPs but others too, is pretty low as repeated surveys show. Indeed, it could hardly be lower. Levels of mistrust are such that one wonders how respondents would answer the question, would you buy a used car from one? Douglas Hurd, retiring as Foreign Secretary, revealed in the Commons that he had once, long ago, sold another Conservative MP his Sprite, but politician to politician is another matter. Linked to a generalised mistrust is the feeling that too many politicians are in politics to pursue their own interests, sometimes put more crudely as to line their own pockets. Put like that, unfair in most cases; but less unfair if one says that too many MPs, notably on the business-culture side of the House, are engaged in money-making activities of which the public tends to disapprove.

Politicians often seem unaware (or deliberately appear unaware, a clever but mistaken ploy) of the depth of feeling reported misbehaviour arouses against them all. Some immediate reactions in the Commons to the Nolan recommendations regarding conflict of interest showed this clearly enough: delayed action while MPs thought it over. When, earlier, criticism in the Scott report of one of his Cabinet members was leaked, the Prime Minister said 'I believe that the people of this country will make up their own minds about that behaviour.' They had already done so, of course, but that is how political leaders speak the world over; though it is never clear whether such statements are rhetorical flourish to impress their colleagues or whether they really do not believe what opinion polls already tell them.

Politicians in all parties are prone to dismiss public opinion that goes against them, but in the nature of things the reaction is strongest on the government side because they have the record of government to defend, unlike the opposition (Mrs Thatcher may have thought reference to what a Labour government did 15 years before a clever answer to criticism at Question Time but members of the public were unlikely to care). Thus the standard answers that public opinion is falsely reported (hence malicious joy when election result predictions turn out a few points wrong) or, if this fails, a discount of public opinion as misguided (how often have we heard ministers say on TV 'we must explain our policies better so that the voters understand them', rather than 'we must listen more closely and understand the voters better'?).

It was said of France's Fourth Republic that its politics was conducted in a house without windows, a reference to behaviour in the National Assembly where governments were made, unmade and remade between elections without much attention to opinion outside. Such inward-looking attitudes describe Britain just as well—though more surprising now than forty years ago, the time of the Fourth Republic, given the multiplication of opinion polls, some doubtless laid on every minister's desk. Some MPs may still believe that they understand 'their people', a finger on the constituency pulse and all that, but it hardly seems true. Most read (or glance through) the day's newspapers, they scan their mailbag (or an assistant's summary). But they rarely address what is reported. They are caught up in the games they play in their club.

When ministers are interviewed on television they run through rehearsed lines, ignoring questions, boasting of achievements they have not been asked about, attacking the opposition about which they have not been asked either. Does no one tell them privately afterwards that the public can recognise stone-walling on questions and believes hardly a word of the sales-talk it gets? This applies as well when charges of sleaze are discussed. The politicians style is as bland, the reaction of the public as disbelieving. Mandy's 'he would say that, wouldn't he' may have been a joke once, but it is a joke no longer. Trust of politicians is not high when that is a commonplace response to any explanation of themselves they offer.

But perhaps it is not that politicians are unaware of public feeling, whether about government policies or personal conduct: their style in answer to interviewers' questions on behalf of the public may be deliberate. In the short term a game of politics is about a politician's standing in the eyes of those on whom his present career depend—impressing a peer group of fellow MPs, the party Whips or the Prime Minister as the case may be. The aim is to show one can 'handle' the situation, say the right things (the line of the moment) or better still say nothing at all. That interpretation is reinforced by a misdirected fax intended for Jonathan Aitken in which a young PR consultant advised the (then still) minister on how to handle a further scandal story about to break in the press: 'The only audience that matters is the MP, the Cabinet, your colleagues in Parliament and your constituency'—the latter meaning constituency party officers.

MPs may be too insulated from the public and thus do not really believe that 'their people' feel the way they tell pollsters; they may sometimes decide to ignore public opinion because it is not the immediate consideration in calculating their careers (what the Whips think matters more). Whatever the reason, the fact is that politicians try to avoid the general issue of sleaze where possible, reinterpret criticism in weaker fashion if a position has to be taken, and as a group reserve the right to handle charges against one of their number themselves. Reactions to Nolan reflected this. If anything was to be done, it would be done by parliamentarians themselves, the people in the dock so to speak. Justified, of course, by phrases of parliamentary sovereignty—a good example of the British constitution's democratic deficit.

Stories of sexual misbehaviour account for some of the disrepute into which British politicians have fallen. These may not count as sleaze as the word is currently used in political commentary, the emphasis there being on dubious, sometimes corrupt, behaviour in the pursuit of material interests. Nevertheless, in ordinary conversation sleazy is used to describe tawdry or (Concise Oxford Dictionary) slatternly behaviour. Adultery need not be tawdry; three-in-a-bed or toe-sucking may simply be good fun for those involved. Taken all in all, however, tawdry does seem to describe many of the affairs. It is hard to say what being an 'honourable' member implies these days in relation to one's family. Explanations are given (even if only on the lines 'I can not explain, it was a moment of folly'); apologies are offered and bravely accepted by wives (no betrayed husbands revealed yet), less bravely by Conservative constituency party officers hoping to minimise embarrassment by ending the scandal and little concerned with the longer-term affects on public opinion of what inevitably appears (wrongly no doubt) as the party condoning misbehaviour.

It is often said that reporting about the domestic as distinct from financial affairs of politicians is a British vice, reflecting a prurient culture not found in France (the country always mentioned) where the privacy of politicians is respected in this regard. If stories about the sex lives of politicians do not surface so often in France, however, it may simply be that readers of its quality press are not interested (the French being more intellectual?), while the popular press has sex stories of greater appeal to retail. The pages in French illustrated magazines devoted to the affairs of British royals and Monegasque princelies is evidence of a prurient interest no different from that of British readers. German illustrated magazines with vast circulations are full of similar stories about personalities in every sphere of life.

The point might be that the public in those countries finds showbiz stars or sporting heroes (tennis for example) more interesting than politicians. But that, of course, is true of Britain also. Much is made of the seeming stream of newspaper stories about the sex affairs of ministers and other MPs. As far as the tabloids are concerned, the column space involved is small compared to stories about more interesting people (and that may include quite minor characters in Coronation Street or Eastenders). Political commentators present a somewhat distorted picture of media interest by concentrating on the stories published in the quality press, where politicians figure more prominently. That is not to diminish the impact of such stories, however, because behaviour the public may expect in showbiz (indeed, may be part of showbiz glamour) it may still find disturbing among politicians and others who present a 'respectable' image (as in the Bank of England).

Are sex sleaze stories related to a decline in public faith in the British system of government? Different stories about misbehaviour by politicians are highlighted in different countries. There is corruption on a grand scale on the one hand, operations quite beyond the scope of ordinary people, involving conspiracies, bribery in high places and millions of pounds taken. Such are the scandals reported in most other western democracies, in Italy, France and Spain, for example. On the other hand, there is unacceptable, sometimes but not necessarily illegal, behaviour by individuals, involving relatively modest sums of the sort that ordinary people can understand, even come across in their own lives. Here the link between sexual misbehaviour and financial misbehaviour can be seen. Great finance scandals can be dismissed as the work of a few 'criminal' politicians. The rest—and those relating to British MPs fall into that category—may seem peccadilloes by comparison. So, returning to sex, politicians' adventures, only a few bizarre, are all trivial compared to serial rapist headlines.

The paradox is that the effect on public opinion can be more serious because small scandals involve so many more politicians, ordinary politicians therefore, than great scandals. They may not rock a government (though Profumo did, the spy element promoting it to great scandal) but they cast doubt on politicians as a class. If people come to believe that politicians as a whole are at best no better than the rest of society (and people know how many of the rest cheat their marriage vows or their income tax returns) and many are probably worse than most of society, then questions about democracy become really serious because removal of a few criminals will not solve the problem.

A different sort of question, now often raised by those with positions to defend, is whether the private lives of public figures should concern the public. Some say they should not, so long at least as they perform their public duties properly. Some journalistic casuists may reply that ministers exhausted by too vigorous a pursuit of a bit on the side will not work well. More seriously, it was argued (notably by secret services during the Cold War) that sexual misconduct placed politicians at the mercy of blackmailers—hence, more generally, exposure is in the public interest. All that is a little unreal. A little more real, perhaps, though not much more, is the line 'if you can't trust him not to cheat in marriage, can you trust him in other matters?' Given the divorce rate, usually involving a 'guilty' party, that would exclude a lot of the population from work in which integrity is required.

More serious, however, is the question whether those who select party candidates, or those who vote for them, have the right to know about the person as well as the person's political views. No, say some; unlike vicars and scoutmasters, a politician's sexual conduct is not relevant to his job, while voters decide on party lines anyway. Others say yes. Selectors take personality into account in their choice of candidates: the fact that Conservative hopefuls are so often accompanied by their wives on the day is evidence of that. And the fact that election literature often has a happy family picture implies that voters too are concerned.

In some ways, moreover, the Conservative Party (more scandals seem to relate to its members than to Labour MPs, for whatever reason) created a problem for itself. Seventy years ago it attacked Socialists as advocates of free love. Mrs Thatcher blamed many of Britain's current problems on the permissive society of the sixties. John Major launched the Back to Basics slogan, a return to traditional morality. Voters can reasonably ask whether their representatives practise the family values their leader preached and journalists are entitled to pick up what appears as another example of politicians' double-talk.

It makes things difficult for democracy if one insists on democratic politicians who are also whiter than white in their non-political lives. Politicians would like voters to accept that so long as they govern well, deliver the goods, their private lives are none of the voters' business. But in a democracy it is for voters to decide for themselves what sort of a person they feel comfortable with as their representative; and to decide that, they have a right to know whatever they feel relevant to their judgement. No one has to stand for election, after all.

Let us turn to sleaze as more commonly used in relation to politics today, that is to say behaviour ranging from inappropriate use of one's position for financial gain to corruption proper. What makes the headlines differs from one country to another as already noted. Great scandals, relatively few in number but involving vast sums of money and considerable ramifications, often involving government itself through its minister, seem to characterise some European states. They become the focus of public attention and subsequently the focus of literature on sleaze. That does not mean there is not also a steady steam of smaller cases in those countries not touching government in the same way, perhaps taken for granted in societies where corruption in daily life is common. Italy might be a good example of that.

The stories that are reported as news of national interest are rather different in Britain. The integrity of individual ministers may be questioned, though rarely in respect of misuse of government office for monetary advantage. Charges relate more often to their time as back-benchers and in any case involve trivial sums by comparison to what has happened elsewhere, the cost of a holiday for example. That is not to say such treats are unproblematic: the issue may well be the relationship with the benefactor and its implications — as in Aitken's nights at the Paris Ritz, apparently paid (though this was disputed) by an Egyptian (owner of Harrods) seeking naturalisation, or in Mellor's Mediterranean cruise allegedly financed by the PLO's treasurer in London. Most businessmen would regard the sums involved as pocket money compared to the profits of fraud in the private sector or the sort of money private intermediaries can make in defence procurement. The nearest one comes to this in Britain may be Mark Thatcher's Gold (a book's title). No public corruption has been involved, but some must have been earned through the mistaken belief of foreign interests that he could influence British government on their behalf.

One may question the appropriateness of former ministers moving to the boards of private companies with which they have dealt in office; their move to the boards of what were public undertakings, where they themselves were responsible for privatisation procedures, is even more questionable. Clearly they now have non-executive salaries, but it is unlikely that this was a calculation in office, hence hardly a misuse of office for gain.

In any case, this is far from the misappropriation of public money found elsewhere in Europe. While most cases reported abroad seem to involve some sort of fraud through which public money is diverted to private pockets, that is not the character of most British complaints about MPs' behaviour. It is hard to think of cases where national politicians have defrauded the public purse; more occur in local politics perhaps—but that said, what is usually involved is false expense claims, travel for example, rather than some complex swindle.

The criticism of MPs is quite different. Some MPs have been discovered willing to take money from private sources in payment for what is essentially part of their parliamentary work, as in the Payment for Questions cases. Of course, since the investigative journalists concerned with the latter only contacted a sample of MPs, the two revealed (a third withdrawing in time) may be the tip of an iceberg of MPs who before the publicity saw nothing wrong with the practice; and since many have regularly put down Questions on behalf of interests which pay them consultancy retainers, it is clear that the practice is well established on a less cash-specific basis. More generally, though, the issue is whether MPs should supplement their parliamentary salaries by consultancy work. Many MPs, more Conservative than Labour but not excluding the latter, supplement their parliamentary salaries. They are paid because interests of one sort or another believe that they have special knowledge to sell or, more serious, may influence government on their behalf. Whether such activities (involving no fraud) are compatible with a parliamentary role can be questioned, but the point here is that this is another issue that sometimes surfaces elsewhere in Europe (and the USA) but catches little attention compared to great scandals there.

The scale and ramification of foreign scandals may seem at first sight to have more serious implications for democracy than what happens in Britain. They can destroy governments, even, as in Italy, a political system. But that is too easy a comparison, nice though it would be to think British democracy safer than others. A steady drip of small affairs builds up in people's minds to a picture that almost all politicians are untrustworthy, as opinion polls show. And, as suggested above, stories about the pursuit of personal interests by ordinary MPs, running a second business in addition to that for which they are elected and for which they collect their salary, implicates MPs as a whole in a way that scandals involving misappropriation of public funds may not. What debilitates a system is sleazy, tawdry, small-scale bad behaviour, 'conduct unbecoming' as it was called by the officers and gentlemen of good regiments in the past. A barrel full of bruised apples may create a worse impression than one of which the vendor agrees that one or two are rotten but can be picked out. In that light, Britain's position looks less healthy.

If it was always thus, politicians enriching themselves in one way or another, what has changed? The career choice of those who enter politics and the climate that surrounds them perhaps. As regards the first, many have noted that Parliament is increasingly dominated by career politicians, that is to say men (mainly) and women whose careers are almost entirely in politics. Their earlier jobs are often chosen as a way into politics rather than as a profession in its own right: work in a party office the bright young Tory's ideal on leaving Oxford. Even employment in a merchant bank, other graduates' dream chance of a real career, may simply be taken as a well-paid staging post where useful contacts are be made while grooming for adoption as a parliamentary candidate. And later, Parliament left for whatever reason, the politicians do not return to professions in which they are qualified by practice before; one networks and gets a job through one's political career. The difference with earlier times, then, is the degree to which politicians depend on politics for their livelihood. The independently wealthy are thinner on the ground on the Conservative side, time-served lecturers or trade union officials on Labour's.

Of course, young politicians may also have chosen that career because they actually want to play the game of politics rather than work in a stuffy office or start as salesmen; they may even have an ideological commitment to the programme of the party of their choice, budding conviction politicians in Mrs Thatcher's phrase. As Peter Riddell put it, however, while they may live for politics, they also live off politics. Is there a chicken and egg question here? Is the early career choice driven by the excitement of politics, the status that comes with membership of Parliament and the power that follows if one manages to climb the greasy pole, even the satisfaction of public service and the possibility of influencing state policy (for one must not be too cynical: politicians are often better intentioned than they are given credit for)? Or is it the other way round. young men (rarely still young women) see politics as a good way of making one's way in the world and pick the party that seems to offer them the best chance?

If one looks at some of Britain's dynamic young ministers (and a little cynicism may be allowed after all), did they chose the Conservative Party in student days (Oxford or Cambridge more often than not) because the Conservative Party offered better prospects for living off politics? It does have better business connections, companies are more likely to look to its MPs than to Labour's (though not exclusively) and if coopting board members, an expressed faith in business as the motor of Britain is more likely to appeal than even moderate Social Democracy. Indeed, if financial rewards are a consideration in career choice, it makes sense to chose the party that emphasises profit motive in its philosophy. That may sound like a politically biased view, but it was a Conservative MP, confronting the fact that accusations of financial misconduct are more often made against his side of the House than Labour's, who asked rhetorically, 'who would employ *them* outside this place?'. And to redress the balance, Socialist Parties offer excellent opportunities in countries where they are in positions of power.

The second aspect of change referred to above was the climate. Public opinion is shaped by a wider range of concerns than the alleged misconduct of MPs or their conflicts of interest. The appointment of MPs (ex-ministers or ministers to be) to well paid board positions is relevant. Networking (acceptable face) or misuse of contacts (unacceptable face) are mentioned in this respect and fuel the belief of many people that insiders—the politico-industrial complex—look after themselves. Often, moreover, non-executive board members seem to get a lot of money (or what looks like a lot to ordinary people) for very little work: sinecure job for the boys almost, since one can apparently receive board papers, even attend board meetings, without knowing what one's company is up to (thus in arms exports). During privatisation, vast sums are paid to merchant bankers and consultancy firms, sometimes linked to politicians' earlier or later careers, costing the taxpayer as much as an enterprise might lose if it remained public. And in recently privatised undertakings there is the spectacle of directors awarding themselves incomes unimaginable to the public except as lottery jackpots. Fat cats is the kindest headline, snouts in the trough also appears. One could go on—and on. The point here is that the image of politicians is caught up in a whole range of perceived scandals.

As Lord Blake, the historian, explained to the Nolan Committee, financial scandals are not new, 'but something has happened more recently and, I think it may be partly connected with the get rich quick mentality which has been prevalent quite a lot in the last 25 years, and this has had a kind of spreading effect.' We live in a society told that individuals are—and should be—motivated by the pursuit of wealth. Even good can not be done unless one pursues wealth first, as Mrs Thatcher claimed about the Good Samaritan in her notorious Edinburgh sermon.

If it is respectable to believe that personal interest comes first, if people are not expected to do a good job as habit or for conscience's sake, it is not surprising that politicians follow suit. And if Thatcherite Conservatism has contributed to that mood, the party can not be surprised if its careerists are more likely to be caught up in new form sleaze than its traditionalist old guard. Public opinion, however, has never really supported the acquisitive individualism implicit in Mrs Thatcher's claim that society does not exist, and stories about MPs money-making activities find an audience unsympathetic to the moneymakers. Another case of a party reaping what it has sown?

Until recently, parliamentary culture expected MPs to present public service as their public face, whatever their private business. The decline of traditional values and the arrival of new values has changed that. The Nolan Report felt that MPs now need guidance because people in public life are not always as clear as they should be about where the boundaries of accepted conduct lie. That, a county Conservative might say, is what happens when Parliament is not composed of gentry or their equivalent. The phrase 'acceptable standards' in ambiguous, however. It could be (and MPs will take it as) what the peer group accepts, as in the self-regulation of established professions. Should it mean, on the other hand, what is acceptable to the public or, a perspective even further from self-regulation, not just what the public will accept but what it wants? In any case, it seems an extraordinary state of affairs when the politicians who make the rules for the rest of society have difficulty in knowing how decent politicians should behave. Most ordinary citizens would have less difficulty in defining the boundaries, even if their definitions are likely to be simplistic (as, of course, were the Ten Commandments).

Public opinion shows that the behaviour of politicians needs to be regulated. In the words of a former *Times* editor, ordinary people find much of what some politicians do 'outrageous and amazing', and when they read that 'many politicians are lining their pockets when they should be minding the public good' it does not need the media to tell them that this is wrong. Blaming the media, accusing it of whipping up public opinion against ministers and MPs, is a misguided defence. Indeed, quite possibly the media have not reported enough. They follow up rumours but often depend on leaks for the evidence their stories need (especially in Britain where libel laws are more restrictive then elsewhere); and some offices are leakier than others.

It is often said, a caveat in research reports especially, that public opinion about politicians is not evidence that most politicians behave as badly as the public thinks. It could just as well be said that what looks like an avalanche of bad news to beleaguered politicians is only the tip of the iceberg, just as drink-driving cases in court are no measure of the problem. Some, politicians in the main, claim that reports give an exaggerated impression of sleaze, the public wrongly extrapolating from a few to the many. The public, for its part, believes that the cases which come to light are a random but typical sample. It is hard to know where along this spectrum the truth lies; but as already said, and it needs repeating, that reality matters less than the reality of public opinion.

What should be done? That now raises issues going well beyond the regulation of sleaze, beyond rules, because fundamental questions are now being asked about the job description of an elected representative in a modern democracy and about who decides it. To take job descriptions first, the current debate in inner circles, Nolan Committee and the House of Commons that is, is largely about conflict of interest and the acceptability of various forms of extra-curricular work. Focus is largely on the register of MPs' interests, the implication being that so long as sources of income are declared, only limited restrictions need be placed on how that income is earned.

MPs who defend consultancy and PR work often put an altruistic gloss on such activity: it keeps the politician in touch with the real world, notably the world of business that creates the wealth of the country. While this appears to echo earlier views that an MP should have the experience of a profession behind him, consultancy is quite different in fact. MPs are not talking of a profession such as law, nor about a managerial responsibility in business outside the House. They want to earn money off politics: it is as MPs that they are paid by outside interests. Given time constraints, of course, one can not hope to have a proper second job outside Parliament these days. Does that mean, as a number of Conservative MPs have claimed, that the professional middle classes would not enter Parliament if all they could get was the salary of an MP? 'To be quite honest, they are not going to come' said one. He was not using profession in the traditional way, of course, unless one believes all business a profession.

If true of them, whoever they are, what does one conclude? Perhaps the businessmen Lord Young thinks Parliament needs to attract by financial incentives are not the sort of people a democratic Parliament should have. If one wants to incorporate the country and run it as UK plc, one should hire managers — though whether elections are the best way of doing this is questionable. MPs are not managers, however, and businessmen's skills are not what is required. Membership of Parliament requires other skills for which there is no obvious market rate. If income considerations outweigh public service as a motive, one is unlikely to avoid sleaze and probably gets inappropriately qualified politicians as well.

There is another aspect to the regulations of MPs outside activities, and that is whether there should be any remunerated activities at all, at least as regards activities which take place inside Parliament or depend on the MP's parliamentary position. In most sectors of employment that is not be allowed. A professor may receive fees for outside work (though substantial consultancies, as distinct from a modest lecture fee require permission); if a professor wrote a note introducing a candidate to the admissions tutors of his university for a consideration from the parents (say a dozen bottles), there would be raised eyebrows at least, disciplinary action more likely. Are consultancy-paid 'facilitators' in Parliament not doing just that when they smooth contacts between a company and a ministry? And remember that not all employers are as liberal as universities. Most will not allow their staff to receive any fees for outside work done in office hours or connected to their office: thus a local government officer giving a a lecture must pay any fee received over to his authority and should share with colleagues any bottles given in lieu. Have the employers of MPs, the public, not the same right to expect the full time of their representatives? Should they claim refund of any outside payments MPs receive for work connected to their salaried employment in Parliament? Of course, MPs would regard that as a vulgar view of their role; the public probably not.

The reactions of politicians to stories about sleaze, misconduct, conflict of interest and the rest may be instinctive self-defence, but they also show a worrying complacency about the extent of public dissatisfaction. British democracy is still proclaimed the envy of the world, the present complaints relativised as only a storm in a teacup. But system politicians are destroying themselves elsewhere, and that is a warning. Politicians repeatedly use the phrase 'last chance saloon' to attack intrusive media, but they too may have reached a point where they need to change saloons. The stable is doubtless less polluted than the public is inclined to think (mixing the metaphor), but it is on public perceptions that democracy depends. And that means a cleansing of the stables well beyond what a rational health inspector might say is actually required.

Adapting the rules, tinkering as it will be called, will not do; nor will fine definitions of conflict of interest. The public makes little distinction between tax avoidance and tax evasion in its judgement of those into such games, whatever lawyers explain, and it will not make many distinctions in the case of MPs and their parliamentary-related outside work either. Having feasted too long, politicians may have to fast seriously for a while if they are to restore public confidence. And they will have to accept that it is the view of the public on what fasting means which must prevail. Parliamentary sovereignty is a formula in law; democracy means the sovercignty of the people.

If idols fall when their feet of clay are revealed, that may be a good thing for democracy, as for religion. Within limits. Democracy does not want leaders held in awe as idols are, but it does need politicians held in respect. In the past, respect (close to awe) came as part of the package; now respect means worthy of respect and has to be earned. As the media cut the distance between MPs and their electors and their searchlight uncovers ever more of MPs' lives, they had better be well shod.

There were no idols in the Temple at Jerusalem, of course, only the Ark of the Covenant, but worshippers needed coins to pay for the burnt offerings made in those days and money needed to be changed. One memorable day, however, the money-changers were chased out. Politicians need to dismantle the market in the Temple at Westminster if public reaction is not to undermine our demcracy. Remember that MPs were also chased out once.

America

BY ROBERT WILLIAMS

POLITICS in the United States has long had a reputation for sleaze. Scandals of both the financial and sexual varieties seem endemic and have contributed to a political environment in which politicians are held in low esteem. Periodically, there are outbreaks of puritanism and moral panic. In such periods, political candidates make a virtue of their virtue. Jimmy Carter, for example, made great political capital out of his personal integrity and by imputation characterised his rivals and opponents as somehow lacking in this crucial respect. The history of sleaze in the United States is complex and colourful, but the concern here is to explain how American attitudes to political office and its abuse have developed and to examine how recent cases highlight important features of the American political process. If the United States really does have 'the best legislature money can buy', it is important to understand both why this has occurred and what impact it has on public expectations and political conduct.

The analysis focuses both on the political framework in which sleaze occurs and on the principles which inform that framework. It draws attention to the fact that, where political authority and discretion are dispersed, it multiplies the opportunities for both corruption and the misuse of office for personal gain or advantage. It also identifies the close historical links between attitudes to public office, the growth of political parties and the ways in which elected officials define their roles. This will draw attention to the possible confusion of expectations which complicate contemporary analyses of sleaze. If what is being done is done by everybody, there is a presumption that what occurs is normal and legitimate. On the other hand, where there is institutional or partisan rivalry, allegations of abuse are rife and, once made, tend to lead to counter-allegations. As the political temperature rises, the need to appease any adverse public reaction or to stave off electoral defeat increases and a puritan plague infects the body politic. Forms of behaviour which were once acceptable are judged by new rules and found wanting. Politicians who fail to make a nimble enough transition from the old practices to the new are those most likely to be identified as associated with sleaze. But this identification may well have more to do with the timing than the substance of their actions.

Sleaze is an all-embracing term and, in the American context, this analysis will try to discriminate between different degrees and levels; the political implications of sleaze clearly vary according to the type and importance of the public office as well as the kind and degree of misuse. It will also attempt to discriminate between misuse and allegations of misuse. While both undoubtedly contribute to public perceptions of political integrity, it may be useful to discern how far the mere suggestion of improper behaviour contributes to the destruction of political careers and serves to encourage cynicism about all holders of public office.

The analysis will be illustrated by a number of examples or case studies of sleaze which will demonstrate recurring patterns of behaviour while identifying the exceptional or deviant. Sleaze is now so well established in the American political system that new procedures and even new public offices, for example the independent counsel,[1] have been invented to deal with it. The role of these new institutions in defining the significance and impact of sleaze will also form part of the conclusion. The initial focus of the discussion will centre, as most analyses of American politics do, on the values and intentions of the Founding Fathers, the framers of the American Constitution.

The political context and its transformation

Where government was both local and minimal and public office was a temporary part-time occupation engaged in by gentlemen who were independently wealthy, the incentives, opportunities and scope for corruption were not great. Conversely, organising for war and subsequently inventing a new federal government multiplied the opportunities for those in power to misuse their offices for private gain. But the Founding Fathers were realists, only too aware that the new political order would be vulnerable to the abuse of power in all its forms, and they were resolved in establishing the political structure, the principle of elections and the idea of term limits to ensure a degree of public accountability and control.

The American political system was designed by men who had few illusions about human nature. They assumed that men were born selfish, acquisitive and greedy and would always be so. To the Founding Fathers, the contemporary European belief in the perfectibility of man and in his innate natural goodness flew in the face of experience. If men were angels, there would be no need of government. But men are conspicuously not angels and government exists to curb their natural, selfish desires and, in particular, to prevent people from taking property that does not belong to them.

If human nature requires governmental restraint, the problem remained of how to control the governors. Politicians and public officials were men like other men and therefore subject to the same vices and temptations as those they governed. The remedy for greed and selfish ambition, or so the Founding Fathers thought, was to separate political authority in such a way as to set ambition against ambition.

They anticipated Lord Acton's famous dictum that 'power tends to corrupt and absolute power corrupts absolutely' and their solution was to divide power so comprehensively that the scope for corruption was severely reduced. While government needed to be able to curb the vices of the general population, to concentrate political authority in any one individual or institution inevitably brought corruption or abuse of power.

The working assumption of the Founding Fathers—that men were not angels—seems to have been confirmed by over two hundred years of political experience. Despite the fragmentation of power inherent in the political structures of the United States, there remained enough power in the White House, in Congress and in the Federal bureaucracy to permit the abuse of public office for personal and party gain. The opportunities, scope and forms of abuse have varied over time and in some cases what was once seen as normal, legitimate behaviour is now seen as improper, unethical, even illegal.

Patronage politics developed in the early nineteenth century and it became an established fact of American political life that the winner of a presidential election would reward his friends, supporters and campaign contributors with jobs in the federal government. At the inauguration of President Jackson in 1829, the White House was besieged by a huge mob of Jackson supporters seeking their due reward in the form of public appointments. While President Jackson is credited with institutionalising the 'spoils' system—the use of public office to reward supporters—he did so on the basis of a political theory which has both historical and contemporary resonances. He argued that anyone who holds public office for any length of time tends both to look upon that office as a form of private property and to see government as a means of promoting individual interests rather than the public interest. He pressed the case for term limits of four years for public appointments in the belief that rotation would help to destroy the perception of public office as the property of the office holder.

The slogan 'to the victors belong the spoils' was thus originally a radical democratic rallying cry and, by the 1860s, the spoils system had taken a firm grip on American life and politics.[2] The strength of this grip is illustrated by the remark of a delegate at a Republican Party National Convention who reputedly asked: 'what are we here for if not for the offices?' The patronage politics which had been introduced by the Jacksonians to destroy the status quo in 1829 later became a mainstay of the new established order. Patronage was now seen as the cohesive force, the cement which bound the organisation of political parties together and which linked the parties to government.

The most bitter disputes over patronage were not over the principle but rather about the respective roles of Congress and the presidency. Congress made repeated efforts, notably in the Tenure of Office Act of 1867, to wrest control of patronage from the Executive and the twenty years before the passage of the first major civil service reform act in 1883 saw a period of congressional supremacy. At this time, the custom of senatorial courtesy (consultation about public appointment in states and districts) became firmly entrenched and the exploitation of the spoils of office became more and more blatant.

The Grant administration (1869–77) was characterised by endemic scandal and thoroughgoing profiteering in all parts of government. The links between business and public officials had never been more intimate and scandal was piled upon scandal. Gold reserves, railroad shares, tax fraud and the sale of offices all featured prominently in the sleaze of the 1870s. Cabinet members resigned and congressmen were indicted. The Secretary of War was impeached for selling public appointments but escaped conviction on a technicality. Both the executive and legislative branches were tainted and in 1873 Congress confirmed its concern for self-interest by voting itself a 50% pay increase and backdated it for two years.

Outside political and business circles, the demand for reform continued to grow and the assassination of President Garfield by 'a disappointed office seeker' compelled the first major reform of the civil service by introducing competitive examination rather than bribery, nepotism or patronage as the principal means of recruiting bureaucrats. But these reforms counted for little in the political arena where political barons dominated the Congress. Congressional giants like Roscoe Conkling and James G. Blaine took the simple view that business corporations existed to subsidise and enrich politicians. Not surprisingly, the classic account of American politics in the late nineteenth century — James Bryce's *The American Commonwealth*, written in 1888 — had a chapter entitled 'The Best Men Do Not Go Into Politics'. This was an era in which many popular jokes about the morality of politicians originated. Henry Adams asked 'If a Congressman is a hog, what is a Senator?', while others defined an honest man in politics as someone who once bought, stayed bought. At the state level, things were even worse; it was said, for example, that Standard Oil could do anything with the Pennsylvania legislature except refine it.

The links between business and politics, their range, frequency and importance have always played a distinctive role in defining the nature of sleaze in the United States. It is more than coincidental that the greatest period of untrammelled economic enterprise and growth coincided with unparalleled levels of corruption and sleaze. Entrepreneurs sought political protection for their huge investments and politicians had clearly demonstrated that bribery was the most effective way of doing business with them. It was not uncommon during this period for Senators and Congressmen to introduce bills designed to restrict business activity with the sole intention of soliciting bribes to withdraw such proposals. While there was land and huge natural resources to exploit, this form of politico-business relationship flourished. The railroads, the oil companies and others were committed to the 'Gospel of Wealth' and were willing to enrich politicans to realise it.

A later period of rapid economic growth, the 'roaring twenties', saw a similar upsurge in sleaze and corruption at the highest levels of government. In the Teapot Dome scandal of the 1920s, the Secretary of the Interior was convicted of accepting a bribe. In another case the Attorney General was charged with trading political influence for cash but was acquitted at his trial—it should also be pointed out that his acquittal has been generally attributed to the bribery of a juror.

To most analysts, 'modern' American politics begins with President Franklin Roosevelt. He not only transformed the role and reach of the presidency but he greatly broadened the responsibilities of government and correspondingly expanded the size of the federal bureaucracy. Big government had arrived and, despite the Republican presidential victories in the 1950s, was clearly here to stay. The creation of new government departments, agencies and commissions, and the new role of government as a big spender, had an impact on the opportunities available to politicians and public officials interested in private gain. It also made government more important to more people. In the nineteenth century the federal government's activities, with few exceptions, had a minimal impact on the lives of ordinary Americans. The sleaze and corruption of Congress and cabinets, while no doubt reprehensible, was not particularly important or relevant to everyday life. But once the leviathan of the federal government began to reach into every aspect of daily existence, the public's interest in and concern about sleaze began to grow; as big government offered greater temptations to more people, public distrust of the federal bureaucracy and of Congress as institutions became a settled feature of American public opinion.

Sleaze in contemporary American politics: from the 1960s to today

In any discussion on sleaze in American politics, it is worth stressing that the two most important political scandals of the last forty years, Watergate and Iran-Contra, had little or nothing to do with sleaze defined in terms of private benefits through public office. The former originated in electoral 'dirty tricks' and ended in a criminal conspiracy to obstruct justice, while the latter arose out of a policy conflict between Congress and President Reagan. There were allegations about Nixon's relations to some rich business friends but they were not part of the Watergate scandal. Similarly, Oliver North was actually charged with accepting improper gifts, but this too was not central to the main Iran-Contra scandal.

The 1960s were famous for the sleaze that never happened. If the public had known then what is known now about the sexual behaviour of President Kennedy, the Kennedy myth might never have captured the public imagination. What media reticence about both Kennedy and

Martin Luther King suggests is that the amount of sleaze uncovered in any particular period depends a great deal on how hard people look for it and how willing they are to publicise it. In this latter respect, there seems to have been a sea-change in media attitudes relating to the private lives of politicians, as both Edward Kennedy and Gary Hart discovered when their presidential ambitions were dashed by media exposure of their sexual behaviour, although less so in relation to their financial affairs.

The most striking publicised example of financial sleaze in American political life in the 1960s concerned Adam Clayton Powell, who represented Harlem in the House of Representatives. Elected black politicians were a rare species in the 1960s and the flamboyant Powell received a great deal of media attention. In 1967 the House of Representatives refused to seat Powell and an investigation found that he had abused his position as a committee chairman to provide pleasure trips for himself and for others at the public expense and had employed his wife on the House Committee payroll. The controversy surrounding his exclusion highlighted two central features of sleaze in Congress: first, that all organisations have some of the attributes of a club, and normally club members look after each other and defend the club against external threats. But Powell was a maverick and not part of the network, so when he got into trouble the normal club loyalties did not apply. Second, he was black. His exclusion was seen as racially motivated, as a way of dealing with a high profile black who had got too big for his boots. Black leaders outside Congress complained bitterly that many white congressmen had behaved in similar fashion to Adam Clayton Powell and had escaped without any disciplinary action, let alone expulsions.

The highest ranking American politician to have been brought down by sleaze was Vice-President Spiro Agnew, who was forced to resign his office in 1973 because of allegations of bribery. Agnew had previously been a county chief executive and then Governor of Maryland, in which capacities it was alleged that he had, over a ten-year period, solicited and received bribes from engineering contractors seeking public contracts. After extensive plea bargaining, he was allowed to plead 'nolo contendere' (unwillingness to contest) to a single misdemeanour charge of tax evasion arising from bribes in 1967. The judge in the case agreed the plea bargain 'in the light of the overwhelming national interest'. Agnew contrived to protest his innocence, claimed he was the victim of publicity-seeking prosecutors and asserted that the so-called bribes were no more than campaign contributions. He further asserted that it was normal practice in Maryland to give public contracts to one's friends rather than one's political rivals or opponents.

From the 1970s onwards, numerous scandals have afflicted both Congress and the executive branch. While there are some similarities in these scandals, there are also institutional differences which suggest that they require separate analysis. Mark Twain is said to have observed 'there is no distinctly native American criminal class, except perhaps Congress'. Students of congressional scandals over the past twenty-five years might be forgiven for thinking that his observation was directed at the late twentieth century Congress rather than its nineteenth century predecessors. The record shows regular eruptions of scandal which have attracted intense media attention and contributed to the dwindling levels of public confidence.[3] From 'Koreagate' in the late 1970s to the Abscam affair in the early 1980s, the impression was given that some members of Congress were prepared to sell their services not only to domestic lobbyists but to foreigners and foreign governments as well. The late 1980s saw a whole crop of examples including the Keating Five and the Jim Wright affair. It seemed that even very senior figures in Congress were unable to resist the temptations of office. In the 1990s, the Rostenkowski affair and the House Banking scandal appeared to confirm what many people already believed, that members of Congress were using their offices to give themselves financial opportunities not available to those who elected them. But this catalogue conceals as much as it reveals about congressional behaviour and it is important to examine the individual cases before any general conclusion about sleaze in Congress can properly be drawn.

One consequence of Watergate was that any conduct with even a hint of impropriety about it had the word 'gate' added to it to facilitate easy public recognition. When a lobbyist, Tongsun Park, working on behalf of the South Korean intelligence agency, was indicted in August 1977 on charges of conspiring to bribe members of Congress, it was inevitable that the media would label the affair 'Koreagate'. Park gave evidence to a congressional committee that he had made gifts and contributions to thirty present or former congressmen. The unusual aspect of this case was that although one former congressman, Richard Hanna, spent a year in prison as a co-conspirator and three others were formally reprimanded by the House of Representatives for failing to report gifts from Park, the public and political reaction was limited. Two of those reprimanded in October 1978 successfully stood for re-election only a month later. The lack of public outrage confirmed the belief that the practice of legislators of accepting money from lobbyists was commonplace.

If those involved in Koreagate mostly escaped public and political censure, the Abscam affair three years later wrought a heavier congressional toll. Abscam was an FBI operation in which agents posing as Arab businessmen offered large sums of money to a number of Senators and Representatives for promises of help in evading immigration restrictions. Abscam (Abdul scam) was a deliberate, conscious effort to identify those members of Congress who were ready to sell their influence if the price was right. In the event, six Representatives and one Senator were caught on FBI cameras accepting bribes and were subsequently sentenced to terms of imprisonment. All seven men had failed to win re-election or had been expelled or resigned from Congress. To save his pension, Senator Harrison Williams resigned just before the Senate voted to expel him. Their defence lawyers argued either that the FBI operation was illegal entrapment or that, although they accepted money, there had been no subsequent unethical or illegal behaviour on the defendants' parts.

The case of the Keating Five brought into sharp relief the importance of context in understanding sleaze in Congress. The Keating Five case served to put public faces to the massive Savings and Loan scandal which lost the American taxpayers billions of dollars. In 1987, five Senators met regulators of the savings and loan industry to ask for favourable treatment for Charles Keating, whose Californian savings and loans failure was later to cost the public purse $2 billion. Mr Keating was a major contributor to the Senators' campaign funds. Constituency service plays a large part in defining what Representatives and Senators do and interventions of the sort described above are not uncommon. What seemed to make a difference is that five Senators from different states do not usually meet together on behalf of one person. There was also a very close proximity between the receipt of the contributions and the Senators' intervention. Even more unusually, the meetings took place without any senatorial staff present. One of the Five, Senator Alan Cranston, admitted that he would not have done for an ordinary constituent what he had done for Keating. The Senate Ethics Committee found that Cranston had continued to intervene on his behalf long after he knew that Keating was the subject of a criminal investigation. It concluded that Cranston's help was effectively bought for almost $1 million in campaign contributions. The Committee's decision not to discipline four Senators but to censure Cranston, who was suffering from cancer and had already announced his decision not to stand for election, was greeted with derision by public interest groups and the liberal press. The *New York Times* added the six committee members to the five Senators and reported the matter as the case of the 'Keating 11'. Keating himself received a term of imprisonment for fraud and, when asked if he thought his contributions had bought the Senators' services, replied 'I certainly hope so'.

If Congress has been inclined to take a generous view of what counts as constituency service, some individual members, including the most powerful men at the House, have been forced to resign as a result of allegations of financial impropriety and breaches of Congress's own rules. In 1989, the Speaker of the House, Jim Wright, was forced to resign.[4] Wright had come under investigation on dozens of charges including influence peddling, accepting a job and a car for his wife from a supporter and violating campaign laws by selling large quantities of a book of his speeches to campaign contributors and keeping the royalties.

In 1994, another congressional giant was toppled. Dan Rosten-

kowski, the powerful chairman of the House Ways and Means Committee, was indicted on 17 counts of fraud and embezzlement. The
indictment claimed he had taken more than half a million dollars from
the public purse 'to benefit himself, his family and his friends'. The
pattern of sleaze included misappropriating public funds, charging
Congress for expensive furniture which was given to friends, cashing in
$50,000 worth of stamp privileges and placing 'ghost' employees on his
payroll.

This review of the most publicised cases of sleaze in Congress enables
us to weigh their significance and the public and institutional responses
to them. Certainly, Congress now treats ethics questions more seriously
than it once did. It has been noted that 'formal controls concerning
congressional ethics before 1977 were poorly understood and little
heeded.'[5] But in the view of at least one 'victim', Speaker Jim Wright,
the pendulum may have swung too far in the opposite direction. In his
resignation speech, he warned his colleagues not to engage in 'mindless
cannibalism' in their panic over the potential political impact of ethics
changes.

The furore over the House Banking scandal in the early 1990s
certainly suggests that even the hint of sleaze can be extremely damaging
to legislators' careers, even where the alleged improprieties appear to be
trivial or unsubstantiated. The Banking scandal revealed in 1992 that
House members enjoyed free overdraft protection for bounced cheques,
a facility which they had enjoyed for about 150 years. The media
criticism this practice attracted made no mention of the fact that the
cheques were written on a pool of funds that involved no public subsidy
or taxpayer loss. Nonetheless, the impact was so great that some 43
members of the House of Representatives announced their retirement.
The 1992 congressional election produced the greatest turnover in the
House since the election immediately after World War II, and a central
cause of this turnover was the banking scandal which symbolised much
that was wrong with Congress. It was not seen as accidental that
Democrats were more likely to bounce cheques than Republicans, but
rather this fact 'was used to illustrate the possibility that long time
control of the legislature by one political party could tempt members of
that party to use a public institution for private gain'.[8] It is also at least
plausible that this same perception helps to account for the even greater
electoral turnover in the mid-term elections in 1994.

Congress is not a popular institution and, viewed collectively, members of Congress are not popular people who inspire public trust. A
1992 survey reported that the percentage of Americans who had a great
deal of confidence in Congress fell from 28% in 1984 to only 10% in
1992. In a Gallup poll, also taken in 1992, which invited respondents
to rank the professional ethics of a variety of occupational groups,
members of Congress did not do well. Their rating score was only a
quarter of doctors and professors, and while their ethics were judged to

be a few percentage points above car salesmen, they were below those of estate agents.

The paradox of congressional unpopularity is the very high re-election rates of incumbent Senators and Representatives. While some observers see Congress as 'the lightning rod for political frustrations, a metaphor for larger ills and a scapegoat for the sins of the people',[7] voters keep re-electing the same people. The paradox is partly resolved by the notion of distance. When constituents have dealings with their local Representative, they are usually satisfied and even impressed and members of Congress give constituency service a very high priority. But viewed from afar and without personal knowledge, the other members of the institution seem much more self-serving, in such circumstances the rational response is to re-elect the one you know and condemn the institution. A further elaboration of this paradox of distance is the notion that voters re-elect the same people for decades yet simultaneously support the notion of term limits[8] These themes also emerge in relation to the executive branch.

Executive branch sleaze

In this section the focus is primarily on the scandals which have afflicted the Reagan, Bush and Clinton administrations. The Carter administration had one high profile case of sleaze involving Bert Lance, whose informal and unorthodox financial stewardship of banks in Georgia made his appointment as Director of the Office of Management and Budget politically unacceptable, but its troubles were as nothing compared to the sleaze which characterised the Reagan administration. In all, more than a hundred members of his administration had allegations made against them. This seems to represent a qualitative as well as quantitative shift, because 'during other presidencies, scandals such as Watergate seemed to multiply from a single cancer; the Reagan administration, however, appears to have suffered a breakdown of the immune system, opening the way to all kinds of ethical and moral infections'.[9]

The attempt by the Democratic Party to make sleaze an election issue in 1984 failed partly because of Reagan's popularity and partly because the Democrats had their own sleaze factor in the form of the vice-presidential candidate, Geraldine Ferraro, whose financial affairs were subject to investigations linking her husband to organised crime interests. Despite the lack of success in using sleaze for electoral purposes, the 1980s saw a whole series of allegations against high ranking officials in the Reagan Administration. The first to fall was the President's National Security Advisor, Richard Allen, who resigned in 1982, having been on leave of absence from November 1981 after facing charges of having accepted gifts including $1000 from a group of Japanese journalists. In January 1984, two other senior figures resigned. The Attorney General, William French Smith, stepped down after persistent allegations of tax evasion. At the same time, Deputy Secretary of

Defense, Paul Thayer, resigned to contest charge of insider trading brought by the Securities and Exchange Commission. In September 1984, the Secretary of Labor, Raymond Donovan, became the first serving Cabinet member to be indicted on criminal charges of fraud and forgery and, despite his acquittal in 1987, his public career was brought to an end.

Ed Meese, Smith's successor as Attorney General, was under an almost constant cloud of sleaze allegations. His confirmation of appointment was delayed by the Senate and although he survived a special counsel investigation, he was unable to shake off a number of allegations of misconduct involving bank loans and reciprocal favours. This had its impact on the Department of Justice and, in 1988, the resignations of several senior staff were an indication of their growing belief that the department was suffering because of the Attorney General's continuing difficulties. Finally, in August 1988, Ed Meese resigned.

The last high profile example of Reagan administration sleaze was the conviction of Michael Deaver in 1987. Deaver had been Deputy Chief of Staff in the White House during Reagan's first term and was known to be exceptionally close to the President. Deaver left the government in May 1985, reputedly for financial reasons, and set himself up as a well-connected lobbyist for corporations as well, it seems, as for foreign governments. His convictions were not for breaches of the ethics legislation relating to lobbying but rather for lying to Congress and a grand jury about his contacts as a lobbyist. In short, he was not convicted for his activities but rather for his lack of truthfulness about those activities. At his trial, Deaver employed the same defence that his old boss, President Reagan, had used during Iran-Contra by claiming he could not remember details.

Below the White House and Cabinet levels, the Reagan administration suffered from other much publicised cases of sleaze. A major congressional report on one government department, Housing and Urban Development, found that 'during the 1980s, HUD was enveloped by influence peddling, favoritism, abuse, greed, fraud, embezzlement and theft. In many housing programs objective criteria gave way to political preference and cronyism, and favoritism supplanted fairness. 'Discretionary' became a buzzword for "giveaway".'[10] It should be noted at this point that whereas political appointees constitute less than 2% of the staff of the executive branch, almost all of the charges, indictments and convictions for corruption which occurred during the Reagan Administration involved this group of political appointees. The significance of this fact will be discussed further in the conclusion to this analysis.

President Bush, having witnessed at close hand the damage done to the Reagan administration by sleaze allegations, was eager to push through reforms to create a cleaner public imaghe, and by the standards of its predecessor, the Bush Administration was relatively free from the taint of sleaze. Its almost conspicuous casualty was the President's Chief of Staff, John Sununu, who resigned in December 1991. Sununu's alleged offences seemed relatively trivial. They involved the use of government planes and cars for his personal benefit; the most publicised example was his use of a government plane to fly to Aspen to give a speech about skiing that was paid for by an organisation that lobbies on behalf of the winter sports industry. Sununu thought the allegations were much ado about nothing but he had played so effectively the part of 'junkyard dog to the president's labrador'[11] that his many political enemies used the sleaze allegations to force his resignation.

President-elect Clinton vowed to clean up sleaze, and immediately following his election, he barred members of his transition team from involvement in public matters that might affect their personal finances or those of their clients. On 9 December 1992, 'Clinton required some 1100 officials in the new administration to sign pledges that they would not engage in either formal or informal lobbying activities with their former agencies for five years after leaving government service'.[12] Similar restrictions were placed on White House staff and, remembering the case of Michael Deaver, a lifetime prohibition was imposed on staff becoming registered lobbyists for other countries.

But Clinton found that pledges and bans were not panaceas for sleaze eradication. Within two years, sleaze allegations were reaching into the Oval office itself. Clinton faced a dilemma in that he wanted to appoint people with relevant experience but he found it hard to identify people who were not, in some way, associated with the sort of lobbying that his pledges and bans were designed to discourage. His initial appointments raised some eyebrows; for example Ron Brown, who was appointed as Secretary of Commerce, was a partner in a law firm that dealt with BCCI, the government of Abu Dhabi, several Japanese corporations, Baby Doc's Haiti and numerous trade associations. It was observed that few of his predecessors had 'simultaneously worn more hats or raised more questions about potential conflicts of interest than Ron Brown'.[13]

Ron Brown's financial affairs have subsequently become the subject of investigation by an independent counsel, but so too have the affairs of several other members of the Clinton Cabinet. Henry Cisneros, Secretary of Housing and Urban Development, was investigated for allegedly lying to FBI background investigators about payments to a former mistress. Secretary of Transportation, Frederico Pena, was investigated over allegations of misappropriating federal funds to build Denver's new airport. The most conspicuous Cabinet casualty to date is Mike Espy, who resigned his post as Secretary of Agriculture in 1994. He was accused of accepting gifts, in the form of tickets to sporting events, travel on corporate aircraft and a college scholarship for a female friend. The alleged benefactor is the Tyson Food Corporation, America's largest chicken producer, whose slaughterhouses are inspected by the Department of Agriculture. The Tyson Corporation is based in Arkansas and has been a major campaign contributor to Bill Clinton. Its legal adviser, Jim Blair, has acted as investment adviser to Hillary Rodham Clinton, the President's high-profile wife.

Bill Clinton came to power promising to clean up Washington, but his administration has acquired a reputation for casual ethics and parochial cronyism. If some of the President's Cabinet appointees have become the subject of sleaze allegations, Clinton is unique among modern Presidents in having serious allegations made about both his own ethical standards and those of the First Lady. The President and Mrs Clinton have been interviewed on more than one occasion by the independent counsel investigating what has become known in America as the Whitewater scandal.[14] If Whitewater narrowly refers to a failed land speculation in Arkansas by the Clintons and its relation to a bankrupt savings and loan company run by a friend and partner in Whitewater, it is used more broadly to refer to a set of Arkansas political or business malpractices, as well as to allegations of a White House cover-up.

Whitewater raises more questions than answers. How did Bill Clinton fund his political campaigns and what is his relationship with his principal backers? How was Hillary Clinton so successful in the speculative commodities markets? More generally, were savings and loans used as piggy banks by the Little Rock political elite and was taxpayers money used to subsidise the Clintons? Have President Clinton and his staff used their official positions to conceal possible evidence and to interfere with investigations? In short, was political influence used to gain personal financial benefit and was political influence used to cover it up? The answers to these questions, which are being sought by an independent counsel and two congressional committees, will play adecisive factor in determining the outcome of the 1996 presidential election. If Watergate was characterised as a cancer on the presidency, Whitewater is more a persistent haemorrhage. The President who promised 'the most ethical administration ever, has been forced to spend a disproportionate amount of time defending himself and his wife from damaging sleaze allegations.

Conclusion

It might be concluded from the numerous cases discussed above that the executive and legislative branches of the national government operate in a lawless and carefree environment. Nothing could be further from the truth. In fact, 'American ethics rules are the toughest in the world'.[15] The centre-piece of ethics legislation is the Ethics in Government Act of 1978, which was effectively a response to the Watergate scandal. Its central provisions are the requirements it places on senior executive branch officials to complete financial disclosure forms for government and public scrutiny and the creation of the office of independent counsel whose responsibility is the criminal investigation and prosecution of senior executive branch officials. It established an Office of Government Ethics (OGE), which was reorganised as a separate agency in 1989. The functions of the OGE are to oversee the disclosure process and to enforce the standards of conduct required by statute or executive order. Many of the recent examples of sleaze were exposed through the disclosure requirement and the activities of independent counsels. President Bush's Ethics in Government Reform Act was passed in 1989 and while it did not achieve its objective of establishing common ethical standards for all three branches of government, it did include more stringent restrictions on post-employment lobbying and bans on some types of honoraria for employees of all three branches.

What is undeniable is that there is a deep-rooted suspicion of government and a widely held perception that politicians and bureaucrats are ineffectual and corrupt. It is important, though, to probe behind the headlines to examine a little more carefully what message is being conveyed. A recent poll reported that public trust in government had slumped dramatically from 76% in 1964 to 44% in 1984 and then to the disturbingly low figure of 19% in 1994. In 1964 and 1984, it was scarcely possible to measure the small number of people who felt you could never trust the government, but by 1994 that figure had reached 9%. This data shows clearly a disaffected· electorate. The rejection of President Bush, the surprisingly strong showing of Ross Perot in the 1992 presidential elections and the Republican capture of Congress in 1994 all point in the same direction: public disaffection with the status quo and a strong anti-incumbent political mood.

What is less clear is whether the evident public dissatisfaction is closely related to sleaze or whether it is more a symptom of America's relative economic decline and the stagnant politics of gridlock between the White House and Capitol Hill. If the causal weights to be attached to competing explanations of the public distrust of government are hard to calculate, what can be measured is the extent to which the public expressions of discontent reflect the behaviour of the wider society. In the 1992 presidential election, Bill Clinton received 43% of the vote, but as only about 50% of the electorate voted, he actually received the support of only 22% of the people. Similarly, in the Republican 'sweep' of the 1994 mid-term elections, Republican candidates picked up just over 50% of the vote but only 38% of the eligible electorate bothered to vote. In short, only about 20% of the electorate voted Republican. One lesson to be drawn from this electoral analysis is that assertions of widespread public outrage need not be accepted at face value.[16] There are many reasons why people do not vote, and while cynicism or anger are undoubtedly among them, so are complacency, satisfaction or indifference.

It is also useful to discriminate between general expressions of discontent and the specific incidents of sleaze discussed above. We have already noted the paradoxical attitude to Congress reflected in institutional condemnation, together with the regular re-election of incumbents, and a similar paradox operates in connection with the federal bureaucracy. Surveys suggest that while there is a public plague on bureaucracy in general, personal impressions of bureaucratic encounters are largely positive. This paints a bizarre picture of a world which is populated by individual legislators and bureaucrats who are honest, caring and effective, working in a political system which is seen as corrupt, remote and incompetent. So far as it is possible to tell, the levels of sleaze in the career civil service are very low, but the excesses of the relatively small proportion of political appointees, especially during the Reagan administration, have given all public officials a negative public image.

Analysis here has focused on American sleaze as primarily financial in character. This is not to suggest that the United States is devoid of the sex scandals which attract so much attention in Britain. Bill Clinton's presidential campaign was plagued by such scandals and his public image as President has been tarnished by subsequent allegations. The popular wisdom is that Presidents are expected to be dignified in their conduct, traditional in their family values and conventional in their sexual behaviour. At the congressional level, the consequences of unconventional sexual behaviour seem to depend more on geography and political culture than on the behaviour itself. Thus, in a liberal district of Boston it was possible for a homosexual congressman not only to 'come out' but to survive employing a male prostitute in his Washington office. In more traditional parts of the United States, for example Mormon-dominated Salt Lake City, a political career can be destroyed by revelations of adultery.

The emphasis here has been on financial sleaze because money is so important in American politics and government. At both congressional and presidential levels, the need to attract private funding is crucial to electoral success, the growth of fundraising and contributing groups, called Political Action Committees, has exacerbated the problem of campaign contributors exercising undue influence over public officials. The traditional distinctions between the roles of political parties and interest groups have almost disappeared as interest groups and their PACs have sought to determine the choice of candidates and the outcome of elections. The dependance of politicians on private contributions means that they are not well placed to resist the demands of institutionalised lobbyists.

If private money in public elections is the major source of sleaze where elected politicians are concerned, the appointment of political executives raises other difficulties. Clearly, if appointees come from the world of business or corporate law, they will have a variety of contacts and connections which may raise questions of conflicts of interest. This is exacerbated by their temporary status, as individuals in public office are not likely to wish to alienate their former and prospective employers. The so-called 'revolving door' through which people move back and forth between the public and private sectors is almost bound to create some ethical confusion.

To understand the emphasis on sleaze in contemporary American politics, we also need to understand the role of the media and the increasing levels of partisanship. The role of the media in American politics has changed dramatically in the past thirty years. In the 1960s, there was little or no coverage either of President Kennedy's liaisons or of the complexities surrounding President Johnson's family finances. The double impact of the Vietnam War and Watergate seemed to have shaken the media into a different role. Instead of accepting what they were told and not prying into private matters, journalists and editors began to see themselves as guardians of the nation's conscience, always on the alert to expose wrongdoing. More recently, the media seem to have become pro-active in that they now create stories as well as cover them. Journalism, like politics, has become more aggressive, less deferential and more attack-oriented. Scandals sell newspapers and improve ratings and it therefore pays to make mountains out of molehills. In so doing, sleaze becomes trivialised and a free ticket to the Superbowl becomes equated with large-scale fraud or corruption.

It would be unfair and inaccurate to claim that sleaze in contemporary American politics is a media invention, but it certainly receives closer, more intensive and extensive coverage than ever before. The disciples and descendants of Woodward and Bernstein, the 'heroes of Watergate', are determined not to miss an opportunity to claim their own Pulitzer Prize for investigative journalism and the new disclosure laws and multiple investigations provide much raw material. The changing role of the media has been described in canine terms as an evolution from the lapdog of the 1960s to the watchdog of the 1970s and ultimately to the junkyard dog of the 1980s and 1990s. Certainly, the media deference, even sycophancy which once characterised relations with the presidency has long since gone and modern presidents have been forced on the defensive by media intrusions and attacks.

On the other hand, if the media have helped to trivialise and publicise sleaze, much of their raw meat has been provided by politicians themselves. Before the passage of the Ethics in Government Act in 1978, the rules about conflicts of interest, the receipt of gifts and the limitations on sources of external income were poorly understood, little heeded and inconsistently applied. In the post-Watergate world, and as a result of growing public and media attention, politicians began to pay serious attention to ethics and rules. Their attention was focused not just by the prospect of ethics charges or independent counsel investigations but, for members of Congress, by fear of retribution at the ballot box.

But the recognition of the potential career damage that could be achieved by sleaze allegations provided opposition parties with a valuable weapon to beat incumbents. In the 1980s and into the 1990s, the Democratically-controlled Congress was able and willing to pursue allegations against the Republican-controlled executive branch. Thus, Congress used the Iran-Contra scandal to beat the Republican White House, but when a Democrat was elected to the presidency in 1992, the majority in Congress showed little interest in pursuing the Whitewater allegations. At the same time, the Republican minority in Congress, especially in the House, felt marginalised and excluded by the Democratic majority, hence Newt Gingrich's concerted and successful sleaze attack on Speaker Jim Wright in the 1980s.

Despite the high profile of sleaze issues in Congress, there is little sign of agreement on the reform of campaign finance laws. Congress continues to regulat and to investigate itself, and the congressional enthusiasm for holding the executive branch to account is not matched by a willingness to address what many observers and politicians recognise as a major source of sleaze—the implicit reciprocity involved in the soliciting and offering of campaign contributions. Within the executive branch, the career civil service has escaped largely untarnished by sleaze allegations, yet there seems no prospect that the sleaze problems of political appointees are likely to lead to an enhanced role for the career service.

Present evidence suggests that the future will be a replay of the present. Strict, even over-strict, ethics laws are in place and will stay in place and this will give further opportunities for organised mud slinging, aided and abetted by a rapacious mass media. We have already seen Newt Gingrich, new Republican Speaker of the House, under attack for sleaze and forced to revise a multi-million dollar book contract with Rupert Murdoch. If they can, the minority Democrats will use sleaze to bring Gingrich down, but at the same time the Republican leaders in Congress are ready to use the sleaze of Whitewater to undermine the Clinton presidency. The interpenetration of business values and public ethics intrinsic to lobbying, the tide of public disaffection, the changing role of the media and increased partisanship in national politics have all contributed to defining the role of sleaze in contemporary American politics. President Clinton's promise to deliver 'the most ethical administration ever' has not been fulfilled and his failure suggests that sleaze will remain an important, negative factor in American politics.

1   See K. J. Harriger, 'Separation of Powers and the Politics of Independent Counsels', *Political Science Quarterly*, Summer 1994.
2   See P. P. van Riper, *History of the United States Civil Service* (Row Peterson and Co, 1958).
3   See *Congressional Ethics: History, Facts and Controversy* (Congressional Quarterly Press, 1992) and *Political Scandals and Causes Célèbres Since 1945* (St James Press, 1991).
4   See J. M. Barry, *The Ambition and the Power: the Fall of Jim Wright* (Viking, 1989).

5   J. Dumbrell, 'Corruption and Ethics Codes in Congress', *Corruption and Reform*, 1991/2, p. 148.

6   C. Stewart, 'Let's Go Fly a Kite: Correlates of Involvement in the House Bank Scandal', *Legislative Studies Quarterly*, 1994/4, p. 521.

7   C. W. Dunn and M. W. Slann, *American Government: A Comparative Approach* (Harper Collins, 1994), p. 494.

8   See H. G. Frederickson and D. G. Frederickson, 'Public Perceptions of Ethics in Government', *The Annals*, January 1995.

9   *Time*, 25 May 1987.

10 United States Congress, House Committee on Government Operations, *Abuse and Mismanagement at HUD*, 1990, p. 3.

11 *Economist*, 7 December 1991.

12 J. P. Burke, 'The Ethics of Deregulation—or the Deregulation of Ethics' in J. J. Dilulio (ed), *Deregulating the Public Service* (Brookings, 1994), p. 64.

13 *Economist*, 19 December 1992.

14 See R. J. Bartley (ed), *Whitewater* (Dow Jones and Co, 1994).

15 *Economist*, 19 December 1992.

16 See B. Barber, 'Letter from America', *Government and Opposition*, 1995/2.

Denmark

BY JØRGAN GRØNNEGAARD CHRISTENSEN

SOME years ago it was revealed how intelligence services in the past bugged leading Communists. In a review of a book on Danish military intelligence, a historian referred to the source of this story as 'an alcoholic former Prime Minister'. With just one adjective, the reviewer brought attention to the ambiguous norms of Danish parliamentary life. The media cultivate their own norms which respect the privacy of Danish MPs. They never report on members' private lives; thus, for example, the drinking habits of MPs and ministers are not a matter of public concern and their family lives, their affairs and their sexual habits are rarely reported. After their death, however, the norms do not appear. Reporters, fellow politicians, former wives and academic historians feel free to reveal their secrets without having to engage in extended discussion of the sudden relevance of this information as belonging to the public domain.

This is not the only inconsistency. News reporters are not bound by the same concern for privacy when it comes to politicians' financial interests and other material interests, as several MPs and ministers over the years have found out. A few nights in the suite of the Paris Hotel Ritz led to the dismissal of a then young and ambitious Minister of Education. That same politician did not learn her lesson: a decade later she rented an apartment in central Copenhagen, belonging to a large Danish bank, while maintaining her official address in the provinces, thus enabling her to cash in the tax-free cost-of-living allowance to which MPs living beyond a certain distance from the Copenhagen central station are entitled. This time she had to resign as president of her party's group in parliament, although once more she had not broken any legal rules.

As a former minister, she has been entitled to a lifelong pension. Like other former ministers, she claims this pension although, as an MP, she is compensated for loss of other income earned at the labour market. However, if a former minister is reappointed to a Cabinet post the pension is suspended; the same applies if the minister should accept a position with civil servant's status. All this is regulated through the legislation on ministers' pay and pension. This act has not foreseen how membership of the European Union has expanded the sphere of operation for national politicians, and consequently, does not specify what happens if a minister, past or present, is appointed to the Commission. However, in the two instances where this happened, the appointee gave up his pension while serving on the Commission. When in 1994 the Danish government made the MP and former minister mentioned above its candidate for the Commission, she did not immediately follow the precedent, nor did she promptly respond to a letter from the Minister of Finance bringing it to her attention. It was only after the incident became public, as news reports over a few days accelerated from brief notes to the front pages and editorials, that she hesitantly sent a letter to the Minister of Finance. She referred to her reluctance to give in to 'people's courts, neither when it concerns travel costs, nor apartments, and not when it concerns pensions. In principle I think that in this as well as in other cases we should follow the rules in force until they are changed. However, as this case has lost any sense of proportion, I will ask you to suspend my pension as a former minister while I am serving as EU-Commisioner.'

There are other cases like these, but relatively few. And as in the cases cited above, it is not so much a breach of rules that has been in question. Where politicians were criticized for their greed, their diversion of public money for private purposes, or just their use of a prominent public position to advance personal interests, they have rarely broken the law. This has not saved them from criticism, nor from more serious consequences.

On the other hand this article claims that Danish politicians are much better than their reputation, which may explain why Danish politics has not been dominated by the types of sleaze found elsewhere in Europe. This may partly be explained by their adherence to a set of norms characteristic of Danish parliamentary democracy which stress modesty when it comes to politicians rewarding themselves. Another aspect of the modesty of Danish politicians is that they are easily caught in a trap if they try to advance their private interests in financial and material terms. In spite of repeated initiatives to revalue their parliamentary or ministerial pay, they run into difficulties that make them cautious and may therefore look for supplementary sources of income, e.g. through positions for which they receive separate and not so visible rewards.

These restraints are not nearly as effective when it comes to other parts of Danish public life. Strong corporatist institutions legitimize close interaction between particular branches of government and organized interests. One corollary in recent years has been the disclosure of several scandals where public funds have been divered from their official, but vaguely defined, purpose to uses favouring the interests dominating, sometimes even monopolizing, the policy implementation stage. In none of these cases have MPs and other politicians drawn any material profit from the misapplication of public funds. However, when issues are moved from the parliamentary to the corporatist arena, they are dealt with according to prescriptive norms emphasizing 'political' rather than legal criteria. At the same time, they are moved from an arena characterized by extreme transparency to an arena closed to either formal or informal procedures of public scrutiny.[1] Corporatist rather than parliamentary democracy is therefore the place to search in Danish politics for private, sometimes even personal, interests served at the public expense.

The virtues of parliamentary democracy

Taken as a whole, misconduct by politicians is comparatively rare. Newspapers do not regularly report on ministers and other politicians taking financial advantage of their position, and neither is it normal for the media to violate their privacy. The separation of parliamentary life and professional politics from the private sphere is supported by the organizational culture of the Danish parliament. Although split in numerous parties, ranging from left-wing socialists through centrist social democrats, liberals and conservatives to right-wing populists, its 179 members are united by shared norms, not very different from the kind of norms accepted by members of professional organizations in both private and public sector bound together by their perception of a common mission or their use of similar techniques in their work.[2]

One dominant trait of this common culture is the emphasis on mutual trust. MPs recognize that the profession of parliamentary politicians relies on negotiation between the representatives of government and opposition as well as between the representatives of political parties. The number of issues on the parliamentary agenda at one time is so overwhelming that within the parties it is necessary to develop a high degree of specialization, with individual MPs delegated to develop, defend and negotiate the positions of their party in relation to other parties. In a parliament with many parties, some parliamentary groups are quite small. In 1994 there were eight parties. Three parliamentary groups less than ten members, another two had 11 and 13 respectively. All have to participate in the same negotiations as larger groups and have to take a policy position on all issues. The organizational culture of Danish parliamentary democracy copes with these challenges. Trust is a much appreciated value in a system where a majority is always constituted by a negotiated compromise. Without the confidence that negotiators speak on behalf of their group and will stick to compromises made, parliament could not operate. Trust is similarly essential when parties appoint MPs to represent them on a committee or in direct negotiations with the government. Members of small parliamentary groups are placed in a delicate position when confronted with an overloaded agenda. But the organizational culture helps them because the bigger parties understand their position and in some routine matters give them a helping hand, e.g. by representing their views on a committee.

A businesslike atmosphere is thus part of parliament's organizational culture and the MPs who enjoy a good reputation among their colleagues are those who play a constructive part in negotiating compromises gaining broad parliamentary support. They are the ones who make parliamentary democracy work, as opposed to some of their more extrovert, publicity-minded colleagues. Such MPs are found in virtually all groups. MPs embedded in this culture, ready to compromise in spite of political divisions, fit into the (self)-image of a parliament dedicated to the common good. It is in accordance with this image that Danish MPs do not receive a salary in formal terms.[3] As representatives of the voters and the servants of democracy, they are still assumed to have an occupation outside politics. The money they receive as MPs is only to be seen as a compensation for the loss of outside earnings (put colloquially, because farmers can not always milk their cows themselves or workers fill their place in every shift). This ideology leaves no place for the career politician. It is deeply rooted in Danish history. In the 19th century, during the formative years of constitutional democracy, the compensation to be given to people's representatives was an issue of intense debate. Bourgeois conservatives argued for low or even no daily allowances because in this way politicians could demonstrate their integrity and altruism (their real goal, of course, was to make it impossible for 'farmers and humble men' to afford election to parliament).[4]

For years there has been a perfect match between this democratic ideology praising the amateur and non-professional status of politicians and the practice of rewarding them as performing a public duty. Compared to politicians in other Western countries, Danish MPs obtain a comparatively modest reward. With their fellow MPs from Switzerland, Norway and Sweden, Danish politicians came out at the bottom in a comparative study covering a number of OECD-countries.[5] MPs serving as Cabinet ministers could add the equivalent to the salary of a relatively low-level higher civil servant. The rules determining pay levels have remained unchanged since 1969. As the same rules apply in other parts of the public sector, politicians have suffered a decline in real terms as the cost of living indexation was abandoned in 1982.

The same democratic ideology applies to politicians elected to offices in local and regional government. Indeed, membership of local and regional councils is defined as a public duty: in principle citizens can not refuse to take upon them the task of local councillor if their fellow citizens insist on electing them. For mayors, and to some extent councillors chairing standing committees of local and regional councils, a full-time job is effectively involved. For this reason they receive payment on which they can live. But again the reward is modest compared to the salaries of senior civil servants, not to mention top managers in private firms. For rank-and-file members of local and regional council the reward is symbolic: it has traditionally consisted of a daily allowance rate, intended as a certain compensation for the loss of income some suffer as a result of doing their public duty.

The modest pay-off of virtue

The organizational culture of the Danish parliament is sometimes taken as evidence of the high ethical standards of Danish parliamentarians. The modesty of rewards, received for performing a public duty in the service of democracy, might support this interpretation but is not accepted without qualification by the electorate. Repeated surveys reveal attitudes among voters that are sceptical and sometimes even critical of the ethical standards of their elected representatives in parliament but this relates much more to political than financial activities. In an analysis of the phenomenon of political (dis)trust, a distinction has been made between three different aspects.[6] One aspect is pragmatic trust, a measure of voters' confidence in politicians' ability to make decisions which cope with the problems of society. Another aspect is moral trust, a measure of voters' perception of politicians as more or less honest and reliable. Finally, there is voters' evaluation of politicians as being more or less responsive to the electorate.

Time-series of survey data going back to the 1960s and surveys from the late 1980s and early 1990s do not lead to unequivocal conclusions. Generally, Danes present themselves as devoted democrats, increasingly expressing their support for the institutions of representative democracy. In terms of pragmatic trust, voter attitudes vary strongly over time. A dramatic decline in voters' confidence that 'politicians make the right decisions' in 1989–90 led to renewed discussions of the voters' lack of trust in their elected representatives. So, between 1986 and 1990 a 20% majority of positive responses turned into a 32% majority of negative responses. Since then, trust has again improved, mirroring the connection between voters' perception of social and economic problems and their evaluation of politicians' ability to cope with them. However, interpretation of trust is difficult because of its ambiguity. Danish voters hardly find MPs and other politicians corrupt, but perception of them as opportunist vote-maximizers is widespread. They are seen as being willing to give up any principle if it does not pay off in terms of votes. There is similar distrust of the electoral promises they make. Thus, when it comes to the morality of politicians, a persistent 70–75% of those surveyed since 1960 do not believe that parliamentarians have a higher morality than other people. A sizeable minority, 21% per cent in 1991, even believe it is lower. According to a majority, politicians' responsiveness towards voters is similarly low.

This data is not as unambiguous as interpreted here. Voters' attitudes towards politicians not only vary over time but also depend on the indicator of trust used. Consequently, there is a fair amount of inconsistency in these attitudes. One cautious proposition is that Danish politicians are confronted with an electorate which clearly supports the representative institutions of parliamentary democracy but is not always convinced that it can trust politician's willingness to solve the problems of society when opportunism prompts them to act otherwise. Part of the explanation for these divided feelings may be due to what voters find confirmed by their own experience; part may also be found in a ubiquitous populism which finds support among people who have difficulty in overviewing the political process and therefore feel power-less themselves.

Do good politicians deserve competitive salaries?

It is within this political climate that politicians have argued that the demands of time and professionalism mean that politics has become a full-time job and should be rewarded accordingly. Popular perceptions, however, make it difficult, probably even impossible, for politicians to get through the message that serving as an MP is tantamount to doing a hard day's work. Neither do they have many chances to convince these voters that political influence and collegial respect presuppose the observation of standards of conduct that in other professional contexts would be proofs of personal integrity. On the other hand, their livelihood depends on the voters. As they realize that this is also the case for their political competitors, little action is taken when the issue of increased pay is opened. Nevertheless, there is a general feeling among politicians that what they earn from politics does not reflect the effort they put into the job. They also feel that professional politicians nowadays take a responsibility for decisions clearly matching those of private and public sector managers.

Thus, in 1986 it was decided to increase the salary of MPs while simultaneously introducing government subsidies for the political parties. The presidium of parliament prepared a proposal for a parliamentary decision together with a bill revising the electoral law to cover the latter. The proposals were balanced in a subtle way. Members of the presidium representing centre parties, commanding an overwhelming majority in parliament, first referred to their intent 'to break the trend towards mass media dominance in the opportunities for political parties to present themselves to the citizens. Acceptance of the proposal will imply that political activities — both on a daily basis and during electoral campaigns — will depend less on private firms and interest organizations subsidizing political parties.' The presidium also found that 'the heavy increase of parliamentary work makes it more and more difficult for MPs to combine it with other work. This, together with the desire that as few people as possible are prevented from standing at elections by financial and job-related reasons, is the background for this bill concerning the improvement of financial compensation etc as well as some of the proposed changes in parliament's mode of operation'.

With this circumstantial argument the presidium declared the traditional idea of the amateur politician performing a public duty defunct. The new professional MP was to receive a salary, still officially referred to as a 'compensation', corresponding to the salary of the mayor of a city with 20–25,000 inhabitants. The bill was introduced at the same time as a proposal to improve the compensation given to local and regional politicians, and among them especially mayors, but here the standard of comparison was to be the salary paid to civil servants. Although neither the leftist Socialist Peoples Party and the Left Socialists nor the right populist Progress Party objected to the proposal of centrist partiest awarding themselves more pay when they were preaching wage restraint to other citizens, it was accepted without much debate. MPs enjoyed a 37% increase in real terms. However, this only compensated the loss in real income they had suffered since 1969. As the salary of ministers is composed of pay as an MP (be they MPs or not) and pay as a Cabinet minister, they were brought to the same level as that of top civil serviants acting as their advisers. With the 1986 increase, MPs received about £30,000, while the full salary of a Cabinet minister increased from about £50,000 to £58,000. In 1995 a Danish MP receives about £34,000 and a Cabinet minister above £70,000.

Nevertheless, an MP's salary does not compare well with the income of private sector managers, nor does it match that of the career-minded high-fliers within the civil service. The latter have been much more successful in their claim that they deserve a salary which allows the public sector to compete with private firms for best-qualified staff. To what extent recruitment is actually a problem for political parties at national level is unclear. However, it is a fact that parties face the problem at local and regional elections. Similarly, politicians generally are confronted with substantial problems if they try to combine their political work, perhaps even a political career, with outside career ambitions, particularly if they are businessmen or employees in private firms. One much debated corollary is that politicians are disproportionately recruited among public employees such as teachers and social workers, because public employees are allowed to retain part-time employment while serving as MPs and are guaranteed return to full employment if they are not re-elected to parliament.

Such concerns have led to several proposals. Some relate to politicians' conditions of work. The president of parliament proposed to increase the resources of secretarial and expert support to individual MPs, as well as the resources of standing committees. Other proposals aimed at improving the financial situation of political parties which suffer from a long-term decline in membership. State financing is also part of the president's plan to strengthen parliamentary work. Notwithstanding considerable opposition, a majority adopted the plan in June 1995. (In local and regional government similar reasons have been given for a restructuring of the political and administrative organization, including the delegation of more tasks to officials and service-providing institutions.)

While improvement of the organizational framework within which politicians operate may alleviate their burdens, it does not improve their income. Repeated attempts have therefore been made to launch another increase in salaries. The president of parliament has supported the idea. The Prime Minister did the same, adding that ministers were not paid according to their responsibilities, especially when considered in relation to private sector managers. Once more, the concern for democracy was given as the principal reason for doing something. There was a parallel move to improving the position of local and regional politicians. With this new policy launched in 1994 it was recognized that it was an illusion to believe that local politics was a public duty which could easily be managed in free time. Parliamentary debates and news coverage show that it is comparatively easy for politicians to deal with the pay at local and regional level. Therefore, local and regional politicians will see a substantial increase, while it remains uncertain to what extent the lot of national politicians will be improved.

Politicians' pension rights is a particular issue. Traditionally, MPs and ministers have had enjoyed liberal pension rights, compensating for the fact that their careers may be brought to an end abruptly. They also obtain temporary compensation while seeking new employment. The rules, however, have come under scrutiny in relation to ministers who receive half their salary for two years following their resignation; after this, they are entitled to a lifelong pension, increasing from 10% salary for ministers with 2–3 years' seniority to 50% for ministers with at least 8 years. Until the late 1980s, the fairness of these rules was not questioned but recent Cabinet reshuffles have given rise to rumours that they were timed to maximize the reward paid to losers in the impending reshuffle. This led the president of parliament to suggest a revision of the rules as part of his package for improving the conditions of parliamentary work. This part of his plan immediately ran into difficulties. His fellow Social Democrats in government said that ministers' pensions was none of his business, while the opposition was reluctant to revise the rules so that ministers would receive the equivalent of their salary for two years on resignation, after this they would not be entitled to a pension until the age of 60. The reform did not find support from a majority in parliament.

The pay of politicians and the cost of populism

Although the 'old' and new centre parties regularly command a comfortable majority in parliament, they are reluctant to use it to improve MPs pay. In 1986–86, when they actually gave themselves a sizeable salary increase, they argued their case in a subtle and circumstantial way. They were at pains to discuss their income in the broader context of a parliamentary democracy allegedly under severe strain. In spite of their care, they still attracted the scathing criticism of especially the right populist Progress Party which, over the years, has neglected no opportunity to bring any issue to public attention which might question the moral standing of the political establishment. The principal strategy for the Prime Minister and the Minister of Finance when confronted with questions concerning ministers' incomes, their financial interests or travel costs has been evasion rather than counter-attack. Similarly, when questions have been raised in parliament concerning the financial compensation of politicians, its president has been reticent in response. His critics in the Progress Party have repeatedly referred to the many letters published in newspapers critical of politicians' salaries. In 1986–86, when parliament voted the 37% increase in MPs' salaries, the Progress Party relaunched its proposal for a 15% cut, also proposing that those appointed to ministerial positions should give up their salary as MPs. Since then, it has changed its proposal to a 20% cut. For as Mogens Glistrup, the party's founder, argued: 'If the salary was reduced to a level which gives no incentive to enter parliament, we would get the idealists who are not deterred by their fear of losing their own ample or fat pay. Thus, the lower the salary, the better the MPs. I think there is a quite unequivocal connection. The higher the salary paid to MPs, the more egoistically do they cling to their benefits, and you get the wrong people seeking election.' This populist proposal, ironically recalling the arguments of 19th century elitists, had no chance of being accepted, but the debate showed how painful the issue is to the majority.

The centre parties have good reasons to watch their step. Opinion polls make it clear that their defensive and prudent strategy is sensible given that voters are sceptical, often even highly critical, of the role of political parties. In a 1995 poll, two-thirds found parties oligarchical, while still less influential than the unions and the employers' organizations. No wonder that a majority did not agree with the proposition that as party members they would be able to influence their party's policies and did not consider joining a party. A majority agreed in the same survey: 'Political parties are only interested in peoples' votes, not in what they think.' A majority also believe that parties should manage without government subsidies; only 2% supported a proposal by the Prime Minister and the conservative People's Party to triple these. The electorate's critical attitudes towards parties coincide with extremely negative attitudes towards any increase in the salaries of MPs or Cabinet ministers. No more than 7–8% support the idea; 86–87% are against it. Even in polls graduating the response, clearly negative attitudes prevail. The same polls reveal an interesting pattern in these attitudes. When asked what a minister deserved, £40,000 turned out as the median income found appropriate. This, respondents thought, treated ministers as equals of managing directors in medium-sized firms. However, £40,000 would only be about a third of what the average managing director earns and a bit more than half of what a minister is actually paid in 1995.

Being caught in this trap between populism, misinformation and their own strategies for political survival in a highly competitive political climate, politicians might be tempted to seek supplementary incomes. No formal rules forbid this. Unlike ministers who are not allowed to have another job or supplementary income, and unlike the strict conflict of interest regulations forbidding local councillors to take part in decisions where they may have a financial interest, MPs are free to engage in whatever business they wish. Moreover, supplementary sources of income have two attractive characteristics. They are not open to public scrutiny in the same way as official remuneration and political parties often control appointments to secondary jobs.

There are a number of positions to which MPs are appointed. Sometimes the law stipulates that the political parties, or at least the larger parties, should be represented on a particular body. For example, government accounts are audited first by the National Bureau of Auditors and then by a political body called the National Auditors whose members, appointed by the parties represented on parliament's budgetary committee, are mostly prominent MPs. Similarly, the Bank of Denmark is supervised by a board on which the same parties are represented. A number of similar positions exist. Others are controlled by the government. There are 'representatives of the public interest' on the board of directors of banks, insurance companies and other financial institutions. The Minister of Industry quite often appoints national and local politicians to the boards of financial institutions and, like other board members, they receive an annual salary. Other positions may be reserved for, at least open to, politicians.

In the populist image of the politician, well-paid service on politically-controlled bodies is a routine ingredient. The Progress Party, in tandem with tabloid papers, has never neglected to draw attention to this side of Danish politics. When a few years ago the Progress Party repeated its proposal to cut MPs pay by 20% it said: 'You forget the tax benefits MPs have. You forget former ministers cashing a pension while serving as MPs. You forget the jobs on the side they give to each other, be it as national auditors, as members of the board of Radio Denmark, as commissioner of the Home Guard, and you could list lots of other profitable jobs. Politically, such arguments are easy to pursue, given the discretion with which governments, together with the parties of the political centre, reveal information on paid secondary positions. One consequence is that nobody has exact information on their incidence although in 1994 parliament introduced rules to create more openness about MPs' extra-parliamentary activities and financial interests. These rules, which were prepared by the standing committee on parliamentary business, set up an open but voluntary registration on MPs' secondary jobs and financial interests. As the rules were not accepted by the Liberal Party, the registration does not give a complete picture of MPs supplementary activities and the level of incomes involved.

The moralising effect of populism and party competition

Openess will not necessarily dispose of populist suspicions. The 1986 increase in MPs' salaries provoked a barrage of questions to all ministers from the Progress Party to discover which offices MPs had been appointed to by them and what they were paid. The answers were disappointing, with only few positions given to MPs, and these were often unpaid. Populism does not recognise that financial reward is only one possible motive for politicians. Influence, or positions paving the way for future influence and political survival, may be just as important to an MP. Nor does populism consider the possibility that politicians are attractive partners for public and private sector organizations.

Danish politicians are modest people. Their income does not compare well with that of other decision makers. They may have opportunities to supplementing it but these opportunities are worse than often assumed in public and political debate. One interpretation might see this as another instance of the comparatively high moral standards characterizing the original culture of the Danish parliament. An alternative interpretation sees these collegial norms as distinctive features of an organization whose members have developed procedures of cooperation to facilitate their parliamentary work, while at the same time allowing them to compete for political positions and for votes.

It is the same competitive climate, made fertile by the existence of many parties, some of them with a strong populist bent, that enforces modesty among politicians, and persuades them to show restraint when it comes to accepting positions that might supplement their income. Not all politicians behave in this way. The irony, however, is that the politicians sticking to their formal right to do more, or occasionally exploiting ambiguities in the rules regulating their remuneration, make it difficult for the rest who repeatedly try to launch reforms that they do not want to risk implementing for fear of hostile voter reaction.

Things are entirely different when it comes to the important institutions of corporatist democracy. Theses are not based on a puritan democratic ideology. Nor are they subject to the constraints of openness and fierce party competition which are the conditions under which parliamentary democracy operates. One might thinks that corporatist institutions compensated MPs for their modest reward from political office. Closed to public scrutiny, they may do so; but given the constant and critical focus on MPs conduct, there is little evidence that this is the case. It is, however, possible to make political career within the partly closed world of corporatist democracy. Trade unions and farmers' organizations have historically played an important role in Danish democracy. Closely related to them are workers' and farmers' cooperatives. In recent decades unions representing a rapidly expanding number of public employees have been added. These organizations have built up huge pension funds. Most public employees work for local and regional authorities which also have their own national associations that control other undertakings. They may provide data services, office material and publishing, road construction, dangerous waste processing, etc. A conspicious trait of current public sector reform, moreover, is the transfer of government functions to public corporations and quango-like bodies.

In all these cases boards are set up with members representing the relevant organizatin or local and central government interests. These members occupy political positions and operate within a universe where decisions are made according to criteria which often combine political with business and/or legal-bureaucratic considerations. This has led to several political scandals. It may also create circumstances where thrifty political and managerial staff can earn rewards which are clearly not within the range of MPs and Cabinet ministers. A recent investigation commissioned by the City of Copenhagen into the financial transactions of a large cooperative housing trust revealed high salaries and pension rights for the managers. Similar transactions have been revealed in another housing cooperative. A few years earlier, Bibliotekscentralen, an organization providing public libraries with books and equipment together with all kinds of administrative services, went bankrupt after a financial scandal involving both its management and its political board of directors. While MPs rarely have positions within organizations like these, operating in the no-man's-land between public bureaucracy and private business, it is not unusual to find local politicians on their elected boards. Sometimes they have made their way into local and regional politics through active participation in corporatist democracy, sometimes they are elected or coopted to the boards because of their background in local politics.

One intriguing question concerns what kind of practices will occur within the expanding sector of quangos and public corporations given that the ethos which has dominated national politics may not be sufficiently strong to constrain the temptations present in this new environment. It is already clear that these new quasi-governmental organizations will not be subjected to the same legal demands for openess as their civil service predecessors, nor is it certain that they will be constrained by the competitive forces of the market. It has to be seen, therefore, whether the traditional modesty of Danish politicians will continue to prevail for the members appointed to their boards, and whether that modesty may itself become eroded if conduct in this new sector extends into the traditional field of national parliamentary politics Modesty in Danish politics has done much to preserve standards not encountered in many other West European states but it may be under threat—not from within but from outside, that is from other public sectors where different attitudes are emerging under the guise of new public management and private sector approaches to the delivery of public services.

1   J. G. Christensen, 'Corporatism, Administrative Regimes and the Mismanagement of Public Funds', *Scandinavian Political Studies*, 16, 1993.
2   H. Nielson, 'Politikersamtalerne', in J. G. Anderson *et al.*, *Vi og vore politikere* (Copenhagen: Spektrum, 1992). T K. Jensen, *Politik i praxix* (Frederiksberg: Samfundslitterature, 1993).
3   See J. G. Christensen, 'Institutional Constraint and the Advancement of Individual Self-Interest in High Public Office: The Case of Denmark' in C. Hood and B. G. Peters (eds), *Rewards in High Public Office* (Sage, 1994).
4   K. Hvidt, 'Politiker—hverv eller erhverv. Vederlag til politikere før og nu', *Økonimi og Politik*, 46, 1972.
5   C. Hood and B. G. Peters (eds), op. cit., p. 229.
6   J. G. Andersen, 'Politikerleden—myte eller realitet?'—in J. G. Andersen *et al.*, op. cit.

France

BY CHRISTOPHE FAY

THE use of their position by politicians to obtain an illicit gain for themselves or their party can easily be distinguished from dubious practices carried out on behalf of the state and in its name. If French political history is mainly characterised by scandals in which the main source of controversy was the existence of dubious state intervention,[1] the last ten years have, on the other hand, been largely dominated by what, in France, is designated by the blanket definition of 'affairs of political corruption'—opportunistic practices which enable political parties or individuals, and often both, to obtain financial benefit. The number of these practices which have been exposed has increased rapidly, and these revelations are considered as the cause for the declining confidence of the public in politicians and even more in the political system. Political corruption goes a step further than dubious state intervention: it is described as 'a flaw in democracy', a process which undermines the basis of the rule of law by negating the principles of equality, transparency and responsibility; and, as such, it is easy to justify the attention to which these phenomena are subject and to understand the judgements they provoke.

At this point, it should be stated that if our subject, political corruption, is not new, the way in which it is manifested today *is* new. Political financial scandals acquired importance in the Third Republic. In 1887 it was discovered that a member of the family of the President of the Republic, Jules Grévy, made money from selling decorations (légions d'honneur). The President, who was not involved in the affair, was forced to resign by public opinion. The large number of scandals which occurred during the Third Republic brought about a strong current of antiparliamentarism. It is during the Fifth Republic, however, that the modern forms of corruption began to develop, as did the role of the media in investigating them, which suggest two important themes.

Firstly, French current affairs in recent years have produced a category, 'political corruption', which is the result of a complex interaction between the multiple actors of a set of agents. The different affairs which appear in the press have given rise to a variety of opinions and declarations, which suggests that, in France, political corruption does not relate solely to specific activities or individuals but also depends for its impact on the circumstances and perceptions surrounding it. Secondly, however, the number of scandals has conferred on the theme of corruption a recognised status in society; this in turn makes the revelation of scandals commonplace and may explain why few affairs now provoke the indignation of the public.

Cause for concern

The first of the major modern cases of political corruption in France was the Carrefour du Développement affair. In March 1986, after the electoral defeat of the Socialist Party, Jacques Chirac was appointed Prime Minister to replace Laurent Fabius. This change of government was the starting point for the scandal. The newly appointed Minister for Cooperation discovered that an association funded by his ministry was on the verge of bankruptcy, with debts amounting to over £1.3m. The Carrefour du Développpment, which was linked to the Ministry of Cooperation, was created in 1983 as an association to channel government aid to Africa and closed down in 1986. It was in fact used to cover up a large number of fraudulent financial transactions (the estimated loss was £2m). Two men were accused during the case; Cristian Nucci, the former Socialist Minister of Cooperation, and Yves Chalier, the finance officer of the association. The transgressions they were charged with were of two kinds: Carrefour du Développpment allowed official or party political activities to be funded and it allowed private individuals to use its funds for themselves. The association's first operation was to finance the Franco-African Summit of Bujumbura (Burundi) in December 1984 but it also contributed to the funding of Nucci's political expenses: £130,000 for a meeting of African ambassadors in the town of Beaurepaire, of which he is mayor; £130,000 to celebrate the anniversary of his appointment as minister; £52,000 for his election posters; £90,000 for media training fees; £120,000 rent for his Paris flat.

Carrefour du Développpment also gave another association (Promotion Française) £650,000 in July 1985 to help it buy a mansion which was to be used as a residence and a training centre for African government officials. But after the mansion had undergone an expensive conversion, which cost the state £320,000, it was sold at the end of 1985 to a company whose shareholders were Chalier and the secretary general of Promotion Française. Additionally, Chalier used association funds to buy a small flat for £52,000 for a friend (an air hostess), lent £26,000 to another woman friend and sent his wife a number of cheques amounting to £117,000.

In August 1986 Nucci was charged. His case had to be tried in the Supreme Court—the Haute Cour de Justice—as the court which could try a minister for offences committed while exercising his ministerial functions. The decision to try him in this court was taken at the end of 1987 and the initial official investigation was resumed in 1988. Nucci's fall seemed inevitable but for a major development in what was to be considered acceptable and unacceptable conduct in French politics. The press, TV and radio reports on the affair emphasised the interdependence of the political character of the fraud by Nucci and the personal enrichment of Chalier, the main defendant. This was the first time that the political and media establishment made a distinction between what some considered 'tolerable' (underhand funding of political parties) and what is 'intolerable' (personal enrichment). Nucci received an official pardon for his fraudulent activities on behalf of his political party but Chalier was sentenced to five years imprisonment.

Confirmation of the unacceptability of similar conduct appears to come from investigations into local politics. One of the most striking examples is the decline and fall of the Médecin 'dynasty'. Father and son, Jean and Jacques Médecin reigned over Nice, the fifth largest city in France, from 1928 to 1990. Their habit of giving jobs to the boys (clientelism) reached a peak in the 1980s, when 'Jacqou' was running Nice. A former chairman of the departmental council of the Alpes-Maritimes and a former Minister for Tourism, he is a colourful personality with some rather shady friends.[2] Money was the key to a ruthless world of casinos, gaming houses, tax evasion and secret overseas bank accounts, fraudulent use of local authority grants and embezzlement. In February 1989 his world collapsed when two opposition councillors accused him of fraud; several associations which were funded by the council were accused of financing a partisan newspaper he owned by buying advertising space at an unusually high price. This was just the first of a series of investigations which revealed that Jacques Médecin possessed houses and land in the USA, two accounts which were in false names, shares in Oppenheimer Inc., eight bank accounts, investments in American food companies, plans to build factories and tourist centres in Haiti, a sum of £650,000 from a Panamanian company and, according to American tax authorities, considerable sums invested in America. Despite that, Mr Médecin had not paid any tax over the previous ten years. In his official statement he declared that he lived on only £1,200 per year and that he gave his wife a maintenance allowance of more than twice his annual income, £25,000. After seeking refuge in Uruguay, Médecin was extradited four years later and ended up in prison. Such misconduct was not confined solely to right-wing politics.

During the first months of 1991, Jean-Michel Boucheron, mayor of Angoulême, a Socialist MP and a former junior minister, was charged with corruption, fraudulent use of municipal funds and embezzlement. Boucheron had been elected mayor of his small town in 1977. The following year he was elected MP. Political promotion was matched by a equally extravagant lifestyle, funded in part at the town's expense. The methods he used were familiar; a number of associations received grants from the town council from which he allegedly benefited, as he did from public contracts through a system of forged invoices provided by a few chosen firms. Even if Boucheron denied the facts, it was obvious that he had derived personal benefit and, in June 1994, he was informed of his four-year sentence in Buenos Aires where he had fled. He was also deprived of his civic rights for five years and fined £130,000.[3]

These two affairs, involving the personal misconduct of a right-wing politicians and a left-wing politician, became synonymous with the public perception of intolerable and unforgivable corruption for which it would be unthinkable to grant an official pardon.[4]

The Amnesty Law

An Amnesty, in the French context,[5] is a law put to parliament by the government with the agreement of the President of the Republic and nullifies minor offences. When a President is elected, it is the custom to pass such a law. This happened in 1969 (Pompidou), in 1974 (Giscard d'Estaing) and in 1981 (Mitterrand). After the 1988 presidential election, the Amnesty Law voted in July contained only five lines concerning the funding of political parties. Using ambiguous wording, it pardoned almost all offences to do with elections. However, it was the second Amnesty Law of January 1990 which was widely commented on in the media. It invented a new concept for France, that of 'personal enrichment' in relation to monies ostensibly for party funding. Paragraph 19 stipulates that 'Except if the offender obtains personal enrichment, all breaches of the law committed before 15 June 1989 in relation to the direct or indirect funding of election campaigns or political parties or groups are amnestied except those offences committed by a person invested with a national parliamentary mandate.' The 1990 Law thus extends the application to all breaches of the law: in France the order of importance of breaches of the law is contravention, délit, crime. Nucci, who had been charged with 'crime', could not benefit from the 1988 Law. The 1990 Law, however, was considered by the media to be tailor-made for him. The MP who presented this 1990 version was J.P. Michel, a Socialist. He was the only MP who had agreed to sign the amendment (amendments are usually signed by several MPs), but it was approved by 283 votes against 168. Part of the right-wing opposition abstained and some even voted in favour, including Gérard Longuet, the Republican Party treasurer, and Raymond Barre, a former Prime Minister.

A year before the 1990 Amnesty Law was passed, two police inspectors had made a discovery of great importance. They were investigating allegations of faked invoices involving a consultancy firm called URBA. When searching its offices, they discovered four exercise books which were to shake the Socialist Party to its roots. The books belonged to one of the managers who, over a period of many years, had kept precise records of what turned out to be a front company whose real purpose was to centralise the secret funding of the Socialist Party. At a time when a criminal enquiry was likely to be opened and when Nucci was under the threat of an indictment, the politicians had to act quickly to bring out the 1990 Law. It limited election expenses, clarified the funding of political activities and pardoned former mistakes by an amnesty. But the Socialists, who did not wish to give the impression that they were indulging in self-protection, nor appear too indulgent towards the mistakes of the representatives of the other political parties, invented the concept of 'personal enrichment' to cover the fraudulent private use of public money, goods or property, and which is therefore morally intolerable.

Nevertheless, this amnesty has hindered or stopped many police investigations. Nucci was the first to benefit from the Law before a legal definition of personal enrichment had been formed. In April 1990, the Supreme Court, with some reluctance, announced that the case was dismissed in accordance with the Amnesty Law. In the official judgement, the Court mentioned Nucci's $2.8m embezzlement and its president made a bitter declaration: 'this is the first time in the history of French Republic that criminal acts have been amnestied.' It caused an uproar in the media and was opposed by a number of magistrates. One of them, Thierry Jean-Pierre, decided to free ordinary offenders in order to show them the same clemency as politicians showed themselves. He went a step further in the URBA affair in 1991 when he signed a search warrant for the Paris head office of the company. He was immediately taken off the case by his superiors and accused of 'personal considerations'. A minister in the Department of Justice even accused him of 'legal burgling'. For the press, however, he became 'the white knight of the false invoices' and the courts upheld him when they approved of his decision to grant the search warrant. Jean-Pierre was the first magistrate to get star treatment and had the support of many of his colleagues, of reporters and of public opinion.

Thus, with the Carrefour du Développement affair political leaders made a distinction between 'good' and 'bad' corruption; and to add weight to these concepts, the latter was clearly typified by two archetypal culprits: J. Médecin and J.M. Boucheron. In this way their demonisation gave, through the distinction with 'good' corruption, the impression that the political class as a whole was honest. There is a price to pay for democracy, and a way has to be found to pay its political parties. And as the Socialist Party was threatened by the URBA affair—which was just an affair of secret funding—it seemed logical to vote the Amnesty Law. But the Socialist Party's hypocrisy and heavy-handedness, the political exploitation by the Right, and the rebellion of a large number of journalists and magistrates had a devastating effect on the image of political parties. This amnesty syndrome was to provide the reference point for many of the debates to come.

Growing public concern: sleaze and scandals

1992 began with the rumbling of the URBA affair in the background. A new magistrate, Van Ruymbeke, attracted public attention when he ordered a search of the Socialist Party headquarters, which had never been done before, and put several people under arrest. Several opinion polls seemed to imply that the number of 'affairs' could be the cause of the lack of confidence in the Socialist Party. In this climate, the new Socialist Prime Minister, Pierre Bérégovoy, used his general policy statement to the National Assembly in 1992 to declare that he would engage his government in a fight against corruption[6] (this was the first time that the term was used in such circumstances) and then set up a Commission Against Corruption which submitted its first report at the end of June that year. The government used the report as a basis for its draft law to prevent corruption. The commission, presided by a magistrate, Robert Bouchery, made proposals in two areas of reform. The first was to institute an active policy of preventing corruption. Codes of professional ethics were to be written, ethics committees set up and public officials receive training in the application of professional ethics. It should be transparent. The management of public affairs should also be open to inspection. This would entail a reinforcement of the power of prefects and ministerial inspectorates, as well as the Court of Accounts. It would also entail the setting up of a central office to fight corruption which later became the Central Bureau to Prevent Corruption (SCPC). Finally, the commission proposed suitable sanctions which could have preventive effects. The second area pinpointed high-risk sectors which would require more urgent action: public contracts, the contracting out of public service, associations supported by public funds, mixed-economy companies (public and private shareholding), companies involved in town planning, advertising and international trade. For each of these sectors, practical measures were suggested to meet the general objectives of the commission. Many of these proposals were adopted in the Law of January 1993 known as the 'Sapin Law', named after the Minister of Justice who introduced it.

The Law established a number of measures which were necessary in the struggle against corruption, although they did not go far enough, and was only one of several dealing with the same area. In 1988 a Law authorised a partial public funding of political parties and set an upper limit for expenditure in parliamentary and presidential elections. A Law of 1990 extended this upper limit to all elections and generalised rules for funding. The Sapin Law tightened the rules concerning the upper limits, advertising and party political broadcasts. Thus it became compulsory to publish the amount of money corporate bodies had contributed to the election campaign. Candidates also had to publish their election accounts. It should be noted that private funding (donations by firms to candidates and parties) was not banned although the government would have liked this to have been included.

The Sapin Law also set up the SCPC which is still working today, but in conditions which are more difficult than when it was founded. In 1993, the Socialist Party was in power. Today the government is right-wing but the rules stipulate that the leading officials of the Bureau are appointed for four years; so for the moment these officials are in an uncomfortable political situation. At the head of this organisation there is a magistrate and there is a secretary general. Its members come from the civil service, one for each service which has to deal with corruption: public works, customs, police, administration, taxes, justice, prevention of fraud. It is responsible to the Ministry of Justice and publishes an annual report. So far, it has published only one report (1993–4), giving an alarming picture of the state of corruption in France and pointing out the weaknesses in the SCPC itself. It deplored the small number of people (nine) working for the Bureau and the limits of its terms of reference. It is not a judicial institution and therefore it has no legal power to call witnesses or demand documents which would assist it in its work; only voluntary testimony is possible. It is an interdepartmental administrative organisation with the following remit: 'to centralise the information which will permit the detection and prevention of active or passive corruption, of trading for favours committed by people holding public office or private individuals, of misappropriation of public funds, collusion and unfairness in the award of contracts. The organisation provides assistance when requested by the judiciary in its investigation of such offences. It advises the administrative authorities concerning measures to be taken to prevent such acts'.

During the same period links between politics and money remained very much in the public eye. Bernard Tapie (a business man and a symbol of the easy money of the 1980s), who had just been appointed Minister for Urban Affairs, was asked to resign before being involved in a civil law case. Then *Le Monde* revealed that the president of the National Assembly, a former treasurer of the Socialist Party, was to be charged with contravening the rules for the funding of political parties; the indictment was duly notified to him some weeks later. The parliamentary session was thus named the 'judicial session', and at the same time the debates about the anti-corruption law revealed the splits in the Socialist Party.

The end of the Socialist period of government took a dramatic turn. The Prime Minister, who had developed an image of integrity, came under suspicion. He was suspected of receiving a £130,000 interest-free loan to buy his flat; the conditions of the loan also seemed rather dubious. After losing the parliamentary elections in May 1993, the country was shocked to learn of his suicide. The political class immediately blamed it on the manhunt encouraged by all those who exploited political scandals: 'If I was a judge or a reporter I would not sleep peacefully' declared Michel Charasse, one of the senior advisers at the Elysée Palace, on the evening after the suicide. Three days later, the President paid homage to Pierre Bérégovoy at his funeral. He praised: 'the integrity of the citizen who preferred to die rather than to face the insult of doubt' and continued scathingly, 'no explanation can justify the fact that a man's honour has been thrown to the dogs, not only his honour but his life. And why? Because those who accuse him have disobeyed the fundamental laws of the Republic—the laws that protect the dignity and the liberty of each one of us.' By accusing those who accuse, by pointing a finger at investigative magistrates who had leaked information and at unscrupulous reporters who had spread these leaks, the political leaders widened the split with a part of the media and the magistrates. The image of the Left, which had come to office in 1981 to fight the power of money in politics, was now broken and public opinion was turning cynical.

An opinion poll in June 1993 asked what the public held the Left responsible for. The amnesty for the faked invoices for party funding came third, after unemployment and immigration; three years after it was passed the trauma of the Amnesty Law was still present. Many other polls showed the decline of the image of French socialism. When asked in 1992 'what would give you a better opinion of the Socialists?', the most frequent reply (48%) was 'a tougher attitude to scandals'. 'Integrity, morality and altruism' were given as values in 1991 which were mainly absent from the 'reality of left-wing power during the previous ten years'. (All SOFRES)

The image the Left gave of itself in its handling of the affairs was suggested by commentators as one of the reasons for its defeat in March 1993. What is certain is the overwhelming nature of the defeat, with the party getting only 17.4% of the vote while the right-wing coalition obtained 44%. This result gave the Socialists 69 seats and the Right 472. The next day, François Mitterrand appointed Edouard Balladur Prime Minister and he announced the following rule to his ministers, which was to prove very useful later: 'Any minister being questioned in a judicial investigation must resign from the government'. The scandals did not stop; with the Right in power, indeed, they became more frequent.

New politicians, old habits

In the June 1994 European elections, the list headed by Phillipe de Villier, whose programme was based on Euroscepticism, the revival of family values and the struggle against corruption, was very successful. The pressures were much stronger than in 1990. Political groups which define themselves by reference to the values of integrity have now joined the ranks of those who keep corruption on the public agenda.

In September 1994, Gerard Longuet, Minister of Industry and Foreign Trade and one of the stalwarts of the Cabinet, was involved in two affairs: the deliberate undervaluing of the cost of building a house for himself and the secret funding of the Republican Party over which he presided. During the previous six months, leaks to the press had prevented the Minister of Justice from hushing up the case. On 19 September magistrate Van Ruymbeke sent a note to the Office of Public

Prosecution which concluded that public money had been fraudulently used in payment of the building work. Twice, on 20 and 22 September, the minister stated his intention of not resigning if he became subject of a judicial investigation. These declarations were seen as time-bombs. On 26 September, the Minister of Justice announced his decision to relax the pressure on Longuet by setting up 'a preliminary enquiry' rather than a 'judicial enquiry' as the magistrates proposed. This caused the media to increase its pressure, while the judiciary was seen as dependent on the government's decisions.[7] The minister was nevertheless forced to resign some weeks later.

This affair destabilised the government as Mr Longuet's personal interest seemed clear. It was this aspect on which public attention concentrated. According to the magistrate, the minister had used his official position to get himself a house built near Saint Tropez by a contractor who often worked for him in his official position. It was said that the house, which cost the firm more than £500,000 to build, cost Mr Longuet only £320,000. Part of the instalments on the loan he obtained were said to have been paid by firms which had already been named in other cases involving faked invoices. On 28 September, the Minister of Justice set up a judicial enquiry and at the same time several MPs of the government parties submitted a bill to stop firms financing political activities. It should be added that two other ministers were already suspected of infringing the law on the funding of parties (infringements which took place after the 1990 amnesty).

Once more, a magistrate had discovered a misappropriation of public money for private purposes at the fringe of irregularities in the funding of political parties. Thus the idea seemed to be confirmed that while it is theoretically possible to distinguish personal enrichment from the secret funding of parties, in practice the two elements are strongly linked. Many examples can be found to confirm this. Thus in underhand negotiations during the award of public contracts there is a 'rule' (known as the 30–30–40 rule) which suggests how the profits of corruption are to be shared out. For example, if a mayor recommends a civil engineering firm for a contract, the firm has to pay a 'commission' between 3% and 7% of its value. For a contract worth £10m with a 'commission' of 5%, £500,000 disappears under the counter to be divided as follows: 30% to the funding of the mayor's political activities, 40% to the political party which initiated the transaction and 30% to refund 'general expenses' in the transaction—i.e. not intended to fund political activities but for the personal enrichment of several intermediaries who may include councillors or MPs.

Longuet's resignation at the beginning of the presidential campaign had several effects. Proposals to stiffen the legislation against corruption became the object of competition between rival groups. In October 1994 Philippe Séguin, the president of the National Assembly and Jacques Chirac's right-hand man in the presidential campaign, chaired a committee to study the relationships between finance and politics. This parliamentary committee presented a report organised around several themes: public contracts, party and campaign funding, the wealth of elected representatives. It made many proposals to change the law. At about the same time, Edouard Balladur asked Simone Bozes, a very senior judge, to chair another committee to investigate corruption. Its report was handed to the Prime Minister in December 1994, containing 27 proposals which corresponded largely to the proposals of the previous committee. Over two months the press discovered more than sixty scandals with judicial implications, involving about a hundred public figures, including 30 members of two chambers of parliament. Comparison with the Italian 'mani pulite' was almost inevitable for political commentators.

The culminating point of this series of events was reached when Alain Carignon was arrested and imprisoned in October 1994. Carignon was the Minister for Communications at the beginning of the Balladur government. He had resigned when he was accused of various dubious deals involving corruption while he was mayor of his home city of Grenoble. The magistrate in charge of the affair then discovered new evidence and so it was decided to imprison him to avoid the destruction of evidence or undue influence on witnesses. Carignon was accused of organising a network which enabled him to receive 'presents' worth over £2.5m from firms whose tenders were accepted for public contracts, including subsidised election propaganda, the use of a large luxury flat in Paris and free travel in private planes. For the first time ever, a leading politician was sent to prison, which had a dramatic impact on public opinion.

The main preoccupation of politicians was to end the idea spreading that all politicians were corrupt. The announcement of plans to stop corruption reached a peak at the end of 1994. Firms announced their intention to stop contributing to party funds until the situation was clarified. In this electric political climate came the news at the end of November that Mr Roussin, Minister for Cooperation, was suspected of collecting cash for the RPR party. He was third minister to resign.

On 24 November a final political manoeuvre to protect the public image of politicians was attempted: a proposal to strengthen the secrecy of civil and criminal judicial investigation, thus limiting the investigative freedom of the press. The main aim was to maintain the presumption of innocence of politicians. The proposal, which included a series of attacks on the 'spiteful little judges', could well have become the solution to the political problem created by corruption. By stopping leaks to the press, the politicians would have been able to decide which cases would be hushed up. The amendment to the law was approved by the National Assembly but rejected in the Senate: 'We should not confuse the protection of the innocent with the hushing of scandals' said one Socialist senator. The official reaction of the right-wing parties was that they refused 'to legislate under the pressure of public opinion'.

The Séguin Law against corruption was passed rapidly in December 1994 and thus ended one of the worst years in the French politics. The Law took up some of the proposals of the committee mentioned above and aimed to provide greater transparency in matters concerning public money. Its main measures were to prohibit the funding of political parties and election campaigns by companies and firms (a highly significant change in French political attitudes), to reduce electioneering expenses, and to introduce strict tender and contract procedures. The main innovation was to introduce a large element of public funding into the financing of political activities and to make the funding by firms illegal. To offset loss of the latter, the upper limit for the refunding of election expenses was raised from 30% to 50% (which cost the state £40m per year), private individuals received tax relief on donations to parties, and the upper limit for election expenses was lowered by 30% for the presidential campaign.

Realising that the eyes of the public were on it, parliament introduced strict legislation but nevertheless managed to push aside the proposals concerning the incompatibility of membership of parliament with certain professional activities and the prohibition of holding more than one elective post, which the Séguin report had described as a deplorable French habit but is an important source of political power and influence.

Election propaganda and corruption

The number of books dealing with political corruption has increased greatly. The authors include the politicians involved, the magistrates who dealt with the affairs, the detectives who led the investigations, the civil servants of the SCPC, journalists, philosophers and sociologists. Corruption has become a subject for small talk in cafés, a source of profit for publishers who compete to produce books faster than their rivals and for bookshops which now have corruption sections. It has become a source of propaganda exploited by politicians such as Philippe de Villiers, Thierry Jean-Pierre or Jean-Marie Le Pen and a subject of thought for the many 'ethics groups' which have been created in companies, as well as for social scientists and public affairs commentators. But if evidence is needed of the emergence of political corruption as a problem of society, it is sufficient to examine the election manifestos which are sent to every potential voter in France before an election. The 'declarations of faith' sent a week before the first round of the 1995 presidential election, when compared to similar literature sent in 1988, show that corruption has become a major theme of political debate and that it affects the way people vote.

From 1986 to 1966, the first cohabitation between a right-wing Assembly and a Socialist President witnessed the emergence of scandals. The Médecin and Carrefour du Développment affairs could have been used as election arguments in the 1988 campaign but they were not. None of the nine manifestos used the term 'corruption', 'affair' or 'scandal'—terms the media used to describe sleaze in politics. Only two made an indirect reference to these questions. The first (Arlette Laguiller of the extreme left) condemned the 'law of money' which gives businessmen a certain influence over politicians and journalists. The second (Raymond Barre of the centre right) wished to establish 'the impartiality of the state'. 'The state', he said, 'should not be the possession of a party. It must not be subjected to the interests of a particular group. It must guarantee the independence of the judges, the freedom of the press.'

The second period of cohabitation, 1993–1995, also witnessed several scandals. But unlike 1988, in 1995 the presidential election rhymed with corruption. There were still manifestos which only raised these problems indirectly; for example Balladur's desire to obtain 'the independence of the judiciary' or Chirac's regret that 'the Republican ideal has been forgotten'. But the other six candidates are explicit. Three made this theme a major element in their campaign, de Villiers and Le Pen representing the ultra-nationalist right and Laguiller the extreme left. The first two condemned corruption in terms of a desire to see the return of traditional values. De Villiers proposed to lead a fight for the integrity of politicians. He was supported by the well-known magistrate Thierry Jean-Pierre who had uncovered the URBA affair and is now a Euro-MP elected on de Villier' list. Le Pen, who boasts of being the only important candidate who has never been a member of a party sullied by sleaze, is virulent in his condemnation of the Amnesty Laws, accusing the more moderate parties of self-interested voting in parliament. For Laguiller, political corruption is now a fact of life. It is not just the money of the ruling class which is to blame but also the politicians. Therefore it is not sufficient to impose controls on the ruling class; 'the sources of revenues, the possessions and properties of all politicians and their families must be open to public inspection' and 'the selfish pursuit of the maximum individual profit' must be stopped. Other parties were more equivocal. The ecologists argued for 'a magic change: we will moralise public life', indiscriminately listing 'the affairs, bribery, phone tapping and corruption'. Hue for the Communist Party and Jospin for the Socialists were more reserved. The former mentioned 'the struggle against corruption', but gave no further details about how he proposed to go about this. The latter merely wished to 'prevent corruption', as if he had to bear the whole burden of the Socialist Party.

Issues and themes

In the past seven years, five laws have been passed[8] to stop political corruption. There have been two Amnesty Laws. In addition three committees have been set up to study the question. Many private members' bills have been submitted for parliament. There have been hours of debate in parliament and on TV and much reported in the press. Scandals have acquired a kind of legitimacy as a theme of political discussion. This new legitimacy helps maintain the spotlight on corruption. It puts the subject on the same level as other issues in political debate. But as this makes discussion of political corruption commonplace, it may reduce capacity of corruption to shock the public. While the subject may continuously be in the news, however, it is impossible to measure the extent of corruption objectively. On the other hand, its affect on public opinion is plainly increasing, with corruption seen as 'sickness' and words like 'epidemic', 'virus' or 'acute gangrene' repeated over and over again.

As concern over corruption developed, new strategies have appeared on the political scene, as have, for example, new issues such as the controversy about the extensive immunity of MPs and the type of court in which a member of the government should be tried (ordinary or special?). Another issue has been the source of the wealth of politicians. During the presidential campaign of 1995 Prime Minister Balladur was accused of making a capital gain of £330,000 on shares. The circumstances in which the deal took place were somewhat mysterious but the subject of concern was not so much the legality of the deal as the amount of money involved. It was as if wealth and political activity were now considered incompatible. What caught the public attention most was that Balladur's income was £1m from 1991 to 1993. As a consequence of this revelation, all the candidates in the campaign felt obliged to publish their income and financial standing to avoid raising suspicions. The media estimated the wealth of candidates, and those who did not possess much were seen as more virtuous.

Another issue has been what incompatibilities there should be between holding certain political and other posts, together with the question of limiting elective functions, possibly to one only. Every committee on corruption has recommended that the number of mandates should be limited, but no important reform has been passed. Other issues include the role of devolution as a cause of corruption; the types of punishment (including ineligibility for public office, prison sentences and the refunding of monies involved); the transparency of the public contracts process. Wider issues raised by the judiciary and the press have focused attention on the question of the presumption of innocence (the Longuet affair), the legitimacy of preventive imprisonment before trial (the Carignon affair), the need for secrecy as regards information obtained during judicial (pre-trial) investigations, and the independence of the investigating magistrates.

A central issue in all these debates in the question of the funding of political parties and that of personal enrichment. What is at stake is the place of political parties in democratic politics. In its attempt to impose the idea that only individual corruption is immoral, the political establishment is seeking to maintain the tolerance of its present funding practices. In a period when there is much talk of crisis in political parties, this strategy is risky. It is difficult to persuade a supporter of right-wing parties that the affairs involving the Left, or the funding of the Socialist Party, are not wrong because they belong to the 'normal' process of funding public activity and are therefore a necessary part of democracy. It is even more difficult to debate the issue with that part of the public which does not identify with the present political system.

1   E.g. the 1985 Rainbow Warrior affair in which the French secret service sunk a ship belonging to Greenpeace in New Zealand territorial waters. The scandalous nature of this affair can be ascribed to the way the government's interpretation of state interest led to an abuse of power, and not to financial misdealing.

2   Especially Urbain Giaume, one of the heads of the 'French Connection', Albert Spaggiari, the well-known burglar of the Société Générale bank and Jean-Dominique Fratoni, the former managing director of the Ruhl Casino in Nice who allegedly had links with the local mafia.

3   On learning the verdict J.M. Boucheron declared dryly: 'I hope this case will be an example for politicians. I hope it will remind them that nobody is above the law and that corruption can not be tolerated' (quoted by G. Gaetner in *Les épinglés de la républic*).

4   In October 1990, Boucheron, who had not yet been charged,was expelled from the Socialist Party; he was charged in February 1991. Nucci is still a member of the party and mayor of Beaurepaire.

5   It is not an exclusively French issue. In Italy, for example, amnesty was applied to offences with a maximum of three years imprisonment; in 1990 the Italian parliament extended this to four to include the illegal funding of political parties but a constitutional law of the same year made it necessary to have a qualified majority to vote an amnesty act which is not the case in France.

6   'France, which is in a strong position, suffers from three ills, unemployment, insecurity, corruption — which demoralise French society. I intend to lance the abcess of corruption ... A group of irreproachable personalities will propose measures which will be applied immediately to moralise the various operations which can be the source of illicit profit.'

7   The Minister of Justice could have closed the affair—which would have put a stop to the investigation but which would also have caused an uproar in the media. Or he could have started a simple 'preliminary investigation' under the authority of the public prosecutor who is himself under the authority of the Minister of Justice. Another possibility would have been to open judicial proceedings, which would have involved appointing an examining magistrate and probably the indictment of G. Longuet, therefore his resignation in accordance with Balladur's rule.

8   Laws of 30 December 1985 limiting the accumulation of mandates; of 11 March 1988 concerning the financial transparency of political activities; of 15 January 1990 limiting election expenses, which reinforces the 1988 Law by imposing ineligibility on candidates who spend more than the upper limit; of 29 January 1993 (Sapin Act) preventing corruption; and of December 1994.

Germany

BY CHARLIE JEFFERY AND SIMON GREEN

ACCORDING to the Society for the German Language, 'Politikver-drossenheit' was the German 'word of the year' of 1992. This was, however, a dubious accolade. The term—literally a sullenness or apathy towards politics—is typically used to describe a deep-seated sense of malaise in the German body politic. It refers to a growing mood of popular disillusionment with, and alienation from, politics and the political system which emerged in the latter half of the 1980s, and which has become even more pronounced since German unification in 1990.

The main culprits in sowing this sense of 'Politikverdrossenheit' are widely seen to be Germany's political parties and politicians. Indeed, as some have argued, 'Parteienverdrossenheit' or 'Politikerverdrossenheit' might be far more appropriate terms to describe the sense of malaise which exists. The level of confidence and trust in political parties—especially the established, 'core' parties in German politics, the CDU/CSU, the FDP and the SPD—has fallen steadily to reach an unprecedented lowpoint by the early to mid-1990s. These parties, along with their leading politicians, are widely perceived as bland, remote from the electorate, self-serving and incapable of resolving the central political issues which Germany faces. The disillusionment that these perceptions have created has had important, wider implications. It has raised sceptical, if rather nebulous, questions about the legitimacy of the broader institutional fabric of the German political system, especially of those institutions most closely associated with party politics. More concretely, it has had a marked impact on voting behaviour. Widespread disillusionment has led voters to distance themselves from the established parties and thereby injected a strong measure of fluidity into German voting patterns which, while not yet fully evident in Bundestag elections, has left a clear mark in the volatility of the Land (regional) elections conducted in the last five years.

A wide range of explanations has been put forward to account for the emergence of 'Politikverdrossenheit'. Common to them all, though, is the negative impact on public perceptions of party politics of a long line of scandals implicating senior German politicians in behaviour which, in a British context, might be termed 'sleaze'. Two forms of sleaze have become especially prominent in the last five years. The first has involved accusations that politicians have individually and collectively voted themselves undue privileges and allowances borne by the public purse, while the second maintains that they are prone to abuse their public position for private gain.

Here we examine the growth and interdependence of sleaze and 'Politikverdrossenheit' in Germany. We begin by sketching out an anatomy of German sleaze. Brief attention is given initially to a number of significant scandals in West Germany in the 1980s which tarnished the image of parties and politicians and sensitised public opinion to political impropriety. Fuller consideration is then given to the apparent proliferation of scandals in post-unification Germany. Given the economic difficulties of the time, these served to intensify the sensitivities left by the scandals of the 1980s: the ritual calls for public belt-tightening made by parties and politicians, apparently beset at the same time by a collective and individual 'self-service' mentality, radically undermined public confidence in them and stoked up feelings of disillusionment to unprecedented levels. We then review the debate about the causes of 'Politikverdrossenheit', seeking to pinpoint the interrelationships of sleaze with the other factors widely seen to have contributed to it. These include the blandness of established party messages caused by an electoral competition to secure the allegiance of a hypothetical 'middle Germany'; the bureaucratic and clique-ridden structures of the established parties, which fail to provide genuine opportunities for new blood or new ideas; and the competence factor, the perceived failure of the established parties to solve the problems of the electorate. Drawing on opinion poll evidence, we argue that sleaze has acted as a focal point to channel and express resentment caused by these other contributory factors; it serves to make concrete and easily targetable an otherwise somewhat diffuse sense. We conclude with a discussion of the wider implication of sleaze and 'Politikverdrossenheit' in German politics; the questions they raise about the broader legitimacy of the German political system and their impact.

Sleaze in the 1980s

Sleaze-related issues were not an especially prominent feature of West German politics before 1980. Periodic controversies about the behaviour of senior politicians did arise, but these were concerned primarily with revelations of involvement in the Nazi state, complicity in the Cold War espionage endemic in East-West German relations, or breaches of constitutional procedure, most notably when the then Defence Minister, Franz-Josef Strauss, overstepped his authority in 1962 by silencing a critical article in the respected weekly, *Der Spiegel*. Then, as now, scandals concerning the sexual activities of leading politicians were extremely rare. The absence of sleaze controversies—the abuse of office for some form of personal gain—was a reflection in part of the extensive state-financing which shielded German parties from reliance on other income sources found in some countries and, more broadly, it reflected an unusual level of trust in the West German political system, promoted so successfully after 1949 by the political parties, which encouraged a generally deferential appraisal of politicians and their activities. The post-war search for a new German identity led to a situation where 'the legitimacy of the state is not superior to, but is identified with, the legitimacy of the political parties'.[1] There were thus a belief, which stood in stark contract to the pre-war Weimar experience, that the political system and its leading party-political representatives were incorruptible.

During the 1980s, however, a number of significant scandals were uncovered which focused attention of the probity of politicians, dissolving the atmosphere of deference and the belief in incorruptibility. The first scandal, the Flick affair, revolved around illegal donations made to political parties, which they in turn used to top up their generous financial grants from the taxpayer. This combined was with suspected corruption on the part of senior politicians in accepting personal bribes. The German industrial conglomerate Flick had, between 1969 and 1980, donated an estimated total of around DM 25m to various charitable-status front organisations, which in turn donated the funds to political parties, thereby making them except from tax. Although the FDP benefited most, the CDU and SPD also profited substantially. When the nature and scale of these donations emerged in 1981–82, mainly as a result of investigative reporting by *Der Spiegel*, there was a public outcry, in part because of a suspected bribe paid by Flick to Bonn politicians to make the proceeds from the sale of its 29% stake in Daimler-Benz exempt from tax. Otto Graf Lambsdorff and Hans Friedrichs, both former FDP Ministers for the Economy were tried in 1986 for bribery, corruption and tax evasion. Although acquitted of the first two charges, they were found guilty of the third charge and fined substantial sums. The resonance of the Flick affair was especially great because it involved all the major parties, including their highest leadership levels, with even the Chancellor, Helmut Kohl, coming under investigation at one stage. As a result, it left a question mark hanging over the credibility of the established parties which was not entirely erased by subsequent legislation to tighten up the rules on private contributions to party funds, especially since the most prominent casualty of the affair, Lambsdorff, was able to rehabilitate himself successfully by assuming the chairmanship of the FDP in 1988.

Similarly damaging, but unsurpassed for its spectacular nature, was the Barschel scandal of 1987. This revolved around the September 1987 Land election in Schleswig-Holstein, where the CDU had ruled without interruption since 1950 but was now faced by a strong challenge from the SPD. The prospect of electoral defeat led the CDU Minister-President, Uwe Barschel, to engage in 'dirty tricks' by hiring a journalist, Reiner Pfeiffer, to organise a negative publicity campaign against the SPD leader, Bjorn Engholm, with allegations about his sex life and claims that the SPD wanted to legalise sex with minors.

Unfortunately for Barschel, Pfeiffer blew the whistle on him a day after the election result had given the CDU and FDP a wafer-thin majority. As Pfeiffer's account was gradually shown to be true, Barschel was forced to resign and a parliamentary enquiry was started. Shortly before he was due to appear before the enquiry, Barschel made an unexplained visit to Geneva and was found dead, lying fully clothed in a bath in his hotel room, having consumed, probably by his own hand, an overdose of tranquillisers.

The combined effect of the Flick and Barschel affairs was to sensitise the German public to the activities of their elected representatives. The combination of electoral dirty tricks with the alleged acceptance of money for favours raised the general awareness not only that politicians were capable of devious, even criminal activity, but also—as the breadth of involvement in the Flick affair showed—that it could happen on an alarmingly wide scale. The more critical attitude towards party politics this generated was further sharpened by the controversy which broke out in 1988 concerning the parliamentary allowances paid to the members of the Hessian Land parliament. The CDU, SPD and FDP had together voted themselves (against the opposition of the Greens) a substantial payrise as well as numerous other benefits, including extremely comfortable pension rights. The justification given was that the pay levels for the Hessian parliamentarians were way below those in other Länder. This, as the crusading investigations of the academic Hans Herbert von Arnim exposed, was patently untrue; Hesse was already near the top of the scale even before the introduction of the new law.[2] The duplicity of the justification for the pay rise (which led to the repeal of the law and the resignation of the president and vice-president of the Land parliament) generated an impression of politicians using the state as a 'self-service shop' for their collective enrichment. The Hessian scandal also underlined an apparent impotence of the citizen. As von Arnim noted, 'whichever party he [the voter] elects, all (with the possible exception of the Greens) are involved in the parties' cartel'. The coalescence of a 'self-service' mentality with the highly limited public accountability inherent in this form of 'cartel' politics created a legacy of public distaste. The immediate effect of this distaste was, however, limited. The course of events of 1989–90 inevitably deflected public attention on to more pressing matters. The legacy of the Hessian scandal was, however, to re-emerge after the euphoria of unification had given way to the more sober mood caused by the problems of transformation in the east and Germany's drift into recession in 1992–93.

Sleaze in the 1990s

The post-unification years have seen an unprecedented proliferation of sleaze-related controversies and a deepening level of public dissatis-faction with parties. This should not be attributed to any suddenly enhanced proclivity towards corruption and 'self-service', but rather to the particular context for public perceptions of party politics in unified Germany. The public sensitivities raised about the probity of parties and politicians by the Flick, Barschel and Hesse scandals were easily mobilised in the difficult period of adaptation which followed unification. High levels of unemployment and social dislocation in the east, together with the rising tax burden and the more general effects of recession in the west, created a climate in which instances of impropriety would assume a particularly high profile. Further impetus was added to the deepening sensitivity towards such conduct by two other factors.

The first was a series of interviews given by the then Federal President, Richard von Weizsäcker, to the prestigious liberal weekly, *Die Zeit*, in 1992. These included a blistering attack on the 'Machtversessenheit und Machtvergessenheit' of the established parties, that is, their supposed 'power crazines's; and their irresponsibility in the exercise of power. Von Weizsäcker was widely respected, particularly because of his open confrontation with the historical memory of Nazism, as a man of great moral integrity. The impact of his attack on the parties was thus all the more telling and, as surveys conducted by the Allensbach polling institute confirm, struck a chord with public opinion. His criticisms, secondly, were reinforced by a growing media concentration on the shortcomings and indiscretions of parties and politicians. An especially important role was played by *Der Spiegel*, which since the Strauss-*Spiegel* affair of 1962 has seen itself as a kind of liberal conscience of the nation. This liberal conscience was reinvigorated in a regular 'affairs' column which persistently highlighted examples of party and politician wrongdoing, including how Hannelore Rönsch, Federal Minister for the Family, financed a class reunion with public funds and of how Monika Griefahn, the Lower Saxony Environment Minister, awarded consultancy contracts to a company run by her husband. It is a moot point whether the *Spiegel*'s revelations merely articulated the resentments of a public eager to focus its dissatisfaction with the economic hardship it found itself in, or whether the *Spiegel* irresponsibly stoked up such resentment as some have claimed. Indisputable, though, is the effect: it served to keep public sensitivities about the sleaze issue very much in the public arena.

There were two main focal points for public and media dissatisfaction: a renewed bout of 'self-service', politicians securing for themselves pay and other financial privileges from public funds, and a series of cases in which senior politicians abused their public position for private gain. 'Self-service' controversies in the Länder have been numerous since unification. Attention was focused on the pension arrangements available to one of the SPD's most senior leaders, Oskar Lafontaine: on becoming Minister-President of the Saarland, he continued to draw his not ungenerous pension as ex-mayor of Saarbrücken. In similarly self-beneficial vein, the Senate members (ministers) of the Land Hamburg awarded themselves a salary rise of over 100% in autumn 1991. More recently, the Bavarian parliament considered a salary increase for its members up to £71,500 p.a., while the Bundestag voted in September 1995 that MPs pay be gradually raised to a staggering £75,000 p.a., marginally less than that of the British Prime Minister.

The typical justification for these self-awarded pay rises was that salaries in public service have to be kept in line with those in the private sector in order to attract individuals of sufficient quality. While this may have contained a grain of truth, it also had an element of the grotesque when the same politicians were ritually emphasising the need for public belt-tightening as compensation for the costs of unification to the public purse. Not surprisingly, public uproar continued, extending seamlessly into the east, where attitudes towards politicians' pay were imported along with the 'Wessis' who took over many key posts in the new eastern provinces at a salary almost equal to western levels. For example, the Minister-President of Saxony-Anhalt, along with three other ministers of western origin had to resign in November 1993 because they had knowingly drawn a salary far greater than that to which they were entitled.

Equally prominent have been cases in which politicians have apparently made use of their public positions to secure some form of private gain. The conspiratorial nature of such dealings would lead one to suspect that the scandals which have come to the fore are only really the tip of the iceberg. Again, prominent politicians have fallen victim to the revelation of such activities: Lothar Späth, CDU Minister-President of Baden-Wüttemberg and once widely tipped as a possible Kohl successor, had to resign in 1992 when the extensive gifts he had received from friendly businessmen became public. Max Streibl, his opposite number in Bavaria, was also forced to resign in 1993 in the now notorious 'Amigo-affair', in which he accepted holidays and free flights from businessmen to such an extent that even in Bavaria, where the distinction between state and party had become especially unclear under the long reign of Franz-Josef Strauss, he was considered an electoral liability by his party, the CSU. In a further highly publicised case of Bavarian elite camaraderie, the Zwick family, which still owes the Bavarian state DM 70m in taxes, has successfully managed to evade prosecution because of its excellent connections to the Bavarian CSU hierarchy. However, the most prominent casualty of this form of sleaze was Jürgen Möllemann, then Federal Minister for the Economy, who was forced to resign in 1993 after it was made public that he had used official notepaper to advertise the shopping-trolley business of his brother-in-law (the so-called 'letter-head affair'). The net effect has been to create an impression—undoubtedly unfair to the majority of German politicians—that the members of the political class are motivated to an unhealthy degree by the prospect of material gain to be secured from their offices.

Explanations of 'Politikverdrossenheit'

It would be stating the obvious simply to say that this accumulation of sleaze has fed into the sense of 'Politikverdrossenheit' in post-unification Germany. It would be surprising if such a catalogue of scandals had not had a severely negative influence on public opinion. Sleaze, though, has not been the sole cause. Other factors have fed into what is undeniably a much wider process of public disillusionment and need to be taken into account. More important, the full significance of the sleaze factor can not be appreciated unless it is seen in conjunction with these other factors: the 'modernisation trap' into which the established parties have fallen, the 'monopoly' position assured by their impenetrable organisational structures, and their apparent inability to devise effective solutions to pressing political problems.

The most fundamental of these additional factors has been described as the modernisation trap into which the established parties have fallen.[3] It is related to the impact of changes in the social structure of post-war West German society on the character of the established parties. Faced by secularisation in society and structural modernisation in the economy, they could no longer rely simply on the traditional support of social groups whose size was now declining—for example the CDU/CSU's practising Catholics or the SPD's unionised manual workers. Electoral competition forced the parties to appeal to new social groups by moderating their ideological heritage. Although the CDU/CSU and SPD—the classic 'people's parties'—did so with great success, the corollary was a blurring of party identity and direction which disillusioned those supporters still attached to the original ideological thrust.

The problem was revealed in particular after changes of government. When the SPD assumed the role of leading coalition partner in 1969, it was unable to meet aspirations for far-reaching political reform. Equally, when the CDU/CSU resumed as leading coalition partner in 1982, the rhetoric of the 'Wende', literally a 'turn-around' in the direction of neo-liberal market reforms, proved by and large to lack substance. In other words, instead of ideologically-driven policy change, party supporters were faced by a technocratically-driven governmental pragmatism. This pragmatic orientation is especially exemplified in the FDP, whose position in the party system as 'majority-maker' has undermined its credibility whenever it has shifted its coalition allegiance in order to sustain itself in office. The FDP as a result has a negligible core electorate and has often depended for its survival on the 'loaned' tactical voters of supporters of one or the other larger parties under the German two-vote electoral system. Its role as majority maker has also served to concentrate the electoral competition of the two larger parties even further on its own moderate centre ground.

The net result, to use an analogy from British politics in the mid-1990s, was to focus party competition on a mythical average voter, the

occupant of 'middle income, middle Germany'. The apparent indistin-
guishability of an established party cartel in which each party was
motivated by overlapping, centrist electoral considerations was the
essence of the modernisation trap. Unsurprisingly, it provoked a process
of alienation among those motivated by ideology or principle: why
support one of these parties if it offers little that its competitors do not?

This process of alienation was accelerated by the nature of the
established parties' organisational structures. These, in essence
unchanged since the establishment of modern party politics in Germany
in the late nineteenth century, were complex and highly bureaucratised,
failing to offer genuine opportunities for new groups or new ideas to
influence the party's established direction. They still exhibited the
tendency to oligarchy identified by Robert Michels. The problem was
exemplified in the SPD when many of those who had joined the party
in the reformist spirit of the late 1960s left again in disillusionment in
the 1970s when confronted with the Social Democratic 'organisational
dinosaur'.[4] More broadly, the impenetrability of party structures has
been revealed in two important ways. First, the established parties were
unable to regenerate themselves by attracting younger members lost to
other, more unconventional and direct forms of political participation.
This problem has been felt most severely by the CDU. According to the
Frankfurter Allgemeine Zeitung, membership in the party's youth
organisations fell from 260,000 to 196,000 between 1983 and 1991,
leaving it increasingly a party of middle-aged and old men. Second, the
established parties have failed since unification to secure effective east
German input into their higher echelons, tending instead to examples of
tokenism.

The outcome of the petrification of party structures has been the
creation of a 'monopoly of power' of a professionalised politician caste
perceived as increasingly remote from the electorate. This has facilitated
the emergence of a closed, self-selecting circle, well described as an
unpalatable combination of 'cliques, cabals and careers'.[5] This style of
politics has infiltrated the wider structures of public service in Germany,
where the 'party book' is a key prerequisite for advancement in the civil
service, the public broadcasting system and scientific research. It has
applied most notably, though, in the various salary and pension scandals
discussed above, which were facilitated by what has been called the
'omnipotence' of a self-interested party 'cartel', and in the composition
of party lists of candidates which form a core part of the electoral
system. Whoever secures a place towards the top of a party list cannot
fail to be elected unless a wholesale rejection of that party takes place.
This has been repeatedly condemned as depriving the voters of the right
to decide who represents them by those seeking to explain 'Politikverdrossenheit'. Without effective routes of input into party life, the
possibility of securing change through the established parties is frus-
trated, and this compounds the disillusion caused by the lack of genuine

choice within an established party cartel which has fallen foul of the modernisation trap. It has also heightened sensitivities about a third factor widely identified to have contributed to 'Politikverdrossenheit', that of declining party policy competence.

There has emerged a widespread perception that while the established parties may hold a 'monopoly of power', they are incapable of using their power to meet the needs of the electorate. This feeling has been encouraged by the impression of policy stagnation which has emerged since unification, particularly as regards economic reconstruction in the east. Only in March 1993, two and a half years after unification, was a comprehensive package for financing economic reconstruction finally decided. Debates in other key areas have also tended to extend over long periods before a clear line was formulated, e.g. whether the Bundeswehr should be allowed to operate outside NATO territory and the reform of Germany's liberal asylum law. While this unimpressive problem-solving record probably has more to do with the dispersal of policy-making powers, the established parties have been the focal points of the public dissatisfaction it has caused.

Sleaze and 'Politikverdrossenheit'

The factors discussed above present a highly unfavourable climate of opinion for the established parties in Germany. We have indicated reasons for the growing dissatisfaction with established parties. That dissatisfaction is given a clearer focus when responses to opinion polls designed to demonstrate the level of public trust in the parties are considered. Both EMNID and IPOS have found that parties had the lowest level of public trust of all political institutions in both east and west in the period 1990–92. In one sense this is nothing new; throughout the 1980s parties were almost invariably at the bottom of the trust league table in West Germany. What is remarkable is the scale of the mistrust they and their representatives have provoked since German unity. Mistrust has increased dramatically. One poll showed that while that 40% of West Germans felt that politicians were 'trustworthy' in 1986, the repeat figures for 1993 were just 15% in the west and 8% in the east, a trend confirmed in a 1994 EMNID survey which suggested that only 7% of Germans felt able to express 'trust' in their political parties.

This terminology of trust—and the extraordinarily high levels of mistrust which have been recorded—inevitably raises questions about public perceptions of the honesty of parties and politicians. These perceptions are not positive ones. They reveal the widespread belief that politicians are not concerned about the view of the 'little man' but are engaged in a 'dirty business' in which the pursuit of their personal interests is paramount. Only 14% of respondents in a 1993 poll believed, for example, that members of the Bundestag first and foremost represented the interests of their constituents, while 73% felt that politicians 'exploited their position to secure for themselves personal advantage', 35% that 'politicians are corrupted by power', and 46% that 'you can count on cases of corruption among politicians'.

This pattern of cynicism about politicians presents an emphatic confirmation of the impact of sleaze on public perceptions of party politics. The emergence of sleaze as a high-profile political issue in the second half of the 1980s and the frequent revelations of impropriety in office in the 1990s have transformed the public image of parties and politicians.

An EMNID survey in 1987 had shown that the top three characteristics associated with politicians were 'eloquence', 'experience' and 'selflessness and responsibility'; the same survey in 1993 revealed the top three characteristics as 'dishonest', 'corruptible' and 'self-seeking'. This mood swing provides a tangible focus for the wider sense of alienation discussed above. Sleaze, in other words, has highlighted the perceived failure of the parties to serve the electorate. It has facilitated the targeting of public dissatisfaction on a party 'cartel', insulated by its 'monopoly of power', which is able to 'look after its own'. The impression of 'self-service' produced by sleaze has placed the failure of parties and politicians into stark relief.

A crucial question for many commentators has been whether the decline in confidence and trust in parties and politicians has had a broader impact on the legitimacy of the German political system as a whole. For historical reasons, this question has a special resonance. A central factor in the legitimacy crisis and ultimate collapse of the Weimar Republic was the massive loss of trust experienced by parties and politicians. Some have pointed to a superficially similar situation in Germany today. 'Parteienverdrossenheit' has undoubtedly had an effect on perceptions of other core political institutions. Indices of public confidence in the Bundestag and the federal government have fallen markedly in recent years, subject to 'guilt by association'. However, the comparison of past with present is somewhat exaggerated. Other institutions—the Constitutional Court and the judicial system or the Bundesbank—remain highly respected. This points to the structural advantages of a system which disperses authority among a range of institutions. It suggests, to use the terminology of political culture analysis, a high level of 'diffuse' support for a political system which is able to absorb lower levels of 'specific' support for certain institutions. Thus the percentage of Germans claiming to be satisfied with democracy (as measured by Eurobarometer surveys) is, at around 75%, consistently amongst the highest in the European Union, and considerably higher than in either France or the UK.

Alternatively, it might be argued that the high levels of 'Politikverdrossenheit' recorded in the 1990s are transitory. It is perhaps no coincidence that the recent prominence of scandals and the associated debate about 'Politikverdrossenheit' has coincided with the deepest recession in Germany's post-war history. The partial crisis of confidence in Germany's political institutions may therefore ebb away when the economic situation improves.

We thank the Allensbach Institute für Demoskopie, the Forschungs-gruppe Wahlen, Mannheim and EMNID, Bielefeld, for the provision of the survey material used in this article.

1   W. Paterson, 'West Germany: Between Party Apparatus and Basis Democracy' in A. Ware (ed), *Political Parties: Electoral Change and Structural Response*, Blackwell, 1987, p.159.

2   cf H.H. von Arnim, 'Entmündigen die Parteien das Volk? Parteienherrschaft und Volkssouveränität' in *Aus Politik und Zeitgeschichte*, supplement to *Das Parlament*, B21/1990.

3   H. Rattinger, 'Abkehr von den Parteien? Dimensionen der Parteiverdrossenheit' in *Aus Politik und Zeitgeschichte*, supplement to *Das Parlament*, B11/1993, following E. Wiesendahl, 'Der Marsch aus den Institutionen' in *Aus Politiki und Zeitgeschichte*, supplement to *Das Parlament*, B21/1990.

4   E. Wiesendahl, 'Der Marsch aus den Institutionen', loc. cit.

5   E. Scheuch and U. Scheuch, *Cliquen, Klüngel und Karrieren*, Reinbek, 1992.

Greece

BY KL. S. KOUTSOUKIS

TWENTY years after its foundation the Third Hellenic Republic is in the midst of a growing crisis. Its political system and the institutions established after the fall of the military dictatorship in July 1974 proved themselves able to face external challenges, to join the European Community, to handle internal terrorism and to live through austerity policies without serious consequences for their stability. It is ironic, however, that Greece now runs serious risks from within the political system. One such risk comes from business, financial and other interests seeking to influence political decisions. A more important risk appears to be that political institutions suffer from a growing perception of sleaze. Although there is concern about probity in the wider public sector, the conduct of politicians seems to be at the centre of this concern.

The rapid diffusion of information which came with the liberalisation of mass media by the end of the 1980s, together with a gradually increased demand for transparency in the public sector, have brought into light unacceptable patterns of behaviour among politicians, including aspects of their private lives. Thus the public began to have an interest in politics and at the same time become gradually critical of politicians' behaviour. Here we examine the impact of their behaviour upon the electorate in this context and note what the political elite thinks about the current political system. Among 324 senior governmental and party figures who were asked in 1993 about the degree to which the political system is satisfactory, only 16% considered it as 'good'. The majority, 62%, thought it had 'deficiencies', and a substantial minority, 22% believed that the system was getting worse (Radio Flash 9.61, 1993).

Corruption and scandal: their impact on political life

Scandals began to appear regularly in the investigative press from the mid-1980s. These included the 1987 'corn scandal' where the Deputy Minister of Finance and the chairman of the State Export Agency were sent to prison in 1990 for several years, together with some officials, for cheating the European Community Common Agricultural Policy by presenting Yugoslav corn as Greek in order to get subsidies. In 1985 the director general of the Public Electric Enterprise was found guilty of receiving kickbacks of almost £1.5m. The then Prime Minister, Andreas Papandreou, said: 'One may expect a director to make himself a gift but not as high as 500 million drachma'.

More serious was the 1988 'Koskotas scandal' involving George Koskotas, a young Greek-American banker, as well as number of leading politicians and officials, businessmen, bankers, managers of state enterprises, lawyers and journalists who in one way or the other were caught up in networks of transactions.[1] Koskotas claimed during the court hearings in 1991–92 that he had the backing of leading figures in PASOK (Greece's socialist party and, at that time, the government), especially its leader Andreas Papadreou and some of his closest associates. In order to cover illegal transactions of his Bank of Crete and to avoid scrutiny by the Bank of Greece, Koskotas persuaded the Deputy Prime Minister to get legislation passed that limited the Bank of Greece's power of scrutiny to those shareholders with more than 20% of the capital while excluding its control of their boards of directors. Koskotas was thus doubly protected: he was chairman of the Bank of Crete and owned less than 20% of its shares. Furthermore, the legislation stated that a bank's documents were enough proof for the origin of funds, without need of verification. This enabled Koskotas to cover up his misuse of bank funds by pretending money had come from abroad, using false documents. Ironically, the law became known as 'Koutsonomos', taking half of its name from the late A. Koutsogiorgas, a powerful member of the PASOK Cabinet, who initiated it, and the other half 'nomos', meaning law. In return, Koskotas alleged in court that he deposited US$2m in a Swiss bank. Through the procedures of the law on ministerial responsibility, parliament filed charges of malpractice, including bribery, damage of state property and violation of laws, against Prime Minister Papandreous, his Minister of Justice Koutsogiorgas, and the Ministers of Finance and Industry. Charges were also brought against the Minister of National Economy, who had been elected to the European Parliament which refused to lift his immunity from trial. Papandreou never appeared in court to defend himself and was acquitted, while the Ministers of Finance and Industry were found guilty of not applying certain legal procedures, thereby damaging the public interest. Koutsogiorgas died during the trial.

Since then, corruption and scandal have been regular features in the media and in political life. It is not surprising, therefore, that corruption appears to be one of the important problems in the eyes of the public, though not as high in priority as many others. In a 1993 survey of the relative importance of current problems of the country (ALCO, 1993), only 7% of the respondents considered corruption as a significantly serious problem that the country faced; unemployment rated 50%, cost of living 40%, crime 26%, foreign policy 19%, pollution 12%, taxation, inflation and national debt each 9% or 10%.

It is significant, however, that other research puts corruption high on the list of problems that need to be addressed within the next decade if the country is to overcome the current crisis (MRB Hellas, 1993). Fighting corruption and scandals by transparency in public life gets one of the highest ratings, 58.1%; this is second only to 58.6% calling for honest, progressive and able politicians. On the other hand, issues such as political stability, modernisation of institutions and parties, and mild political climate get lower ratings, ranging from 44% to 25%. Indicative also is another questionnaire distributed randomly among 139 officials in 1994, asking how important the issue of corruption was in the public service: 27% consider it non-existent, 34% negligible, 15% serious and 25% very serious. Thus about 40% of public servants think that corruption is, at the least, a serious problem.[2]

The politics of corruption

Corruption in politics has been used by the political opposition as an effective weapon against the government. Serious political scandals that concern mismanagement, corrupt practices and the integrity of government ministers provide a means to criticise the integrity of government ministers, while press reports and opinion polls can be seen as indicators of the society's sensitivity to ethical matters; as such, they may also cause shifts in support from the government to the opposition party. Since the mid-1980s political scandals have been used by the opposition for this purpose. This led to a polarisation of political life in which the two big parties, PASOK and the New Democracy, monopolised political power, succeeding each other in government and, if one adds the personal animosity between their leaders—Papandreou and Mitsotakis—until 1994, produced what looks like games of 'bad and good guys', who's who depending on who is in power and who in opposition.

The New Democracy party in opposition in the 1980s was able to draw attention to a serious number of cases involving corruption (fifty were reported to parliament, such as those involving defence procurements). After it won the elections in 1989–90, it was able to file charges of misconduct against PASOK's leader, Andreas Papandreou, and have convicted a couple of ministers as well as several high officials (particularly managers of state enterprises such as post, telecommunication and Olympic Airways) for depositing large amounts of their agencies' money in the Bank of Crete, either with no interest or with lower interest than that offered by all other banks. Public opinion at that time (1989–90) was divided. As many as 56% of respondents believed that Papandreou should be put on trial, while 53% were convinced that his former ministers should also be tried. However, only 44% believed that those really responsible would be punished (MRB Hellas, 1989).

While in opposition between 1990–93, PASOK challenged the New Democracy government on mismanagement and integrity, targeting particularly the Prime Minister of the time, Mitsotakis. Thus when PASOK came to power by the end of 1993, it proceeded to file charges against the former Prime Minister and two of his former ministers, the Minister of Finance (who had meanwhile become an EC Commissioner) and the Minister of Trade and Industry. The charges concerned the sale of the biggest state-owned cement company (AGET-Hercules) to the Italian Ferruci group at a price lower than could be got in the international market, thus damaging the interests of the state. (Separate charges on suspiciously high and probably illegal profits were filed against the vice-chairman of AGET and the brokers in this sale, but this case is still pending.) The hostility of public opinion towards the cement scandal a few months before the elections of October 1993 is shown in a survey: 25% said the transaction was done on a manner which raised serious questions, 40% that it constituted an economic scandal (MRB Hellas, 1993).

Besides the cement scandal, private properties of the former Prime Minister were also under scrutiny by PASOK, including land in the Savoy region in France. The issue was settled when it was shown to be only a procedural matter, connected with the annual property declarations that all politicians submit to parliament. Another inquiry concerned the private collection of several hundred antiques which Mitsotakis had donated to the town of Chania in Crete where he was born and where a special museum was established. The investigation conducted by the prosecutor's office, at the request of the late Melina Mercuri, Minister of Culture, found no illegal holdings or transactions in respect of this collection.

Other charges against Mitsotakis involved spying on the PASOK leader by tapping his telephone conversations. A few years earlier the former Prime Minister had charged Papandreou on the same grounds but, while in government, obtained a parliamentary resolution suspending further prosecution; Papandreou returned the favour by introducing a parliamentary resolution in January 1995 to suspend further prosecutions of Mitsotakis and his ministers as regards the ACET-Hercules scandal. The PASOK government's action was disapproved by a considerable majority of respondents, with only 28% in favour. When asked if the approval of the resolution by parliament would affect the credibility of political life, only 18% believed that it might benefit the credibility of politics, whereas 78% believed that it would hurt that credibility (MARTEL, 1995). These answers indicate that the electorate disagrees with parliament's decision (or at least PASOK's initiative), a fact that one might expect to have further consequences for public attitudes to the political system.

The impact of political scandals seems to have been an influential factor in the shift of government in 1989–90, when elections were conducted with 'Catharsis' as a slogan against PASOK. 'Catharis' is an essential element of tragedy according to Aristotle, appearing as a way out of tragic events or the purification of spectators 'with incidents arousing pity and fear wherewith to accomplish its catharis of such emotions'. In modern Greek, the meaning of the term is cleaning something or, allegorically, bringing someone back clean, free of charges of immoral or dishonest behaviour. The latter was the meaning that politicians gave to it in their attempt to counteract general public accusations that all politicians were corrupt. Indeed 'Catharsis' was one of the main election campaign slogans adopted by the opponents of PASOK. PASOK lost the elections in June 1989 and a coalition government of the Left and New Democracy was formed, primarily on the basis of their common goal of 'Catharsis' under the then leadership of the New Democracy MP, Tzannetakis. In 1993, when New Democracy's mismanagement in privatising the economy was put under scrutiny, the same 'Catharsis' slogan appeared in PASOK's election campaign and contributed to its victory.

The importance to the electorate of honest behaviour in politics is reflected in the answers given to the question on how the respective scandals affected them: 60% agreed that the economic scandals which approved under the PASOK government destroyed its credibility; 67% agreed that the Prime Minister's inability to eliminate corruption and scandals was one of the main problems of New Democracy (MRB Hellas, 1993).

The ethics of politics: a framework

To understand why politicians behave as they do, the Greek term 'idioteles society', composed of the word 'idion' which means 'its own' and the word 'telos' meaning purpose or goal, has been utilised elsewhere to describe the nature of Greek politics.[3] It describes the motive for which an act is committed, or the reason for a certain behaviour, in a society where particularistic interests outweigh the public interest. Thus members of such a society tend to act in ways that go against virtues which strengthen the collective good or social values. Certain characteristics may be indicative of its existence, including the ineffectiveness of legislation or institutional processes, and an imbalance of values between specific interests and wider societal values. The members of different particularistic interests may not have strong ties but tend to come together for specific actions serving their mutual interests. They may follow parallel behavioural patterns without forming a unified group but, by resembling each other's behavioural patterns, reinforce their appearance as a distinctive group with its own subculture. When the group uses social and political processes for its own sake, and fails to respect established values or national aspirations for example, it weakens the spirit of community that holds the members of a society together. The higher in the sociopolitical ladder members of such interests are found, the more influential their behaviour and the greater the impact upon society.

It may not be accidental, therefore, that the present crisis in Greece is centred around politics and the behaviour of these practitioners. The law 'for the protection of the honesty of politicians', introduced in 1964 by the late George Papandreou, then Prime Minister, established a practice whereby every year MPs submit a statement of their property and income from all sources. They must report changes from one year to the next and specify the source of anything new. By an amendment introduced in 1987, the accuracy of statements is examined by the deputy chairman of the parliament. If he finds some irregularity, he sends the matter to the Supreme Court prosecutor's office. In 1994 the leader of the opposition, Mr Evert, asked the deputy chairman to follow that procedure for the Prime Minister's annual statement. When he did not do so, because he saw no irregularity, Mr Evert and some colleagues signed a petition to the Speaker of the House asking for an ad hoc parliamentary committee to examine the annual statements of all who had served as party leaders since 1985. In a special debate in February 1995 he questioned less the accuracy of Andreas Papandreou's statement than whether it was appropriate for the Prime Minister to build a luxurious villa in a period of austerity with money accrued beyond his current known income. He then queried how morally acceptable it was for the Prime Minister to borrow money from three of his ministers — which the opposition leader said could make him beholden to them — as well as from three other friends, of whom only one (a foreigner) required repayment with interest.

The PASOK majority in parliament voted against the New Democracy's proposal. It is noteworthy, however, that the leader of the second largest opposition party (Political Spring) asked, during the debate, for the examination to include the statements of all the party leaders since 1974. Furthermore, he asked that it should be conducted each year by the appropriate tax authorities under the supervision of the Court of Accounts instead of a parliamentary committee. Although the proposal was overruled by PASOK's majority, one consequence of the debate has been an inquiry by the prosecutor's office into the opposition allegations about breaches of law in the issue of the building licences during construction of the Prime Minister's villa.

Having in mind the sensitivity of the public to ethical behaviour of politicians and with the past use of scandal as an effective means to criticise the government, Mr Evert demanded a special session of parliament devoted to the ethics of politics. In doing so, he attempted to describe the public's criticism of the ethical standards of politicians and to encourage politicians to think seriously about certain aspects of their behaviour. In the debate that took place in January 1995, Andreas Papandreou accepted that politics was on trial. He stressed the need for political life and political parties to be independent from the influence of outside interests, and that transparency and scrutiny needed to be established to end the cynicism and disillusionment about public life of the country. To achieve this, he proposed four institutional arrangements: a new law about the responsibility of those who serve as ministers; a law that would settle the problem of financing political parties; the modernisation of public administration; and amendment of the constitution. The Prime Minister stressed the fact that individuals could not always distinguish the collective need from personal goals in society, while, in politics, the choice was often for the 'temporary today' for the 'dominant personal tomorrow' and not 'the collective effort for the needs of the country'. There was a positive reaction to his proposals; all the parties in parliament agreed to cooperate within the committees that would draft the various bills. It may be noted, however, that amendment of the law on ministerial responsibility and the law on financing of the political parties has been demanded for a long time, while the need for a second amendment of the constitution (the first was in 1986) was proposed in early 1990s by the New Democracy party.

During the debate Mr Evert, the opposition leader, stressed the responsibility of political leadership and of politicians in general to set an example for the rest of the society, and not add to the atmosphere of sleazy behaviour, citing circumvention of law, avoidance of taxes, contempt for official institutions, use of parliamentary immunity and clientelism in the public sector. It is indicative, for example, that merit appointments and the abolition of clientelism in the public sector received high support, 61% and 56%, among the respondents in one 1995 survey. Mr Evert confessed that 'we have created an impression that politicians legislate with an admirable agreement for projecting their personal interests; we have reached the point where members of parliament give the sense of a small, closed society which fights anxiously for the preservation of its privileges'. He stressed the need 'to stop such an impression and reconstitute the credibility of politics and politicians', to resist acting in accord with prevalent public belief that 'all politicians are the same, they all steal, all are unscrupulous, all are inefficient'. Consequently, he argued that many privileges of MPs were unjustified and should be abolished, making it clear that he would support any action in that direction.

These special privileges for MPs have become a matter of public debate. Recently, judges appealed to the Supreme Court for equal treatment with MPs on a 50% tax exemption of their salary. The Court's decision was positive. Since then, a generalised discussion has taken place in the media, informing the public that certain professional and social groups also have privileges similar to tax exemption. Because of this, an ad hoc committee has been established at the Ministry of Finance to examine all these cases and suggest which of them will be cut off. After the debate on ethics in politics, special attention, however, has been given to the politicians' privileges which, according to the press, include: extra remuneration for participation in standing parliamentary committees and in the summer sessions; free telephone calls and postage up to a certain level; the right to buy a car (up to 2000 cc) tax and customs free every four years; the right to employ up to five secretaries paid by state, two coming from the civil service and two working at his or her parliamentary office; policeman as personal guard;

a number of air tickets for visiting constituencies; a special housing facility in Athens four days a week during parliamentary sessions for those residing outside the city; assistance in renting a building where the MPs from regional constituencies have their offices; and a pension after serving for one period in the parliament. There is also concern about the immunity of MPs from legal action for behaviour which does not fall in the domain of their political activity.

In his letter to the Speaker proposing the abolition of all special privileges, Mr Evert stated: 'Greek society needs an example to be provided by its leadership and not be fed with behaviour that scandalises the public.' Subsequently, all the parties in parliament agreed to proceed in eliminating certain of the above privileges in order to diminish protests of the public.

Electoral reaction: a new factor in political life

Although without further research it is not possible to establish a direct causal link between the growing dissatisfaction of voters and the behaviour of politicians in Greece, opinion polls and recent debate in parliament indicate that a considerable part of public alienation from the parties may be attributed to sleaze politics.

The widening gap between the electorate and parliament has been confirmed by research which indicates a widening gap of credibility separating the public from politics and politicians. Earlier research suggests that abstentions or void ballot papers in elections may be interpreted as a gradual manifestation of this credibility gap. In 1993 the abstention rate in the parliamentary election was 26%. Further research on voting patterns shows a higher incidence of potential blank voters, or voting for the opposition.

Discussion of ethical matters concerning the behaviour and perform-ance in office of politicians (and the ruling party) seem to validate the hypothesis that scandals raise ethical questions and cause a shift in the electorate in favour of the opposition party that initiates such debates. Nevertheless, it is critical public opinion, through the media, that is the force for change rather than the politicians.

Apart from the 'Catharsis' campaign, the concerns expressed over scandals have led to the adoption of various anti-corruption policies and institutional changes for reducing corruption in the public sector of Greece. These include: (a) the establishment of the Corps of Public Administration Controllers in 1987 and 1991 to eliminate improper behaviour by public servants towards citizens and to promote principles of equality and merit systems in the public sector; (b) a bill in 1995 introducing social control and procedures of transparency in the critical area of state procurements; (c) the establishment in 1991 of a new agency for controlling economic crime, the laundering of money, narcotics and the arms trade, as well as fraud in relation to European Union subsidies for agriculture exports. Above all, one may not disregard the state campaign to call upon the citizen for help in reducing tax evasion and the underground economy which absorbs about 40% of national income. The degree to which such cooperation will take place and the conscience of citizens expand will show whether civil society is strengthened. Despite all efforts to reduce corruption, there is still a considerable distrust of politics and politicians.

To a certain point this distrust and disappointment may have its roots in the lack of exemplary behaviour by politicians who appear to the public as members with particularistic interests. It is obvious, however, that Greek society has now entered a period of serious discussion about its problems, its future course and long-range perspectives. The present multidimensional crisis is caused by several factors such as internal corruption, sleaze, ineffectiveness in government and dysfunctional institutions, the lack of exemplary behaviour on the part of national leadership. The ongoing discussion will be complex and will take time before reaching a point of agreement on a new social contract.

1   More about this scandal in K.S. Koutsoukis, 'Corruption and Reform: "Catharsis" and Anticorruption Policies in Postsocialist Greece', paper present at the ECPR workshops, Leiden 1993.

2   K.S. Koutsoukis, 'The Problems of Public Administration from the Public Servants' Perspective', *Information*, April 1995. For the comparative level of corruption in Greece see L.W.J.C. Huberts, 'Public Corruption in Europe: A Sketch of the Problem', paper presented at the IPSA congress, Berlin, 1994. For Greece see K.S. Koutsoukis, 'Patterns of Corruption and Political Change in Modern Greece 1946–1987', *Corruption and Reform* 4, 1989.

3   K.S. Koutsoukis, 'The Good, the Bad and the Ugly in Society: The Idioteles Institution in Society as a Source of Corruption' in U.Berlinsky, A Friendberg and S B Werner (eds), *Corruption in a Changing World* vol 1, Jerusalem: International Society of Etchics in Public Service 1994.

Ireland

BY NEIL COLLINS AND COLM O RAGHALLAIGH

THE question of standards in public life has been a political issue in Ireland for some years, but particularly since a series of scandals concerning politicians and business people in 1991. The topic was given even greater prominence by a tribunal of enquiry which sat between May 1991 and June 1993 to examine the irregularities in the beef processing industry. At the turn of the year 1994–95, a change of government was forced in part on the issue of ethics and standards of truthfulness in public life. By the summer of 1995, new legislation governing behaviour in public life and giving Dáil (parliamentary) committees effective powers to investigate matters of public disquiet was in place. Politicians recognise a growing public cynicism about their conduct and are attempting to respond by tougher, more transparent rules. The Ethics in Public Office Act 1995 covers all ministers, parliamentarians, public servants and board members of state-owned companies. It marks a significant change in Irish public life.

Though the word itself does not have much currency, the issue of sleaze has never been more evident in a country where politics is a spectator sport with a major public following. Political figures generally have a high public profile, if not nationally, then at least in their constituencies. This visibility of politicians reflects among other things the keen interest in politics of the electorate. It is also a product, however, of the Irish electoral system which pitches politicians of the same party into competition against each other. The single transferable vote system of proportional representation means successful candidates must have a significant personal vote. This extra-party support is usually garnered by assiduous constituency service. Much of what outside observers may identify as sleaze in the politics of the Republic of Ireland is a product of the rivalry between politicians for perceived influence or 'pull'. In Ireland, however, the use of 'pull' is generally within the catalogue of tolerated conduct. Here, therefore, we seek to define the phenomena of sleaze with reference to Irish political culture, recent examples of controversy and the bounds of acceptable behaviour by politicians.

Irish political culture

In general, the word sleaze is has become popular with headline writers in Ireland 'in search of something that crosses a blast of moral outrage with a puppet show hiss' (*Irish Times*, 26 April 1995). On the other hand, social attitudes are now more liberal than the laws governing divorce and abortion would suggest. For example, marital separations which were once the subject of social sanction are now frequently cited by estranged politicians themselves as evidence of the strains of public life or tokens of solidarity with others in marital difficulty. In the absence of divorce legislation, the leader of Fianna Fáil is openly living in an adulterous relationship. His election as leader was taken as a sign of the tolerance of the public generally. In his address to the party following his victory, he pointedly referred to his marital status and openly acknowledged his situation. His willingness to do so was greeted enthusiastically by the party faithful.

To understand what sleaze means in the Republic, it is important to appreciate the significance of particularism or personalism, localism and clientelism in its political culture. These elements set the parameters within which judgements are made by the electorate about what kinds of behaviour are an unacceptable intrusion of private interest into public life. In recent years there has been a gradual narrowing of the aspects of Irish politics which the political science literature classifies as sui generis. The analysis of Ireland now relies less on comparisons with it nearest neighbour, Britain, and places the Republic more in the category of small continental European Union states. Ireland is, as a result, less 'distinctive' but more easily understood. Thus, for example, the assertion asserts that 'Irish parties are *not* peculiar—they are common or garden European varieties, rather than the weird and wonderful mutants that some would have us believe.'[1] Similar statement could be made about Irish voting behaviour or public policies.

The parallels to Ireland are often found in the Mediterranean countries, so it is not surprising that clientelism is considered an important feature of politics. In the Irish case, the term 'brokerage' may be more accurate because the resources which are the subject of the exchange between citizen and politician are usually under the direct control of a third party, generally an official of the state bureaucracy. The key to holding office for most politicians is a reputation as a political 'broker'; that is someone who can provide privileged access to state services as well as favourable consideration from important private sector bodies. To do this, politicians must develop extensive networks in the state bureaucracy, public bodies, local authorities and significant local employers.

Much of the brokerage activity of members of the Dáil (TDs) is little more than advice about the benefits to which people are entitled; help with access to information about public services and clarification of the sources of help. Such constituency service is uncontroversial, though politicians often complain about the amount of it they are expected to do. The extension of this facilitating work into appeals to bureaucrats and others on behalf of disappointed constituents is potentially unsavoury, implying that the politically-assisted applicant is gaining unfair advantage and that other citizens suffer. The evidence, however, suggests that, in most areas of the public service, few real distortions of the pattern of provision occur. The politicians are really marketing their specialist knowledge of state services and ready access to bureaucrats to the bureaucratically illiterate.[2]

Major allocative decisions, long-term plans and fiscal arrangements are the responsibility of the government or senior public officials. Local politicians avoid association with broad policy because it may compromise them with their own local following. For example, it is difficult for Irish politicians to support publicly changes of policies for the housing of problem families, the siting of refuse facilities or refusing planning applications on aesthetic grounds because of their vulnerability to electoral pressure. There is always somebody else in their own party who, by playing the local or NIMBY (Not In My Back Yard) card, can displace them without changing the partisan balance. The politician is not acquiring something which the citizen could not have, rather he or she is getting it much more readily. The TD or councillor is a resource which is available to the constituent at no cost and, therefore, political intermediaries are used by many people. In a 1991 poll, a quarter of respondents had contacted their councillor since the previous local elections. Contact was highest among rural and working class groups.

Politicians are thus unquestionably very busy making representations on behalf of constituents. In most cases, however, they are querying a delay in provision rather than a bureaucrat's judgement on entitlement. On other occasions, the politician is providing additional information about the personal circumstances of the citizen which may be relevant to the official's decision and thus expediting a favourable outcome. This kind of low level brokerage may be a waste of the time of legislators and/or bureaucrats; it may signal a low level of civic skills on the part of citizens; but, it does not amount to sleaze. In contrast to their counterparts in other 'civic culture' countries, politicians in Ireland are expected to be brokers and the rewards they get in terms of votes and local prestige are quite legitimate where localism is a persistent feature of politics, especially outside Dublin. Ireland is a small country with a very centralised system of government. Neither the public service nor the political elite are characterised by social distance from their fellow citizens. There is no equivalent to Oxbridge or the Grandes Ecoles of France. Indeed, for politicans especially, the social and electoral pressures emphasise approachability, local loyalty and visibility. Almost all TDs live in their constituencies; most were born, raised and educated there; and 90% are or have been members of the local council. Many TDs have extensive family connections in their local base and almost a quarter are related to previous or current parliamentarians. It is thought useful to a political career to be active in local voluntary organisations: 'political leaders lack credibility if they are not local'.[3]

The individualised nature of intra-party electoral competition forces candidates from the larger parties, that is, those with more than one candidate per constitency, to resource personal campaigns in addition to the general party effort. Personal campaigns receive assistance from volunteers, such as members of the legal profession, which may hope that their association with a particular candidate will offer some return in the form of briefs or reputation in political circles. Some established or promising politicians may also attract support from individuals who aspire to appointments on committees of enquiry, the boards of state-sponsored bodies and similar patronage positions.

The candidate's own election efforts may receive material assistance in the form of cars on polling day, use of commercial-standard phone-banks for campaigning, audio and other media equipment, and, importantly, money. For most business people such help can have no real prospect of direct reward because the ratio of candidates to ministers or other decision-influencing politicians is very unfavourable. Nevertheless, the possibility of sleaze is real in the sense that some electors feel that those who do help politicians may benefit unfairly from insider knowledge, preference as supplies or lax application of state regulations.

It is hardly surprising that, given the importance of brokerage and localism, the Irish political culture has also been characterised as particularist or personalistic. The literature offers a 'vast array of evidence which reveals how politically relevant grievances are often processed in a particularistic or personalistic fashion'.[4] Some observers, most notably have presented the particularism of Irish culture as inimical to the development of democratic institutions and the pursuit of collective interests.[5] Suggestions of brokerage in politics extending to corruption are seldom made and are hard to sustain; some claim that TDs seem to exert considerable power from their influence on local government appointments.[6]

Local appointments, however, are governed by an independent commission which was set up in 1926 to end corrupt personnel practices, the Local Appointments Commission, which is generally regarded as immune from political pressure. There are, however, some documented cases of political interference in posts outside its control. A former senior civil servant cited an example in his memoirs of a candidate for a post of immigration officer who an interview board had placed fourth being appointed by the relevant minister, Charles Haughey, following representations by a fellow minister in 1962. Other examples from 1982 and 1984 of ministers appointing candidates who were not the first choice of interview boards have been given.[7] In relation to sleaze, however, the most important feature of particularism is that it could act as a constraint on universalistic and rationalist criteria for behaviour in the public domain. The safeguard against this is the virtual exclusion of all but the most senior politicians from any signficant power in a highly bureaucratic and centralised state. Although politicians remain primarily supplicants for their constituents, they are rarely seen to benefit personally or financially. The one area of generalised controversy is planning.

The centralised, bureaucratic nature of the Irish state is reflected in the independence and power given to the city or county managers (i.e. chief executives) relative to their elected councils. The divisions of functions between politician and bureaucrat is, in practice, useful to them both as it allows each side to operate effectively in areas close to their main interest. The politicians are generally content to allow the manager to make individual case and planning decisions as it removes them from direct public accountability. They are, however, able to reverse managerial decisions as they impact on individual citizens in particular cases using a residual power known as Section Four. Typically, Section Fours are used in relation to planning control, e.g. to overturn refusals which have been made on general planning criteria. Councillors are also able to rezone areas of land as they appear on the local authority's development plan from 'agricultural' to 'residential', thus significantly altering the commercial value. Many poor planning decisions have been made using this procedure, so in 1991 the law was significantly tightened and Section Fours are now more difficult to pass. Nevertheless, there is a widespread public belief that corruption, involving money being paid by developers to councillors, is 'widespread and serious'. Indeed, 65% of respondents agreed with this description in a December 1991 opinion poll. No legal cases have been brought against councillors, and the only one brought against an official failed. While councillors come under tremendous pressure, especially in the Dublin area where property prices are very high, there is only rumour to back up allegations of sleaze in this area of public life. All planning decisions, in Dublin at least, are the subject of intense public scrutiny. Disquiet is widespread but proof of malpractice is not available.

Because almost all Irish parliamentarians are or have been local councillors, public attitudes make few distinctions between deputies and others. Significant national power, however, is concentrated in the hands of a small group: the 15 Cabinet members and their 15 junior ministers. These senior politicians are given substantial help from within their departments to handle constituency work. Being a minister is a considerable advantage to a politician in terms of the brokerage system even though he or she is obliged to relinquish any local government position. Politicians are also required to distance themselves from their business interests when holding ministerial office. The rules governing ministerial conduct have been put on a statutory basis in the Ethics in Public Office Act 1995, though this is less detailed than the Cabinet procedures which have been developed over many years and remain in force. The legislation extends the requirements of disclosure of interest to ministers' political advisors; that is, appointees whose tenure is dependent on the minister remaining in office. Nevertheless, there have been incidents involving ministers with questions being asked concerning their links between public allocations and private interests. For example, the granting of an Irish passport to a foreign investor under an established scheme to encourage job creation in Ireland came under scrutiny in 1994 when it was revealed that the investment had been in the Prime Minister's family firm.

In the same government, another minister, Brian Cowen, was revealed to have a small personal shareholding in a mining company that was seeking planning permission from his department. In 1995, a senior minister in the new coalition government resigned after it was established that he had spoken to the chairman of a state-sponsored body in relation to an upcoming contract in which the minister's family company were interested. Public reaction to this latter incident was muted. It is possible that the public's view is jaundiced by cynicism about the motives of senior politicians. In opinion polls, taken shortly after the revelations, 50% were dissatisfied with Mr Reynold's explanation of the passport affair, but only 35% felt Mr Cowen should resign.

In a broad sense political culture in the Republic is influenced by the attitudes of a 'colony'. Under British rule, power was centralised both legally and symbolically in Dublin Castle. It was exercised primarily by an alien or 'arriviste' elite or 'ascendancy'. The people were attuned to dealing with a formidable bureaucracy through intermediaries and to regarding public moneys or other benefits as prizes to be gained. Levels of fiscal morality were low. While replacement of the old order by native government in 1922 has slowly changed these attitudes, strong elements of 'incivisme' remain. This popular culture coexists with the highly bureaucratic and legalistic administrative system inherited from the British. Many citizens continue to regard public officialdom with distrust as possibly malevolent and certainly fair game. A recent tax amnesty, which brought in many times more than expected, underlined the routine level of tax evasion and avoidance. Its success followed an aggressive and high-profile campaign which targeted particular types of business and was the occasion of much political protest, especially in peripheral areas away from Dublin where state bureaucracy enjoys a markedly lower level of public esteem.

The Irish public administration is in many ways like the British system. This is not only because the institutions were modelled on the lines of the British apparatus they replaced but also because the founders of the state established a very puritanical regime. The 'rebels' and their supporters in government departments, courts and other institutions were keen to prove that the new government matched in probity and efficiency that which had gone before. Ironically, they needed British approval or, at least, they were sensitive to the criticism that they would not be able to equal the standards of their former masters. Thus the Irish Free State set itself high standards of public honesty: 'radical though some strands in the independence movement may have been, it was the more cautious, conservative wing that ultimately won power in the new state and shaped its character in the early, formative years.'[8]

Since its earliest days, the Irish state has played a direct role in the economy through state-owned or sponsored companies. There are more than a hundred of these and they operate over a wide field, though they are primarily providers of essential infrastructure services. Each company is set up by legislation and most have a part-time board of six to twelve directors whose appointments by the relevant minister is frequently an area of controversy. The Ethics in Public Office Act 1995 extends to the boards of state-owned companies and, in future, all members will have to make an annual statement of their interests to safeguard against undeclared conflicts of interest.

The remuneration for state-sponsored company directorships is modest by the standards of private enterprise but they are often seen as prestigious positions of influence. For example, board members may decide investment patterns, strategic business alliances or the appointment of key senior personnel. Ministers are generally anxious to ensure that they will be able to cooperate closely with boards and frequently appoint party supporters. There is an inevitable tension between politicians and the boards of the companies they 'own' because of the differing time-scales and priorities of business and politics: e.g. plans for commercial rationalism, job shedding or price increases have sometimes been delayed for electoral considerations; rural post offices have been saved from closure because they happen to be in the Prime Minister's constituency. Members of the Irish and the European Parliament are debarred from board membership. In May 1995, two Fianna Fáil county councillors were asked to resign from the board of ACC Bank, formerly the Agricultural Credit Corporation, by the Minister for Finance, but both refused and the minister backed away. A gradual change in the character of the boards of state-owned companies is likely to occur as a result of the Ethics in Public Office Act 1995. Many current and potential members may be reluctant to make an annual public declaration of their economic interests and may find the tighter rules on conflict of interest onerous. Further, there are EU codes of conduct which come into play when European financial assistance is obtained and these, in some respects, are more restrictive than Irish regulations.

The only bureaucratic innovations the new Irish state produced were designed to remove administrative discretion from all but the most senior politicians in the decade after independence. New mechanisms for public service recruitment, codified versions of Whitehall minister/civil service relations and strict systems of public service accounting were introduced. The main criticisms of the Irish public service focus on its caution, insularity and narrow intellectual perspective. The impression gained from academic studies, political memoirs and contemporary accounts is that 'the general probity of officials is not in much doubt.'[9]

Recent political controversies

In general, therefore, the particularistic political culture, acceptability of brokerage and systemic personalism and localism found in the Republic of Ireland narrow the parameters of what may be recognised as sleaze. Nevertheless, recent controversies have further illustrated the extent of sleaze and refined the public's understanding of what conduct would be considered a matter of concern in public life. Relations between politicians and business has become an area of particular concern. A number of events in 1991 seemed to suggest the existence of a 'golden circle' of businessmen which commanded large amounts of public money for private interests. Each incident would have been a source of public disquiet on its own, but coming together very seriously undermined the general assumption in Ireland that sleaze was not a major political problem.

The first incident concerned the Irish Sugar Company which was about to be privatised. This loss-making public enterprise had become profitable under the tough management of Chris Comerford. Mr Comerford was allegedly involved in a company which had been lent money by Irish Sugar to buy 49% of another company of which Irish Sugar already owned 51%. This was later sold to the parent company at what was perceived to be an inflated price that could not be sustained on the subsidiary's performance. A group of managers, including Comerford, realised a profit of IR£7m in what was seen to be a risk-free transaction. The scandal was seen to arise from possible conflicts of interest between the public duties and private interests of the chief executive of a state-owned company.

Another state-sponsored enterprise, Telecom Eireann, was at the centre of a row in 1991. The company board paid IR£9.4m for a property for its new headquarters despite a valuation of IR£6m by the State Valuation Office. The allegations of impropriety arose from the suggestion that the government-appointed chairman of Telecom had links with United Property Holdings, the company selling the property. The official report into the affair found that, while the chairman did have a shareholding in the company concerned, he had not exercised any undue influence in Telecom's purchase of the property. The matter created a serious scandal at the time, the allegiations appearing to gain currency when the Prime Minister of the day requested the chairman to 'stand aside' pending investigations.

Some of the same names were put into the public domain by each of these incidents. One in particular, a stockbroker, Dermot Desmond, was further implicated in another. This centred on information of a sensitive commercial nature about the helicopter business of Aer Lingus, for which his company was acting as an advisor, which came into the possession of a rival, Celtic Helicopters, owned by the son of the Prime Minister, Charles Haughey. When the incident became public, it was clear that Mr Desmond's actions had been discovered when he had sent the information he was giving to Celtic Helicopters to Aer Lingus through a 'postal error'. He was further embarrassed by the revelation that while acting for a large French company in a take-over bid for Irish Distillers, he had cited in a letter to the French his ready access to very senior politicians as one of his advantages.

The Irish Sugar, Telecom Eireann and Celtic Helicopter incidents each contributed to public unease, not just with businessmen but with politicians. This was reflected in a public opinion poll in December 1991 in which 65% of respondents thought 'corruption was a widespread and serious problem amongst our elected politicians'. Most important of all, however, was the unfolding story of the relationship between politicians and the dominant company in the beef processing industry, Goodman International.

In August 1994, a report from a Tribunal of Inquiry was issued concerning the Irish beef processing industry. The industry, which accounted for 34% of the Republic's agricultural output, was by 1991 dominated by Goodman International and its associated companies. Larry Goodman had, however, suffered several major business set backs and was, in 1991, in deep financial trouble. The Report was called for by the Irish parliament following allegations, in an ITV *World in Action* documentary broadcast in May 1991, of irregularities in the administration of export credit guarantees. Many serious charges were made in the Dáil before the Inquiry, and criminal charges have since been successfully brought against certain employees of private companies. The central political figure was the Prime Minister, Albert Reynolds. He assumed full responsibility for decisions made on the allocation of export credit insurance on consignments of beef for Iraq by which Goodman benefited immensely while he was Minister for Industry and Commerce in 1987 and 1988. The Tribunal found that Mr Reynolds was legally entitled to make the decisions he did and that he had acted in good faith, and there was no suggestion of personal financial gain by any politician involved. Nevertheless, the Beef Tribunal does highlight some areas of concern in the way politicians and private companies relate to each other in the conduct of Irish politics.

Fianna Fáil had been in power during most of the period of Goodman's success. While in government under Charles Haughey, it identified Mr Goodman as the linchpin in its plans to create new jobs in food processing. A much-heralded and grandiose scheme never materialised but the media coverage surrounding it identified Haughey and Goodman as close confidants. The Tribunal, however, found no evidence of any wrongdoing, describing their friendship as business-like. The promise of massive investment in a major Irish industry may have contributed to politicians' making poor judgements in an effort to support Goodman's business but they were motivated, according to the Tribunal, by their interpretation of the national interest rather than

personal gain. Nevertheless, its revelations did show that Albert Reynolds and other senior Fianna Fáil politicians had acted in a way which
undermines confidence in the process of public administration when
laws, procedures and expectation of caution were disregarded. The
Tribunal also followed up accusations that Larry Goodman profited
from advance business information which he acquired because he was
on the 'inside political track'. Clearly, early commercially-useful intelligence could have allowed him to take risks with greater confidence than
rival firms. It found that Goodman 'had reasonably ready access to
members of the government . . . for the purpose of discussing his plans
for the development of his companies and his exports. It is clear that he
had similar access to previous governments'.[10]

While Goodman's ready access was regularly used by the company,
no identified political links or personal friendships were relevant to this
business advantage. Rather, it reflected ministers' assessments of the
commercial potential of its operations and the contribution these could
make to the national economy. Ministers took huge risks with public
money but they did so in the 'national interest'. They also overruled,
ignored or misunderstood the advice of officials and junior ministers.
The report did not allocate blame to anyone for the staggering irregularities which it uncovered in the way employees of Goodman International conducted their business, nor did it seek to pin responsibility
for the inadequate control exercised by government departments. The
proceedings of the inquiry, however, with seemingly daily revelations of
malpractice and systematic fraud in the handling of beef exports, the
bitter personal accusations made by the most senior of political figures
about each other, and the depressing catalogue it provided of incompet-
ence in the management of public affairs, did seriously damage the
standing of the political process.

The Beef Tribunal brought to prominence the financial links between
businesses and politicians. Private companies in Ireland are free to give
money to politicians and political parties. It was suggested that Larry
Goodman had been given special treatment because of contributions he
had made to Fianna Fáil, the largest party in the Republic. The record
of his companies in terms of investment, job creation and increased
market share had been spectacular. The basis of this success had been
exporting to new markets. The report accepted that Goodman had not
been shown favouritism by Fianna Fáil alone and that he had equal
access to the previous Fine Gael/Labour coalition government. Private
companies, it emerged, make donations to all the major parties without
expecting particular benefits. There is, however, an easy assumption
shared by the political and business elite that what is good for Irish
companies generally, and specially in the export field, is beneficial to
the Republic as a whole. This outlook is thought to be particularly
prevalent in Fianna Fáil, a party which has dominated government since
the 1930s and which pioneered Ireland's development strategy in the

late 1950s and early 1960s. In the mid-1960s, Fianna Fáil organised its business supporters in a body known as Taca, which acquired a reputation for influencing ministerial decisions. Fine Gael also had a specialist Business Election Committee. Despite all the efforts of the Beef Tribunal, the link between business contributions to parties and 'favourable treatment' is far from clear.

All the political parties continue to solicit and accept support from business by, for example, holding fund-raising dinners. The relationship between governments and business is so complex, however, that it is hard to pinpoint specific benefits to either companies or individual politicians. More likely is the explanation that, given the corporatist element in Irish policy making and the relative size of government as a purchaser of goods and services, political contributions are seen as a form of public relations. Nevertheless, in what some have called the 'biggest scandal in Irish political history', the Beef Tribunal inquiries suggest that, from 1987 to 1991, 'the relationships between the Fianna Fáil government and Goodman International became inextricably inter- twined' with contributions of all the main companies in the beef industry to Fianna Fáil's election campaign in 1987, amounting to 10% of party headquarters' spending. Several other parties, however, also received sizable contributions from Goodman International and other beef industry firms.[11] The Fianna Fáil government did reverse decisions on export credit finance which very directly favoured Goodman but the reasons appear to be linked to poor judgment by Albert Reynolds, then Minister for Industry and Commerce, about Goodman International's potential as a contributor to 'kick-starting the economy', rather than more serious behaviour.

In the 1990s several state-sponsored bodies have been brought to a condition of commercial crisis because of long-term mismanagement and lack of political will by past governments. Despite their political sensitivity, the state-sponsored bodies have been remarkably sleaze-free. Even the area of appointments is likely to get less controversial as corporatist arrangements between the government and interest groups reduces the scope of effective ministerial autonomy and the trend to neo-liberalism impacts on Ireland through privatisation and other changes.

Conclusion: tolerated conduct

As discussed above, the political culture of the Republic of Ireland and recent controversies help to define the extent of sleaze. Less identifiable changes in attitudes and expectations, however, have caused the events of 1991 to be seen as more damaging to the political and business community than early events which hit the headlines. In the autumn of 1982, especially while Seán Doherty was Minister for Justice, allegations of senior politicians and police colluding in tape-recording ministers' telephone calls with journalists were made. The bugging was part of

Doherty's attempts to identify the source of Cabinet leaks at a time of intense internal wrangling in Fianna Fáil about the leadership of the party. Doherty later admitted that the then Prime Minister, Charles Haughey, had known of the bugs, though at the time it was denied. This admission subsequently led to Haughey's resignation. Haughey's position had been threatened in the summer of 1982 when a notorious murder suspect, Malcolm McArthur, was arrested in the house of Attorney-General Patrick Connolly. Neither Haughey nor Connolly seemed to have appreciated the seriousness of the incident and, initially, it appeared Connolly would continue a prearranged holiday in America. The Attorney-General did resign on his return to Ireland, but Haughey's style of government was criticised as encouraging what would now be termed sleaze. In another case involving court proceedings against Seán Doherty's brother-in-law, himself in the police, a witness for the prosecution was detained by the police in Northern Ireland just long enough to prevent him giving evidence. This series of events gave rise to the term 'GUBU' (Grotesque, Unprecendented, Bizarre and Unbeliev-able), coined by Conor Cruise O'Brien from the words used by Charles Haughey in explaining the strange unfolding of scandals.

It is important, however, for comparative purposes, to understand the kinds of behaviour which are tolerated in Ireland but which may not be elsewhere. Tolerated conduct is understood to be that which causes little adverse comment although it may be of public interest. This category is widening as more liberal attitudes to many areas of social life develops. Again, a broad analysis of Irish democratic development suggests comparisons for Ireland may be found in southern European countries where personalism and clientlism are marked aspects of the political culture.[12]

Ireland exhibits a culture of ambiguity where what is said is secondary in some ways to what is not said. It possesses an ability to cope with seemingly contradictory messages without needing to draw absolute conclusions one way or the other. This tolerance for ambiguity may encompass certain scandals, without demanding full exposure. Given the conservative nature of the dominant Catholic mores, such ambiva-lence is surprising. The emphasis, however, would appear to be on condemning the sin, not the sinner. Thus, for example, the minister cautioned by police for meeting male prostitutes, appears to have escaped a harsh judgment by 'confessing his sin' and acknowledging the error of his ways. He has yet to face his electorate but his chances of success are reasonable. The minister, Emmet Stagg, remained in office and has since been reappointed by a subsequent coalition government. It is interesting to note that in making an open and frank statement, covered live on television, the minister in fact gained enormous sym-pathy from the general public. Despite the embarrassing nature of the allegations, there was no clamour for his resignation.

The Stagg incident became public because the politician himself made a statement confirming that he was the unnamed TD referred to in a newspaper article. It is quite possible that his identity would not have become public otherwise. Press exposés are much more likely in Ireland following evidence of supposed haughty or extravagant behaviour by politicians. Excessive use by ministers of the facilities available to them; for example the government jet, chauffeured cars and expensive hotels when travelling abroad, are highlighted regularly. The foreign travel of Members of the European Parliament or local councillors is frequently censured. In the parochial and egalitarian political culture of the Republic, the press adopt a particularly strident tone when reporting stories of alleged extravagance. A recent delegation of eight MEP's to Guadaloupe generated much publicity when it was revealed that six of the group were Fianna Fáil. Any lasting adverse impact, however, may be mitigated by the public being 'sneaking regarders' of people who manage to live the high life.

Sleaze, as understood in the Republic of Ireland, has largely been confined to unacceptable conduct in the public domain by public and private sector interests and associated senior politicians. Some conduct, which in other jurisdictions may be considered suspect or an unreasonable use of the office for personal gain, is tolerated in Ireland. The question about the pervasiveness of sleaze can only be answered with reference to what the Irish public or informed observers would regard as dubious behaviour which brings the conduct of public affairs into disrepute. Such judgements are not, of course, absolute and, they change over time.

While events since 1991 have heightened public awareness, it is not clear whether they will open the door to further re-evaluations of standards in public life. The Beef Tribunal was an important marker in Irish politics. Despite a largely inconclusive report, it did succeed in exposing the nature of some business and political relationships. Its impact has been to suggest that such dealings will no longer be tolerated: a clearer line will almost certainly be drawn in the future between the interests of the state and those of any business, no matter how large.

The media and their handling of issues plays a key role in determining the impact of sleaze. Journalists have shown a reluctance to expose what are perceived to be personal indiscretions. Thus, while individuals remain consistent in terms of their political stance and personal behaviour, it would appear that the media are tolerant. The consensus among journalists on the reporting of scandals is reinforced by practical considerations. Libel laws in the Republic are relatively stringent. The costs of legal actions are high and, therefore, considerations of risk are important. The Irish market is small and the newspapers do not have the financial strength to absorb regular losses in the courts even if their circulations were to rise as a result of a more liberal policy on exposés. RTE, the national public service television and radio system, often clashes with politicians on the subject of supposed bias or unbalanced coverage. The consensus on personal privacy, however, is rigidly observed. There would appear to be a genuinely-held intention of not descending to the levels of the imported UK tabloid press. Whether this is in fact a moral position or a reflection of a comfortable competitive structure between publications is unclear.

The institution which should act as a safeguard against sleaze in the Republic is parliament. Its importance in the prelude to the Beef Tribunal and the enormous cost of the enquiry have radically changed the way parliamentarians now see their role. The 1995 legislation on ethics and public conduct, as well as the new powers given to Dáil committees, are signals of an intent to make parliamentary scrutiny more effective. The question remains, however, as to whether the elements of personalism, particularism and clientelism in Irish political culture examined here will allow the time and freedom from electoral pressure to combat sleaze.

1   M. Laver, 'Are Irish Parties Peculiar?' in J. H. Goldthorpe and C. T. Whelon, *The Development of Industrial Society in Ireland* (Oxford University Press, 1992).

2   M. Gallagher and L. Komito, 'Dáil Deputies and Their Constituency Work' J. in Coakley and M. Gallagher, *Politics in the Republic of Ireland* (Folens, 1993).

3   J. P. Carroll, 'Strokes, Cute Hoors and Sneaking Regarders: The Influence of Local Culture on Irish Political Style', *Irish Political Studies*, 1987.

4   P. Mair, *The Changing Irish Party System: Organisation, Ideology and Electoral Competition* (Francis Pinter, 1987).

5   D. Schmitt, *The Irony of Irish Democracy: The Impact of Political Culture on Administration and Political Development in Ireland* (Lexington, 1973). R. J. Carty, *Party and Parish Pump: Electoral Politics in Ireland* (Wilfrid Laurier Press, 1981).

6   M. Bax, *Harpstrings and Confessions: Machine-style Politics in the Irish Republic* (VanGorcum, 1976).

7   Gallagher and Komito, loc. cit.

8   J. Coakley, 'The Foundations of Statehood' in Coakley and Gallagher, op. cit.

9   E. O'Haplin, 'Policymaking' in Coakley and Gallagher, op. cit.

10 L. Hamilton, *Report of the Tribunal of Inquiry into the Beef Processing Industry* (Dublin: Stationary Office, 1994).

11 F. O'Toole, *Meanwhile Back at the Ranch*. London (Vintage, 1995).

12 B. Kissane, 'The Not So Amazing Case of Irish Democracy', *Irish Political Studies*, 1995.

Italy

BY HILARY PARTRIDGE

IN February 1992 investigating magistrate Antonio Di Pietro, with a few officers of the carabinieri, arrested his first politician: Mario Chiesa, Socialist director of a Milanese nursing home. The politician was charged with extortion of a £2,700[1] kickback on a cleaning contract for the institution. In March 1995, after three years of extensive investigation, Di Pietro accepted the Freedom Prize, offered by two Scandinavian journals to honour those who have fought for freedom and previously awarded to Walesa, Havel and Mandela. He turned the prize money over to the residents of the home, in recompense for lost charity income following the case. Despite his modest claim that he had done no more than his duty, the investigations of Di Pietro and the so called 'Clean Hands' pool of Milanese magistrates had been responsible for triggering a regime crisis comparable in the minds of the awarders to those in the former East European regimes and apartheid South Africa. Chiesa's confessions had set off a chain reaction implicating other political and business leaders in kickbacks on public work contracts, illegal party financing, tax fraud, embezzlement and other crimes. As confessions drew in an ever-widening circle of the political and business elite, such practices were exposed as the unwritten rule rather than the exception. At time of writing, about 3,500 investigations into politicians, businessmen and professionals have been opened by magistrates such as Di Pietro and the 'Clean hands' pool. By the March 1994 general election, triggered off by two years of corruption scandals, five former Prime Ministers and nearly a third of outgoing members of both houses of parliament had been investigated on various charges. Although Di Pietro was not in fact the leader of the Milan team, his sensational court performances had given him a high-profile role in the collapse of the main regime parties and elevated him to the status of national, and indeed international, hero.

Italy and sleaze

In the light of the recent deluge of corruption scandals across Europe and elsewhere, it will be useful first of all to characterize the public perception of sleaze in Italy. Sleaze might in fact be a misnomer in the Italian context given its connotations of distasteful personal behaviour, including sexual hypocrisy. In Italy, public anxiety has focused more on the systemic nature of corruption and the role of political parties in its perpetuation. It is not easy, in fact, to separate the appropriation of money for individual purposes from illegal party financing: the distribution of kickbacks is often complex, part of the funds going to the party and the remainder being shared out, sometimes across party lines, among a wide range of politicians and administrators to ensure their complicity in the system. Furthermore, channelling funds to the party ultimately enhances the politician's career prospects within the party or the entrepreneur's business prospects, augmenting the personal resources of both. The focus of public opinion at the level of the party system rather than the individual is further reinforced by the nature of the Italian political system. Until very recently, a multiplicity of parties competed for a portion of political influence, with the electorate's choice based more on party than on perceptions of individual politicians. If the recent electoral reforms ultimately create two broad, moderate and relatively cohesive forces competing for the control of the executive, public attention may focus more closely on the personal attributes and behaviour of leading politicians. Indeed, the close scrutiny of former Prime Minister Silvio Berlusconi, the leader of the new centre-right grouping, may reflect such a trend.

It is difficult to make cross-national comparisons of corruption, since what has not been exposed can not be measured. It is, nevertheless, generally conceded that the Italian political system—designated by some political scientists as a 'particracy'[2]—has actually encouraged the pragmatic politician to seek advantage over competitors through corrupt practices. Corruption has long been endemic in Italy, especially in the agrarian South. In conditions of abject poverty, individuals attempted to secure family livelihood by reference to a hierarchy of power whose higher levels reached into the heart of the state.[3] In the party system newly re-established after the second world war, the chain of patronage was replicated within, especially, the Christian Democratic Party (DC) which dominated governing coalitions until the collapse of the system in 1993. The DC understood that the Southern vote could be maintained by the exchange of political protection for electoral support, even if it failed promises of good government and reform. It was thus able to use the resources of the state, further centralized under fascism, to 'buy' the vote of the Southern poor in exchange for jobs or benefits and to establish the South as its main electoral heartland. Up until the late 1970s relatively stable voting patterns enabled the DC to dominate coalitions. But by the 1980s the DC's successful strategy had been emulated by competing coalition parties, most notably by the Italian Socialist Party (PSI) under the leadership of the now disgraced Bettino Craxi, who displaced the DC from its monopoly of the premiership in 1981.

An example of the widespread use of patronage in the South concerns the allocation of civil service jobs. Sabino Cassese explains that temporary jobs, usually in perphery field offices, were regularly made permanent by special laws, thus bypassing ordinary recruitment procedures based on competitive examination.[4] He estimates that between 1973 and 1990 about 350,000 people were recruited into public administration without regular procedures, as against some 250,000 recruited regularly. This process has led to a profound 'Southernization' of the civil service: again according to Cassese's study, between 80 and 90% of high-ranking civil servants were born and had studied in the South. Further examples of clientelistic exchange aimed at maintaining electoral support among the lower and middle classes are, respectively, the widespread use of disability pensions, which, particularly in the South, became a practical alternative to a universal system of income support, and the lax collection and inspection of income tax, especially with regard to the self-employed and small or medium businesses. In yet another variant, state money, for example from the fund for Southern development, is invested in what often turn out to be white elephants. A rolling mill at Bagnoli, near Naples, was built by the state-owned steel company ILVA to create jobs in a depressed area where the DC was strong. The plant took nearly ten years to build and was never used.

The system of clientelistic exchange was reinforced by the institutional and particularly the electoral arrangements of the Italian political system. A very pure system of proportional representation, chosen by the Constituent Assembly of 1946–47 to guard against the rise of another authoritarian leader, gave rise in a rather fragmented society to a very large number of parties. In the Cold War atmosphere, the outcome was coalition governments dominated by the largest party, the DC, and excluding the Communist Party (PCI). The PCI, together with the other 'antisystem' party, the neo-fascist MSI, was thus permanently consigned to the role of opposition (although the recent revelations demonstrate the PCI members were willing to use the bargaining power given to them by their weight in parliament, participating in the spoils system, and even accepting kickbacks to fund the party as financial support from the former Soviet Union began to dry up).

Whilst the continued dominance of the DC, latterly with the PSI, was thus assured, the actual composition of the government was determined by intense competition among and within the parties of the coalition, a competition in which a handful of politicians could make or break the majority necessary for a vote of confidence. The fragility of the executive (52 governments from the formation of the 'First Republic' until its collapse in 1993) was intensified by the poorly disciplined nature of the parties and the frequent emergence of 'snipers' — MPs who voted against their own party in secret ballots. The road to an important ministerial post, then, was not patient and unswerving loyalty to the party but the marshalling of a faction and its astute management. Power within the party depended strongly on the number of votes (parliamentary and electoral) an individual could muster. This was especially true when the system of preference votes was in force. Under this system, removed following a referendum in 1991, voters could arrange candidates in order of their preference, thus allowing politicians to demonstrate an individual packet of votes, enhancing their position in the fierce internal rivalry.

In this situation of overall political stability, with the entrenchment of a group of 'acceptable' parties in permanent power but also in a permanent condition of internal rivalry, there was increasing pressure to control state agencies in order to gain access to their resources. As the frontiers of the state were expanded, so more and more areas were taken into the public sector, allowing further possibilities to exchange public resources for the party financing which was so necessary to generate votes in increasingly expensive electoral campaigns, or sometimes simply to enrich influential politicians and their supporters. The parties of government appointed supporters to manage public firms. These 'apparatchiks' would then use the state companies to channel funds to the parties, often syphoning off a proportion of the proceeds for their own use. The money was raised mainly through the award of contracts in return for kickbacks, a mechanism facilitated in Italy where, since 1919, public sector companies were able to reach agreements with suppliers without competitive bidding. The exchange of public contracts for kickbacks extended even to money earmarked for aid to developing countries. Companies wishing to undertake work on foreign aid projects were required to make payments for 'consultations' amounting to 3 or 4 % of the total cost.

One major case that illustrates the role of money in politics and the political penetration of the sprawling 'sottogoverno' of public agencies concerned the giant Ente Nazionale Idrocarburi (ENI), the state energy company. In March 1993 the company's top executives were arrested and charged with fraudulent accounts to create slush funds that were used for at least a decade to channel money to the political parties. The company's former chairman, Gabriele Cagliari, an appointee of Bettino Craxi, described to the investigating magistrates the flows of ENI money to the PSI and DC through secret Swiss bank accounts. The owner of the bank used by the ENI, the Italo-Swiss Pier Francesco Pacini Battaglia, another member of Craxi's circle, was also arrested. According to the banker's lengthy confessions to Di Pietro, public money was illegally channelled to the political parties through three ENI subsidiaries: AGIP, a Socialist-controlled petrol company, the DC-controlled SNAM (a gas company) and SAIPEM (a machine plant agency). Other funds were apparently delivered directly to the PSI by a Milanese businessman. An even more sinister aspect of this story is given by the involvement of the Banco Ambrosiano—whose president, Roberto Calvi, was found hanged under Blackfriars Bridge in London in 1982— and the shadowy P2, a secret brotherhood of the powerful linked to politics and terrorist outrages. It is alleged that ENI money flowed into the bank for use by political parties of Calvi's choice.

Not all of the money, however, was destined for party use. In March 1995, as the ENI investigations were drawing to a close two years after the arrest of the management group, it has emerged that of the approximately £190 million milked from the company books, only about £15 million went to the parties of government. According to the managers, the remainder went to middle-men of international trade, £77 million, for example, going to a certain 'Omar' in Switzerland in connection with the renewal of a contract for the supply of Algerian gas. The magistrates remain unconvinced: regardless of the legitimacy of such payments, there is no evidence that the money did not go directly into the managers' pockets, leaving them open to the more serious charge of embezzlement.

If corruption in Italy had become systemic—the rule rather than the exception in politics and in business, in the public and in the private sector—so its use was condoned or at least tolerated at every level of society, including those institutions charged in liberal democracy with the role of watchdog of the public interest.

The media, in the Italian 'First Republic' of 1947–1993, were not an effective critical force. There are few independent publishers, and commercial viability of the printed press has typically been subordinated to opinion-moulding aims. For industrialists such as FIAT's Agnelli, the influence offered by newspaper-ownership offset poor financial returns even in times of declining circulation figures. Owners are not ashamed to use media outlets to shape public opinion on issues affecting their interests. For example, the media-mogul and ex-Prime Minister Silvio Berlusconi was able in the 1980s to exchange support of the PSI for a weakly regulated environment permitting virtually unrestricted market activities. At time of writing, magistrates in Naples are investigating claims that a private television company financed by Berlusconi's giant holding company, Fininvest, was the mouthpiece of disgraced politicians Paulo Cirino Pomicino (DC), Giulio Di Donato (PSI) and Francesco De Lorenzo (liberal) in the late 1980s and early 1990s. According to the magistrates, the politicians received control of news services and choice of editors, plus financing of the TV to the tune of roughly £380,000 a year. In return for this, they helped recruit parliamentary support for legislation favouring the expansion of Berlusconi's media empire.

Public sector television is equally enmeshed in the hidden exchanges of the party system. The main public sector TV channels were shared out among the parties, according to the spoils system, with the DC and PSI controlling the two best-resourced channels, RAI 1 and RAI 2. In exchange for not obstructing the deal, the PCI was offered control over RAI 3. Given the cosy relationship between parties and media, it is unsurprising that tough investigative journalism did not emerge to rock the carefully balanced boat.

At the other end of the scrutiny spectrum, the judiciary in Italy are on paper comparatively independent. The magistrates' ability to investigate the activities of politicians is enshrined in the constitution and given substance by the creation, in the 1950s, of the Superior Council of the Judiciary, responsible for the professional functions of the judiciary, including recruitment, training, posting and discipline. Judges are thus not political appointees. But the judiciary, at least up until the early 1990s, remained very heavily influenced by the party system. Its association, like other Italian professional associations, was also divided according to the party-political identifications permeating society, and these divisions were reflected within its highest body. Promotion, for example, frequently depended not only on seniority and merit but on negotiation between the different party-political currents, the outcome depending on their relative strength. According to Carlo Guarnieri, the case of the Italian judiciary is somewhat paradoxical, showing a high degree of institutional independence but limited individual independence.[5] Once again, party-membership and influence within the party could be a crucial factor in prospects for promotion. Thus, with exceptions, the judiciary continued to tolerate the status quo until the collapse of Soviet block communism took away the underpinning of the 'particracy', introducing a new element of unpredictablity into Italian politics.

Politics of change

By the early 1990s, crisis was threatening the relative stability of the Italian party system. Five days after the fall of the Berlin wall the PCI leadership announced its intention to change the party's name, and in 1991 the Communists exchanged the hammer and sickle for an oak tree, in the process shedding its 'hard left' component to the breakaway Communist Refoundation (RC). The metamorphosis of the PCI/PDS may or may not have been sufficient, eventually, to break down the psychological and material barriers holding the Communists under an electoral ceiling of just over 30% of the vote. Such an outcome would doubtless have posed a serious threat to the 'particracy'. But in the meantime, another development had immediate implications for the old balance of the party system. A new party, standing on a regionalist, populist, anti-Southern and anti-corruption platform, was seriously threatening the DC vote in the North, particularly since the main reason for voting DC—to keep the Communists out—had diminished. The Lombard (later Northern) League's dizzying rise tore through the fabric of the old party system. Business interests, no longer automatically supportive of the old regime, felt freer to speak out against the widespread and increasingly expensive requirement of kickbacks for public works contracts.

In the new post-Cold War climate, a determined group of investigating magistrates were at last able to blow the whistle on systemic corruption. An important weapon in their battle was their power, like their French counterparts, to arrest and hold suspects before conviction.

Pampered members of the political, business and professional elites, faced with the prospect of months of imprisonment even before coming to trial, were quick to cooperate with the magistrates, implicating former friends and associates in ever-widening circles. The exposures proved fatal to the already weakened party system.

The Italian regime, in fact, has never received a strong legitimation from its citizens. Responses to the Eurobarometer question measuring satisfaction with democracy show Italians with positive attitudes towards the democracy of the 'old' regime at 28% in 1985, 26% in 1987, 27% in 1989 and 21% in 1990 (all-EC figures for the same year were 58, 57, 66 and 62%). Even prior to the exposures of the magistrates' 'Operation Clean Hands', there had been considerable public disquiet about public corruption. An electoral reform campaign led by Mario Segni, a dissident Christian Democrat appalled by the DC system of power, had already scored a notable success against the old regime, obtaining a 62.5% turnout for a referendum in June 1991 to end the preference vote, despite Craxi's notorious invitation to the electorate to 'go to the seaside' on the day of the ballot. The reformers won the day, with a remarkable 95.6% voting in favour of the reform, aimed at reducing competitive pressures within the parties and the associated corruption. Such a strong public interest in a seemingly minor aspect of electoral reform was even more remarkable given the role played by the media. RAI 1 and RAI 2, which, as we have seen, were controlled respectively by the DC and PSI, virtually ignored the referendum, while only two major newspapers campaigned for a 'yes' vote.

In the general elections of April 1992, before the full extent of the scandals was known, the voters punished the old parties without as yet destroying them. The DC poll dropped from 34.4% in 1987 to 29.7% — below 30% in elections to the Chamber of Deputies for the first time in its history. The PSI poll dropped from 14.3% to 13.6% — a small decrease, but significant in the light of the consistent upward trend in its support since 1976. At the same time, new secular and 'protest' parties, perceived as outside the 'particracy', received public endorsement. Support for the Northern League, whose appeal was to a large extent based on its anti-Southern and anti-particracy rhetoric, rose from 0.5% to 8.7%. Its share of the Northern vote was, naturally, more spectacular. Despite this electoral earthquake, the parties of the old coalition were still able to put together a parliamentary majority.

As the stories of corruption broke on a virtually daily basis through 1992, however, public pressure for change became inexorable. Segni's reform campaign gathered further momentum, becoming a cross-party movement, almost unthinkably embracing former Communists and Christian Democrats. The necessary signatures were collected for a further series of referendums aimed at breaking the stranglehold of the 'particracy' and undermining the bases of public corruption. Central among these was a referendum to repeal the law requiring proportional representation to be applied to elections to Senate (technical reasons prevented a more wide-reaching reform being put to the electorate, as referendums in Italy may only repeal existing laws or parts of them, not propose new ones). It was nevertheless the reformers' assumption that a resounding success on this seemingly minor issue would force parliament to enact more thorough-going reform. By this point, the parties of the old regime could no longer afford to align themselves in defence of electoral and institutional arrangements widely perceived by the Italian public as responsible for the perpetuation of the 'particracy' and the associated abuses of power, and the main parties of government joined in the campaign for a 'yes' vote.

At the referendum, held in April 1993, 77% of the Italian electorate turned out to vote—as it turned out—on the fate of the regime; 82.7% voted for the reform. Faced with this massive vote of no-confidence by an outraged electorate, the government of Giuliano Amato resigned and was replaced by a caretaker government presided over by the ex-Governor of the Bank of Italy, Carlo Azeglio Ciampi. Under this government, new electoral rules were approved. In general elections, 75% of seats were to be attributed by a first-past-the-post system and 25% by proportional representation. In local elections, the mayor was to be chosen by a two-ballot system designed to pit the two leading candidates against one another in the final ballot. The first application came with local elections in June and December 1993 and the results were a catastrophe for the parties of the old ruling coalition. For most voters, the exposure of the corrupt practices of the old coalition parties had made them ineligible. The DC secured only 9 of the 221 mayoral offices up for re-election, the overwhelming victors were the left, allied in a loose electoral coalition dominated by the PDS, while the Northern League also scored notable success, as did the neo-fascist Italian Social Movement in its traditional stronghold in the South.

But despite the collapse of the old centre, the government that replaced it was not one of the left. In the few months separating the last round of local elections from the general elections of March 1994, a new force had arisen to fill the political space vacated by the disgraced parties. Silvio Berlusconi's Forza Italia! (Come On Italy!) is not so much a party as a movement whose electoral support may be explained by two main negative aims: to prevent the election of what is still seen by many as the Communist successor party and to prevent the return of representatives of the 'old' regime. He was able to market a brand new political formation, to an electorate avid to bury the old regime with the aid of his virtual monopoly of commercial television. The FI and its unlikely coalition partners—the federalist Northern League and the nationalist MSI—were swept into power on the promise of economic, and above all, political renewal.

But despite the presence in parliament of large numbers of business and professional elites new to politics, it soon became apparent that Berlusconi and his associates were not as 'new' as they wished to appear. Allegations that Berlusconi's holding company, Fininvest, was engaged in the creation of slush funds, gained substance. The creation of slush funds, or money that is 'off the books', is the necessary first step in the bribery, kickbacks and, indeed, illegal party financing characteristic of the old regime. The allegations mostly concern Publitalia, the advertising sales agency that is the Fininvest empire's main source of profit. One story relates to Romano Comincioli, a Fininvest consultant, old friend of Berlusconi's and founder of Forza Italia in Sicily. In late January 1995, a warrant was issued for the arrest of Comincioli, who was accused of collusion in fraudulent bankruptcy and fake invoicing. The bankruptcy in question related to a small Milanese firm, European Group Services (EGS). The magistrates contended that EGS was involved, with Publitalia, in a labyrinth network of fake invoices. Following the arrest of the EGS owners, Comincioli disappeared. The owners' confessions confirmed that the company had issued invoices to Comincioli for goods and services never actually delivered. The issue of such fake invoices is a common method used for the creation of slush funds, or money that can be used for illegal purposes such as bribery. The magistrates' investigation also revealed a transer of money from Fininvest to Comincioli when the latter was already on the run from the police.

A rather similar story, again involving Publitalia, began to emerge in mid-February, when an arrest warrant was issued in Turin against a high-ranking manager of the company, Gianpaolo Prandelli. Prandelli became a key witness in investigations into fake invoicing involving the sponsorship of motor-racing and power-boat racing teams, arranged by two agencies owned by Giovanni Arnaboldi which handled publicity for the sports teams. The alleged mechanism of this scam if fairly straightforward. Clients of Publitalia paid sponsorships to have their company logos emblazoned on Arnaboldi's power-boats. However, although the sponsorships were recorded as an expenditure, only 20–30% of the money actually went to the sports team, the rest returning under the table to Publitalia and its clients as money now off the books and available as a slush fund. Arnaboldi is alleged to have issued fake invoices to a value of about £27m, £4m of which were to Publitalia. Arnaboldi went on the run from police in the summer of 1994 but was arrested in Florida, where he was questioned by the Clean Hands pool of magistrates, to whom he has talked freely. He claimed that Publitalia gave him £58.000 in the form of cheques issued by Istifi (a kind of internal bank for the Fininvest group which receives money taken by subsidiaries and then distributes it for the payment of wage bills, etc.) to go into hiding. He also claimed that Prandelli and another Publitalia associate told him they would be able to let him know in time if an international arrest warrant was issued because 'the diplomatic channel was in their hands'. Prandelli, under arrest since early May 1995 after a month on the run, has so far claimed responsibility for the scam. However, the president of Publitalia, Marcello Dell'Utri, was arrested later in May. The main accusations against him concern a cheque, originating from Arnaboldi, which he turned over to the architect restoring his Lake Como villa.

Suspicions that Berlusconi's business empire, if not Berlusconi himself, may have been involved in the large-scale creation of slush funds were further raised by the discovery, in February 1995, of 35 or so special savings accounts made out to 'the bearer' and claimed by the company to represent personal savings of the Berlusconi family. The advantage of this sort of account is that anyone (the bearer) can carry out banking operations with them. Multiple accounts also allow large movements of money to be subdivided, making them harder to detect. With the exception of four accounts (named summer, spring, autumn and winter), the accounts were in the names of Fininvest employees and associates. About £27m had been deposited in them during the period 1989–90, which then trickled out over a longer period, mostly to Istifi, Fininvest's 'internal banker'.

If Fininvest has been involved in the creation of slush funds, what was their purpose? Some light may be thrown on this by the trial of General Giuseppe Cerciello and other high-ranking officers of Italy's special tax police, the Guardia di Finanza. The officers are charged with accepting bribes in return for lax and irregular inspections of company accounts. It has emerged during this trial that large sums of money were paid to tax police who inspected Fininvest companies between 1989 and 1992. Fininvest employees are also accused of having obstructed enquiries into the bribes, attempting to buy the silence of one officer. Fininvest has admitted to having 'submitted to the demands' of the tax police, paying out bribes on the occasion of tax inspections at some of its companies. Responsibility for this has been claimed by Berlusconi's brother Paolo and Salvatore Sciascia, the head of Fininvest fiscal services. Sciascia claims that he paid the bribes on the instructions of Paolo Berlusconi. However, the magistrates believe their investigations show that Sciascia was directly responsible to the company president, who, until January 1993, was Silvio Berlusconi himself.

Whatever the truth in Berlusconi's protestations that he cannot be expected to know of or take responsibility for the actions of all Fininvest employees, there can be little doubt that Fininvest, from within whose ranks a large part of the leadership of Forza Italia had been recruited, was operating according to the old informal rules of the 'hidden exchange'.

Controlling the investigations: limits to sleaze?

The demise of the main parties of the old regime and the political death of individual politicians most implicated in the scandals do not, therefore, constitute grounds for complacency. Serious concern must be raised by the continued influence of those who benefited from the spoils and kickback system in the processes both of closing the investigations and completing institutional reform to prevent further abuse. Whilst a complete renewal of Italy's old political class, comprising some one million full-time politicians,[6] may be impossible, collusion to defend the 'new' one from the attentions of the judiciary might be taken as evidence of a lack of the all important political will to clean up the system.

In fact, the attempt to bring the turbulent magistrates to heel has been a feature of both 'new' and 'old' regime. As the Clean Hands investigations proceded, in the last stages of the old regime, a number of suicides by prominent corruption suspects (including Gabriele Cagliari, the ENI chairman mentioned earlier) prompted arguments that the magistrates were abusing their powers to jail unconvicted persons where there is danger of the suspect fleeing, tampering with evidence or repeating the crime, and were using prison to wring confessions out of them. Cagliari, who committed suicide after 133 days in prison awaiting trial, accused the magistrates in a note of using prison as 'a tool for psychological torture'. The government of Giuliano Amato used public sympathies aroused by such cases to argue the need for a political solution to the corruption crisis triggered by the activities of the Clean Hands pool, in which pardons were offered in exchange for confession, resignation and restitution of embezzled funds. On March 5 1993, the government approved a package prepared by the Minister of Justice, Giovanni Conso, including limitation of the use of preventive custody, pardons on the above conditions and changes in the (severe) rules on party financing. Part of the package was made law by decree, to become effective that very night. Public outrage was immediate and led to spontaneous demonstrations in several cities. Shamed, the city of Milan withdrew its bid to host the Olympic games in the year 2000. Gherardo D'Ambrosio, head of the Clean Hands pool, declared that 'the political class in power has absolved itself, by itself.' The Amato government hurriedly retracted the decrees amidst a clamour for its resignation. By this date, the magistrates calculated that the cases under investigation involved £70bn pounds bribes, 65% of Italy's public debt.[7]

The Berlusconi government, elected on a wave of public repugnance to give a fresh face to Italian politics, continued the attempt to restrain the activities of the investigating magistrates. The new government argued that its own election showed that the corruption crisis was over. In June 1994 Berlusconi's Minister of Justice, Alfredo Biondi, removed from office Mario Vaudano, a magistrate responsible for clearing the way for investigations into foreign bank accounts: this move, it turned out later, closely followed Arnaboldi's flight from Florida and the issue of a warrant for his arrest by Turin magistrates. According to the latter, Vaudano's removal set back their investigations by at least seven months. This was an early shot in what was to become an enduring battle between the government and the Clean Hands proponents. In July 1994, after just ten weeks in government, Berlusconi and Biondi attempted to rush through a decree curbing the magistrates' powers of arrest. Di Pietro countered by using his strong personal appeal to make a resignation threat on television. The decree was issued as Italy was playing a World Cup match. Despite the Italian people's well-known passion for football, newspaper fax machines were immediately jammed with messages of protest and support for the magistrates. Berlusconi's coalition partners began to distance themselves from the decree, the Northern League threatening to withdraw its vital support for the government. The decree was quickly retracted. Suspicions were aroused that the decree had been designed to benefit Berlusconi's old friend Craxi and other business and political associates under investigation on a variety of charges, and such concerns were sharpened when, a few days later, an arrest warrant was issued for Paolo Berlusconi, who was to be investigated for collusion with Fininvest employees who had already confessed to bribing the tax police. The decree predated the public emergence of the allegations, discussed earlier, that would implicate Fininvest yet more deeply in the creation of slush funds.

In early October 1994, the chief of the Milanese Clean Hands pool, Francesco Saverio Borelli, escalated tensions with a statement that corruption inquiries might soon reach 'very high financial and political places' — a transparent reference to the Prime Minister. Berlusconi's Cabinet responded with a letter to the President of the Republic denouncing Borelli for attempting to undermine constitutional organs and asking Scalfaro to take formal action against him. When news of the government's attack on Borelli was broken on the evening TV news programmes, a wave of faxes expressing solidarity with Borelli and the pool once again inundated newspaper offices, just as had occurred for the Biondi decree. Again, the government was forced to moderate its position.

Later in October, in an effective disciplinary action against the magistrates, Minister of Justice Biondi sent inspectors from his ministry to look for evidence of irregular procedures, including the use of preventive detention as a threat to extract confessions from persons under investigation. The legitimacy of this action was strongly contested by the magistrates, as internal discipline is the responsibility of the Superior Council of the Judiciary, not the ministry. In the event, however, the report of the ministerial inspection team exonerated the magistrates of malpractice.

On 21 November 1994, while Berlusconi was in Naples attending a UN conference on international organized crime, the investigating magistrates leaked to the press the news that the premier was himself under investigation concerning the bribes paid by Fininvest companies to the tax police.

In late November, the Court of Cassation (Supreme Court) removed the trial of General Cerciello and other top-ranking tax police, which included the accusations against Fininvest employees, from the jurisdiction of the Milan pool, transferring it to Brescia on the grounds that the policemen's investigation by former colleagues created a conflict of interest. This was a very positive outcome for Berlusconi. The Brescia magistrates are working on the basis that the cases involve extortion, in which case the tax police (especially lower-ranking officers, against whom such allegations are easier to prove) will be accused of blackmailing companies to extort bribes. The Milan pool, on the other hand, believes that the companies were actively bribing the tax police to turn a blind eye to irregularities in the books—in other words, the firms were not submitting to threats but participating in the general back-scratching. Berlusconi and his supporters pointed to the Court's decision as a vindication of the argument that the Milan investigators are politically motivated.

During the month of December 1994 both Di Pietro and later Berlusconi resigned their offices, each after longstanding complaints that it had become impossible to do their job. Di Pietro's intentions were the subject of much speculation. He then resigned from the magistrature altogether, possibly to free himself for a political career. Berlusconi's downfall was caused by his inability to create the necessary consensus to address Italy's mounting public debt crisis, compounded by the mounting evidence of illegal practices within his empire. However, he continued his campaign against the Clean Hands pool from the sidelines, as well as mounting unsuccessful campaigns to prevent referendums that could lead to tightened media regulation and the break-up of his TV empire, and to hold a new general election before such regulation could take place.

Although the Berlusconi government was replaced by a 'non-party' government headed by Lamberto Dini, it is still not clear that those who most benefited from the practices of the old regime, or their representatives, have been divested of influence over its reform. The attempt to discipline the Clean Hands pool, for example, continued even under the new government. In early May 1995, the new Minister of Justice, Filippo Mancuso, ordered a fresh ministerial inspection of the Milan pool, implying that the favourable conclusions of the inspectors' earlier report were due to intimidation of the inspectors by members of the pool. Although the move was applauded by Forza Italia and AN MPs, the Prime Minister distanced himself from the decision, stating that it was the minister's responsibility. Officials involved in the earlier inspection, outraged by the questioning of their report, threatened to resign. In the face of parliamentary outcry against his unilateral action, Mancuso was forced to back-pedal, indefinitely postponing the inspection.

Cause for concern may also be found in less high-profile events suggesting the continued influence of those who seek to defend the practices and practitioners of the old regime. An example is raised by Antonio Di Pietro himself, in an article published in *La Repubblica*, on 28 May 1995, in which he expressed concern over the fate of the Merloni Law, a complex package reforming the system of tendering for public works contracts. The law had met with repeated criticism for its supposed effects in killing off enterprise initiative and limiting free access to contracts, and was suspended until April 1995, when it was reintroduced in a modified form. Whilst Di Pietro applauded some positive aspects of the law, he also pointed to loopholes that 'could compromise the clarity of the relationship between public administration and enterprise' and questioned the postponement of the enforcement date of part of the package.

The sustained attempts to limit the autonomy of the magistrates, coupled with the sabotage of reforms intended to limit the hidden interdependence of public and private power, do not bode well for an emergent 'Second Republic' and raise wider issues in relation to the focus of political reform which, in Italy, broadly follow two approaches. The first, historically embraced by the right, attributes the ills of the Italian political system to its 'ungovernability' and the opposition's ability to derail government policy. The prescription of this approach is a majoritarian electoral system with direct election of the head of government and the strengthening of executive powers in relation to other branches, including, of course, the judiciary. The other approach concentrates on the need to destroy the spoils-sharing machine driven by intra-party and inter-party rivalry. But as Angelo Panebianco notes, achievement of the first objective may not lead to the elimination of the 'particracy': reform in a majoritarian direction could simply cut the opposition off from state resources, delimiting the 'particracy' to the parties of government.[8] If the representatives of the majority in government should also retain a virtual stranglehold over the media, the development of an eligible opposition to replace them may prove difficult.

Given the systemic exchange of influence for money in Italy, it may be assumed that many have much to lose from reform that effectively dismantles the mechanisms of the 'particracy' and regulates relations between the public and private sectors. While Belusconi's political star appears to have faded, it is improbable that the ranks of the aspirants to political power have been purged of conservatives. The struggle to defend old privileges may continue in attempts to shape reform, resist effective reform and tame or control newly independent spirits, unleashed by the end of the Cold War, especially within parliament, the judiciary and the media. In this context the 'easy' solution of majoritarian reform could have the effect of locking the exponents of the old regime into the sweetshop, where they can continue to fill their pockets with public goodies unrestrained.

1 All money figures are roughly calculated on the basis of an exchange rate of 2,600 lire.
2 See e.g. M. Calise 'The Italian Particracy: Beyond President and Parliament', *Political Science Quarterly*, 1994, pp. 441–79.
3 For the origins of clientelism see S. Tarrow, 'Peasant Communism in Southern Italy', Yale University Press, 1967.
4 S. Cassese, Hypotheses on the Italian Administrative System, *West European Politics*, July 1993.
5 C. Guarnieri, Magistratura e politica: Il caso Italiano, *Rivista Italiana di Scienze Politica*, April 1991.
6 F. Sidoti, The Italian Political Class, *Government and Opposition*, 1993 3.
7 *The Guardian*, 10.3.93.
8 A. Panebianco, 'Riforme contro i partiti? Un commento', *Rivista Italiana di Scienze Politica*, December 1991.

Spain

BY PAUL HEYWOOD

IT is difficult to dissociate sleaze in Spain from the wider concern over corruption which has dominated Spanish political life during the 1990s. Indeed, since the general elections of June 1993 corruption has become the single most salient issue in Spanish politics. The catalyst for this development was the so-called 'Guerra case', which emerged in early 1990 and eventually forced the resignation of the Deputy Prime Minister, Alfonso Guerra, following allegations about his brother's misuse of party facilities and influence-peddling. Added impetus was subsequently provided by the remarkable revelations which began to emerge from Italy in 1992: in common with their counterparts throughout much of Europe, Spanish political commentators were tempted to seek domestic parallels to the 'tangentopoli' ('bribesville') culture, sparking discussion of the so-called 'Italianisation' of Spanish politics. However, it was the dramatic events of April and May 1994 which really opened the floodgates of investigative reporting on corruption. In the space of just a few weeks, the Socialist government was rocked by a series of major scandals which ultimately led to the resignation of five ministers.

The two principal scandals surrounded the activities of the former Governor of the Bank of Spain, Mariano Rubio, and the former head of the Civil Guard, Luis Roldán, who escaped and went into hiding after being arrested on suspicion of fraud and perversion of the court of justice. The activities of Rubio led to the resignation of Carlos Solchaga, former Minister of the Economy; those of Roldán resulted in the resignations of Antoni Asunción, Minister of the Interior, and his predecessor, José Luis Corcuera. In addition, Baltazar Garzón, an investigating magistrate who had been elected to parliament as an independent on the Socialist slate and given responsibility for drugs control, resigned in protest at the government's failure to act against corruption. Finally, Vicente Albero, Minister of Agriculture, resigned to forestall further scandal (see below). Most damaging of all, however, was renewed interest in the government's alleged involvement in setting up the Grupos Antiterroristas de Liberación (GAL), death squads which waged a dirty war against ETA activists between 1983 and 1987.

Although less obviously damaging than major corruption scandals, sleaze operates in a more insidious manner to undermine confidence in the political class. Sleaze is a somewhat amorphous concept with inescapably normative connotations (for instance, unlike Britain, there is little concern in Spain over the sexual exploits of leading politicians), but a sense that sleaze is widespread in Spanish politics has existed for some years. This sense of sleaze is perhaps best encapsulated in the phrase 'la cultura del pelotazo', which has become widely used by political commentators to refer to the scandal-ridden atmosphere in contemporary Spain. It has no precise translation. Although 'sleaze culture' probably comes closest to capturing its sense, the expression also has a wider resonance. The word 'pelotazo' literally means 'a kick', which has overtones of the 'in your face culture' familiar from the British context; 'darse un pelotazo', however, means to get drunk or high (usually on drugs) and links in to the activities of the so-called 'beautiful people' who came to prominence in the mid-1980s under the Socialist administration of Felipe González.

The politics of the beautiful people: scandals and sleaze

'Los beautiful'—a group of closely interconnected and very wealthy individuals (many with connections to the Socialist Party) who are highly influential in the financial world—became the focus of much attention in Spain after the spectacular economic takeoff prompted by entry to the European Community in 1986. Together with the 'la jet [set de Marbella]'—international socialites who congregated in southern Spain's most exclusive resort—they became virtually emblematic of Spain's dynamic economic development during the latter part of the 1980s. For all that more traditional PSOE (Spanish Socialist Party) activists felt uncomfortable with, or even betrayed by, the Socialist government's apparent courting of the world of high finance, 'los beautiful' seemed to capture the public imagination, featuring regularly in Spain's ubiquitous weekly glossies, such as *¡Hola!*. No individual was more representative of the interconnections between the Socialist Party and the financial world than Miguel Boyer, Minister of the Economy between 1982 and 1985. Married to the glamorous former model, Isabel Preysler, Boyer subsequently became chief executive of the Banco Exterior de España and then of the investment company, Cartera Central. The rapidity of his appointment to head the Banco Exterior after leaving ministerial office certainly raised eyebrows in Spain. Cartera Central had been created with capital provided by the fabulously wealthy Koplowitz sisters, Alicia (Marchioness of Real Socorro) and Esther (Marchioness of Casa Peñalvar), who were married respectively to 'los Albertos'—the cousins Alberto Cortina and Alberto Alcocer. Plans by 'los Albertos' to expand their business empire ultimately foundered, along with their marriages, following episodes of infidelity. Nevertheless, Socialist Spain in the late 1980s seemed synonymous with the high-life, symbolised by the self-confident vibrancy characteristic of the 'yuppy culture'. Indeed, Boyer's successor as Minister of the Economy, Carlos Solchaga, made the infamous boast that Spain was the European country in which you could get rich quickest.

Whilst socialism and wealth are in no sense necessarily incompatible, the growing divorce between the social democratic rhetoric of the PSOE government and the reality of Spain's social structure contributed to a sense of disillusion, if not distaste, amongst Socialist supporters. When the economic boom of the 1980s turned to recession in the early 1990s, criticism became much more widespread. Many of the self-appointed heroes of the 1980s turned out to have feet of clay: a seemingly never-ending series of scandals, many involving figures closely connected to the Socialist administration, generated the impression of a government mired in sleaze and corruption. Although there had long been accusations that the Socialist Party had abused its hold on power, the charges only really began to stick following the protracted investigations which commenced in early 1990 into the activities of Juan Guerra, brother of the then Deputy Prime Minister. The 'Juan Guerra case' centred on his illegal use of PSOE offices in Seville for private business purposes. During the Socialist government's period in office through the 1980s, Guerra went from receiving unemployment benefit to amassing a considerable personal fortune—the result, it was alleged, of 'influence trafficking'. Although the case remains under investigation, the majority of charges against Guerra were either dropped or not proved. So far, he has been found guilty only of inflicting bodily harm on his wife and incitement to pervert the course of justice.

Following the emergence of the Guerra case, the number of scandals began to snowball. Significantly, they encompassed not just the Socialist government but all the major political parties, as well as leading figures in the financial world. By 1995 the list of scandals either proved or still under investigation in Spain had reached remarkable proportions: over twenty separate major cases contributed to a generalised air of disillusion with the political class. The international edition of *El País*, Spain's leading newspaper, began in April 1994 to include a regular section on 'political scandals', usually running to some two pages; by mid-May the section had become 'scandals and crisis' and by October it was headed 'corruption and political turmoil'.

One scandal in particular symbolised 'la cultura del pelotazo' and the fall from grace of 'los beautiful': the Ibercorp case, which first emerged in 1992, involved several leading figures in the world of finance, including Boyer and the former Governor of the Bank of Spain, Mariano Rubio. Ibercorp had been created in 1986 by Manuel de la Concha and Jaime Soto, two prominent figures amongst 'los beautiful', and rapidly developed into a financial empire built around the Ibercorp bank, established in 1987. After heady expansion, the group fell into spiralling crisis following the Gulf War and subsequent slowdown in world trade; in March 1992 the Bank of Spain was obliged to intervene and trading in Ibercorp was suspended on the Stock Exchange. Ibercorp's main debts were to other financial institutions, including the Bank of Spain itself, but one of the most significant aspects of its downfall concerned the activities of Sistemas Financieros, a company which originally specialised in office furniture and which had been bought by De la Concha from the Banco Urquijo Unión. After the furniture business had been sold on, Sistemas Financieros was floated on the Stock Exchange, where its value sky-rocketed—largely, it was later alleged, as a result of insider dealing by certain shareholders with access to privileged information. Amongst the names involved in the alleged insider dealing were Mariano Rubio, Miguel Boyer, Isabel Preysler, and a former Minister of the Economy under the previous centrist UCD government, Juan Antonio García Díez. Rubio, who had been appointed to head the Bank of Spain by the Socialist government, was cast under further suspicion as a result of the fact that his sister, his cousin and his brother-in-law were all connected to a Luxemburg-based company, Schaff Investments, which was involved in selling shares in Sistemas Financieros. Even more damaging, however, was the revelation in April 1994 that Rubio had operated illegal accounts in Manuel de la Concha's investment agency whilst Governor of the Bank of Spain. The scandal, which at the time of writing remains under investigation, led to the resignation of the PSOE's parliamentary spokesman, Carlos Solchaga, who had been Minister of the Economy between 1985 and 1993 and a staunch defender of Rubio when the Ibercorp scandal first broke in 1992.

The Filesa and Naseiro cases, which involved the alleged illegal funding of the PSOE and the right-wing Partido Popular (PP) respectively, are on the borderline between sleaze and corruption.[1] Although they revealed a cynical disregard for public probity, the two cases fall into a pattern which has become familiar in several European democracies whereby political parties have sought to by-pass official channels in order to secure funds as the cost of the party machinery and media advertising outstrips membership income.[2] Their importance in Spain lies in the fact that they focused public attention on the existence of graft at the highest political levels. Filesa was the name of a holding company established in February 1988, under whose auspices it is alleged that various front organisations (amongst which the most important were Time Export and Malesa) engaged in parallel financing of the PSOE through the preparation of bogus reports commissioned by major banks and energy companies. The Filesa case came to light following revelations to the press by a disgruntled former employee of Time Export, the Chilean Carlos Alberto Schouwen, who had been offered one month's severance pay (some £500, Pta 90,000) in lieu of the Pta 25 million he had demanded. When the investigating magistrate, Marino Barbero, sought evidence of the reports commissioned from Filesa (usually at a cost of some Pta 200m each), the vast majorty had mysteriously disappeared. Investigations into the Filesa case brought to light the activities of other companies connected to the PSOE through the offices of Aida Alvarez, a senior figure in the party's administration. Along with other figures involved in the scandal, such as the MPs Guillermo Galeote and Carlos Navarro, Alvarez was obliged to resign her post. However, by early 1955—four years after Marino Barbero began his investigations into the case—no prosecutions had taken place.

The Naseiro case emerged in April 1990 when the judge Luis Manglano ordered the arrest of a number of individuals connected with the Partido Popular in Valencia. Principal amongst them was the PP's treasurer, Rosendo Naseiro, and Salvador Palop, a regional councillor, who were accused of involvement in illegal financing of the party via the payment of commissions by construction companies to win public contracts. The case had come to light as a result of an entirely separate investigation into drug-trafficking, during which bugged telephone conversations between Palop and other party members revealed (often in explicit, if colourful, detail) the existence of a well-established system of parallel financing in Valencia. The case was brought to trial but dismissed on a technicality: the taped telephone calls were ruled by the Supreme Court as inadmissible evidence since they had been authorised for a separate investigation. In June 1994 the tapes were destroyed, but their contents had by then been widely disseminated in the press. The scandal effectively ended the political careers of Naseiro and Palop, as well as another MP, Angel Sanchis, Naseiro's predecessor as PP treasurer.

In December 1994 Naseiro appeared before the parliamentary committee established earlier that year to investigate the financing of political parties and denied any illegal activity. He cited ill-health in his defence: he had earlier undergone open heart surgery, and his appearance before the committee apparently went against doctors' advice. However, that same month Angel Sanchis admitted to the same committee that he had actively engaged in fund-raising through the use of intermediaries connected to the CEOE, the Spanish employers' organisation, although he vehemently denied that any favours were ever offered in return. In fact, Valencia came to represent something of a nightmare region for the PP. In June 1994 another taped telephone conversation revealed that the right-wing party's regional leader, Vicente Sanz, claimed that he was in politics only for the money. On the night of the PP's victory in the European elections, Sanz declared that 'now we're really going to make a packet' and spoke of plans to use official posts for personal ends. In a damage-limitation exercise, the PP leadership moved quickly to dismiss him.

The Socialist government similarly found itself embarrassed in May 1994 by the activities of an MP from Valencia. In the midst of the Rubio and Roldán crises, Vicente Albero, appointed Minister of Agriculture just five months earlier, admitted that he had been guilty of fraud whilst working for a private company in the early 1980s. Albero not only left his ministerial post—thus becoming the fifth minister to leave the government in the space of a few weeks—but also resigned from Parliament and from the leadership of the regional party in June 1994. Although the Albero case involved straightforward personal dishonesty which was unlinked to political favours, the cumulative impact of scandals involving leading figures in the Socialist Party was to convey the impression of a government steeped in venality.

Amongst other noteworthy examples of sleaze were the Renfe and Salanueva affairs. The Renfe affair cost the political career of Julián García Valverde, Health Minister from March 1991 until his resignation in January 1992. García Valverde had previously been in charge of Renfe, Spain's national railway. It emerged in October 1991 that Renfe had been involved in land speculation around San Sebastián de los Reyes, a dormitory town for Madrid. In order to finance the construction of a railway link to the town, a company called Equidesa borrowed Pta 1.8bn from Renfe to buy up land cheaply prior to the granting of permission to build on it, which would then allow the land to be resold at a considerable profit. Such a move was a familiar, if perhaps questionable, means of raising capital. However, it turned out that a series of other companies had been tipped off to purchase the land in question before Equidesa's intervention, allowing them to inflate the price that Equidesa—and therefore ultimately the state—had to pay. Moreover, the purchases also entailed a massive VAT fraud. Similar operations were discovered in Zaragoza, Seville and Barcelona, and it was also revealed that Renfe had paid two companies of dubious provenance, Syop and ABC Empresarios, Pta 50m for what proved to be non-existent feasibility studies. The Spanish parliament set up an investigating commission, but García Valverde was not formally charged with any wrongdoing.

The 'Salanueva case', which first emerged in 1990, involved Carmen Salanueva who had been given responsibility in early 1985 for production of the *Boletín Oficial del Estado*, the state's official journal of record. A facelift for the journal, agreed upon in 1986, entailed the purchase of new supplies of paper, which provided Salanueva with the opportunity to engage in major fraud. Full autonomy over the journal's budget allowed Salanueva not only to create false invoices when purchasing paper and pocket the difference but also to favour companies in which she was a direct beneficiary. Moreover, along with three colleagues, she engaged in a remarkable number of overseas trips in the course of official duties. Again, the presentation of false invoices enabled her to benefit personally, a fact which contributed to a lifestyle which was quite out of keeping with her official salary. When the scandal broke in late 1990, Salanueva offered her resignation but was allowed to remain in post until the end of May 1991. Following a lengthy investigation by the magistrate, Ana María Ferrer, she was finally arrested in November 1993 but released from prison on bail. The following month she was rearrested, but this time on an entirely different charge which related to using the names of Queen Sofia and

Carmen Romero (wife of the Prime Minister, Felipe González) to obtain discounts on works of art.

Sleaze, politics and public concern

The Salanueva case is perhaps most indicative of a perceived inability by leading public figures to distinguish between what they are entitled to in their public and private capacities. Part of the reason for this lies in the weakness of anti-corruption legislation combined with poorly developed systems of investigation—a legacy, to some extent at least, of the Franco dictatorship. Yet the Socialist government showed little inclination until recently to confront a situation which led the World Economic Forum to conclude in 1991 that Spain was second only to Italy in the developed world in the inadequacy of its anti-corruption measures. In fact, the boundaries between public office and private gain appear to have become increasingly blurred as Spain's economic fortunes have prospered. Graft, kick-backs and bribes, often tied to property speculation as prices soared in the heady 1980s, came to seem endemic in Socialist Spain.

Even in Catalonia, which has always prided itself on a sense of thrift and efficiency in contrast to what was seen as profligate waste in the rest of Spain, sleaze and corruption scandals have undermined confidence in the political class. In the BFP case, the credibility of Jordi Pujol, president of the Generalitat (Catalan parliament), was called into question. Pujol, leader of the right-leaning nationalist party Convergència i Unió (CiU), came to power in 1980 on the slogan 'Let's get to work' and is often seen as representing traditional Catalan attributes of sobriety, financial acumen, devout Catholicism, and pride in the Catalan nation and its culture. BFP was a finance company named after the initials of its founders, Joan Bassols, Salvador Forcadell and Jordi Planasdemunt—the last of whom was simultaneously in charge of the Institut Català de Finances (ICF), a body responsible for promoting Catalan enterprise which was directly dependent on the Generalitat. In late September 1992, shortly after the Barcelona Olympic Games, Planasdemunt and his two colleagues were arrested on suspicion of a major fraud racket whereby BFP sold fake promissory notes in major firms, such as Repsol, Cepsa or Telefónica. It was estimated that the fraudulent transactions eventually amounted to some Pta 6bn, and that many of the investors had used co-called 'dinero negro'—that is, money which had never been declared to the tax authorities. It further transpired that Planasdemunt, a long-time close friend of Jordi Pujol, had authorised an ICF loan of some Pta 40m to another company headed by Bassols, his colleague in BFP. Moreover, it emerged that Planasdemunt had also been involved with several other private sector companies at the same time as he was discharging his official responsibilities as head of the ICF. The CiU, which enjoyed an absolute majority in the Generalitat, refused to establish a parliamentary committee to investigate the affair, a move which was widely seen as reflecting poorly on Pujol. The Catalan president's continued backing of the Socialist government throughout the crises of 1994 contributed to the belief in some quarters that he was anxious to avoid a thorough investigation into political corruption.

There can be no doubt that the PSOE is the party which has suffered most in terms of image and voter response as a result of sleaze and corruption scandals. Felipe González acknowledged that the Socialist Party's poor performance in the June 1994 European elections — the first national level elections it lost to the right-wing Partido Popular since the return of democracy — was largely attributable to corruption scandals.[3] Survey evidence indicated that more than half the voters who had abandoned the PSOE cited corruption as the main reason for doing so, compared to just 2% who were disenchanted by the government's informal pact with the right-of-centre Catalan nationalists (CiU) led by Jordi Pujol. This confirmed poll findings prior to the European elections which indicated that 82% of PSOE voters and fully 65% of PP voters believed that if the Partido Popular were to win, it would be due more to Socialist failures than the PP's own merits. A Demoscopia survey in early June 1994 indicated that 80% of the electorate expected the European election results to be affected by corruption scandals. Yet, although the Socialist Party has undoubtedly been the main focus of sleaze and corruption allegations in Spain, all political parties are seen by the electorate to be implicated in underhand activities; 52% of respondents to Demoscopia's Winter 1994 barometer of public opinion believed that all political parties were equally involved in corruption, as opposed to 29% who felt some parties were more involved than others. The corresponding figures for Spring 1992 were 62% and 21% respectively, indicating that suspicions over the activities of the PSOE had increased. This was confirmed by the responses to the further question put to those respondents who believed that only some parties were involved in corruption or that some parties were involved more than others: 82% said the PSOE was the most corrupt, followed by the PP (17%), no response (13%) and CiU (5%).

In spite of the fact that the Socialist Party has been the most deeply implicated in sleaze and corruption, levels of support for all political parties appear to have been affected in a similar way. Expressed support for the four main parties in Demoscopia's quarterly opinion barometers has on the whole tended to rise and fall together. The one clear exception occurred in the wake of the Rubio and Roldán crises of early 1994, when the PP opened a clear lead over the PSOE. Even so, the one-off 23 May 1994 survey, which centred specifically on the issue of how political corruption was affecting voting intentions, showed a clear drop in support for the PP also, as well as a narrowing of its advantage over the PSOE from the Spring 1994 survey. By Summer 1994 the lead had widened again, as support for both parties rose, and since Autumn 1994 the two main political parties have been much closer together in terms of expressed support. These figures probably reflect less on attitudes towards sleaze and corruption than on the relative support for party leaders. In spite of the PSOE's travails, José María Aznar (in contrast to the Communist Party leader, Julio Anguita) has never outscored Felipe González in evaluations on a scale of 1–10 of national leaders. Nevertheless, when respondents are asked likely, as opposed to definite, voting intentions and 'don't knows/no answers' are excluded, the PP has enjoyed a clear lead over the PSOE since early 1994 of between 5% and 8%. The regional and municipal elections of 28 May 1995 confirmed this finding: although the PP won a comprehensive victory, taking control of ten out of the thirteen regions in which elections were held and winning an absolute majority in five of them, the PSOE vote held up much better than had been predicted in the polls[4]

The emergency of sleaze and corruption scandals has undoubtedly changed the landscape of Spanish political life. The dominance enjoyed by the Socialist Party throughout the 1980s has been shattered, and there now exists the real prospect—inconceivable a few years ago— that the Partido Popular will form the next government. For many commentators, this would represent a healthy development for Spain's still young democratic system, completing a stage often seen as vital in the process of consolidating democracy: the peaceful transfer of power between established political parties. The risk, however, is that the sense of sleaze and corruption will contribute to an undermining of confidence in the probity of the political class as a whole. There are clear indications that the rise in support for the PP is to some extent negative insofar as it represents an anti-PSOE response more than a positive endorsement of the right-wing party; to this extent, it mirrors the ABB vote ('Anyone but Bush') which helped ensure Bill Clinton's election in the US presidential elections of 1992. There is certainly little evidence of enthusiasm (even amongst PP voters) for the prospect of José María Aznar becoming Prime Minister, as opposed to relief at the prospect of an end to the Socialist grip on power. Indeed, many Socialist strategists believe that the next elections are effectively already lost, and the most urgent task now facing the PSOE is to avoid the devastating scale of defeat suffered by the French Socialist Party in the 1993 general elections.

That the Spanish political class should have fallen into such low public esteem in large measure reflects the ineffectiveness of some key institutional structures. In particular, the Spanish parliament has long been criticised for being unable to act as a proper check on a very powerful central executive. Spain's constitutional architects deliberately created a weak parliament, anticipating that coalition governments would be the norm in democratic Spain: the design of parliamentary rules was meant to encourage a 'pactist' style of decision-making. The minimum size of parliamentary groups was set at 15, and strict controls were placed on individual MPs—for instance, only parliamentary groups are allowed to introduce legislation, and MPs who wish to leave their own party may only switch to the 'Mixed Group; rather than to another party. Parliament was designed to serve as a chamber in which negotiation between well-matched forces would act as a symbol of tolerance. A well-balanced parliament would then serve as an effective check on a secure Prime Minister, who would have to consider a wide range of interests. The reality turned out very differently, for the prestige of Spain's parliament has been steadily eroded since the election of 1979. Under the centrist UCD's second administration, it was criticised for its incapacity to stop agreements being reached without reference to parliamentary procedures. Thereafter, the PSOE's absolute majorities between 1982 and 1993—an unanticipated electoral outcome when the 1978 constitution was framed—further reduced the role of parliament in terms of policy-making. The search for consensus could be ignored by a government which enjoyed an overwhelming majority. Parliament has tended to follow government in a docile manner, and investigative committees have rarely been established. Only with the loss of the PSOE's absolute majority in the 1993 general elections has it been able to start regaining some of the initiative it had lost during the preceding fifteen years, although so long as the government can maintain sufficient discipline to put together a majority on any specific item of legislation, parliament's real power is limited.

Another feature of Spain's political system which has been altered by the emergence of sleaze and corruption scandals concerns the role of the judiciary. In spite of provisions in the constitution for an independent judiciary charged with upholding the 'state of law', in practice Spain's legal structure has been subject to virtually unremitting criticism since the restoration of democracy. In particular, judicial independence has been questioned: the Socialist government has been accused of appointing party sympathisers to leading posts in the Constitutional Court, the Supreme Court and, especially, the General Council of the Judiciary, which has overall responsibility for Spain's legal system. As a result, the judiciary has often been seen as ineffective, incapable of acting to prevent abuses of power by the government. The sleaze and corruption scandals which emerged in the 1990s went some way towards altering that picture. Indeed, as in Italy, judges and investigating magistrates have become key figures in the political process, several of them assuming a prominent public profile. Of no one has this been more true than Baltazar Garzón, whose investigations into the GAL affair in the late 1980s led to his being dubbed 'Super Garzón' in the press—an image he was happy to cultivate during his rapid rise to political influence. Garzón, who revelled in the public limelight, was co-opted by Felipe González as number two on the PSOE list for Madrid in the 1993 general elections, but growing disillusion with the government's failure to tackle corruption scandals prompted his resignation in

May 1994. Thereafter, he became a major thorn in the government's side, taking charge of reopened investigations into the GAL affair and the related Roldán case. Although the judiciary is still often subject to criticism over the slow progress of investigations and the lack of successful convictions of political figures, its role as upholder of the rule of law in democratic Spain has come to assume signal importance.

Conclusion: politics, culture and sleaze

The question which inevitably emerges is how and why Spain's political class has become embroiled in the 'cultura del pelotazo'. A number of reasons may be adduced in explanation. One factor may be longevity in power, which in the case of the PSOE has been seen to breed a certain arrogance and even contempt for opponents. Political parties which repeatedly win elections can easily believe themselves invulnerable, and the lack of any obvious challenge to the Socialists' dominance throughout the 1980s undoubtedly contributed to such a sense of superiority. The boundaries between government and state unsurprisingly became blurred, leading to the impression on occasion that the Socialists had 'become' the state, accountable only to themselves. Yet, while such an explanation may provide insight into some of the activities of the PSOE, it fails to account for the existence of sleaze and corruption in other parties and other spheres of public life. A second key factor which must therefore be considered is opportunity, which was largely provided in the Spanish case by spectacular economic growth in the second half of the 1980s. It was this economic take-off, linked to massive overseas investment attracted in part by high interest rates and a strong currency, which promoted previously unknown levels of speculation in stocks and shares. Vast sums of 'dinero negro' were used to engage in speculation, further encouraged by financial deregulation measures consequent upon Spain's entry to the European Community. It was the opportunities provided by this new financial environment which led to the emergence of 'los beautiful' and the ever closer interconnections between the worlds of high finance and politics.

Alongside opportunity, motive is also a necessary factor. In many cases, of course, the motive to engage in sleaze was sheer greed: the desire to accumulate wealth and, significantly, to flaunt it. Much more than in the case of 'yuppies' in Britain and North America, Spain's 'nouveaux riches' came to be closely associated with style, glamour and, ultimately, power. More prosaically, though, many of the most notorious examples of sleaze and corruption—such as the Filesa and Naseiro cases—were motivated less by the desire for personal enrichment than the need to secure funds for political parties. Politics in the mass media age has become an ever more expensive business, leading political parties constantly to seek out new avenues of funding. Favours for finance has become a standard feature of the party system in many democratic polities.

That some—albeit, just a few—European democracies appear to have largely avoided sleaze and corruption scandals points to a final factor which should be considered: the efficacy of anti-corruption measures. This refers not just to formal legislation but to the institutional structure of the democratic state. Democracy needs to be safeguarded through the effective functioning of mechanisms of accountability: the checks and balances familiar from any constitutional textbook. These mechanisms of accountability not only have to be in place, but they need to be enforced. In a young democracy like Spain's, which provides for a very high degree of executive power, the risks of institutional degradation are high. Perhaps the one positive aspect which has emerged from the sleaze and corruption scandals of recent years is a renewed sense of the need to defend Spain's democratic institutions, to ensure that the political class is indeed ultimately held to account.

1　The distinction between sleaze and political corruption is not clear-cut. Consideration is given here to some prominent cases which involve parties and individuals, as opposed to government-related scandals such as the GAL affair and the activities of the former head of the Civil Guard, Luis Roldán.

2　In June 1994, the PSOE owed Pta 11.7bn., the PP Pta 5.9bn, the PNV Pta 2.8bn, and IU Pta 1.5bn. Between 1977 and 1994, Spanish parties had received a total of Pta 83.3bn in state subsidies (74% going to the PSOE and PP), with a further Pta 28.2bn in electoral expenses (67% going to the PSOE and PP).

3　In the European elections, the PSOE won 30.7% of the vote (comapred to 39.6% in 1989) against the PP's 40.2% (compared to 21.4% in 1989). The distribution of the vote meant that although the PP gained 13 seats to reach an overall total of 28, the PSOE's 22 seats represented a loss of just five. González's comments were made at the PSOE's annual 'Jaime Vera summer school' held at Galapagar, near Madrid.

4　In the regional elections, the PP won absolute majorities in the Balearic Islands, Castille and Leon, Madrid, Murcia and La Rioja. The PSOE was able to retain control only in Castille-La Mancha and Extremadura. In the municipal elections, the PP won absolute majorities in 32 out of 54 provincial capitals, including Madrid, and won most support in 17 of Spain's twenty leading cities. Overall, the PP took some 35% of the vote compared to 30% for the PSOE. Prior to the elections, opinion polls had predicted a winning margin for the PP of some 15 to 16%.

The Politics of Fasting and Feasting

BY CHRISTOPHER HOOD

Feasting in public: the rulers' dilemma

WEST African kings once ate in secret, to avoid reminding their people that they too were flesh and blood. The rulers of the former communist empires in effect did the same. And those who hold high office in today's affluent 'liberal democracies' face a dilemma that is not so different. They too need to eat. But they are fearful of living too visibly off the fat of the land at the expense of the hard-pressed taxpayer. And if Tocqueville's reasoning is correct, such a fear is far from irrational, because most voters will want to see their masters on the political equivalent of the Flat Stomach Plan.

In *Democracy in America* Toqueville argued that democracies would be dangerously parsimonious with the pay of those in high public office. The parsimony would come about because few voters hold such office (or can reasonably expect to do so in the future), so there will be effectively no votes in paying high public officials well. The danger would lie in the paradoxical result of such 'rational' self-serving behaviour on the part of the voters, namely that democracies would tend to turn back into de facto aristocracies. Only those with access to substantial personal or corporate wealth could afford to hold high public office on anything but a corrupt basis. But even if not all voters are as narrowly selfish as Tocqueville expected, those at the top are still likely to be expected to practise some of the self-denial and public virtue that they so often demand of everyone else. Being seen to feast while others fast remains a problem, and not just in West Africa.

Indeed, as many of the contributions to this volume show, it seems to be becoming an increasing problem, and certainly not just with the 'sleaze backlash' against the Major government in Britain since the 1992 election. Related issues, often in much more dramatic form, have come to the surface in many of the established OECD democracies. The famous Fitzgerald report on corruption in the Australian state of Queensland in 1989 (revealing widespread corrupt protection by the police and the state government of illegal casinos, bookmakers, massage parlours and brothels), leading to the electoral defeat of the National Party government which had held office since 1957, was a foretaste of things to come elsewhere in the early 1990s. The most dramatic cases were the seismic shift in judicial willingness to take on political corruption which started to bring down the Italian 'partitocrazia' regime in 1992 as described by Hilary Partridge in her account of the 'Clean Hands' group of Milanese magistrates, and the contribution of the Recruit and other scandals to the electoral defeat of the Japanese Liberal Democrat Party in 1993 after four decades in office.

Even the long-established French tradition of close ties between the business and political elite, with no finicky Anglo-Saxon concerns about conflicts of interest, has suddenly been challenged by a series of corruption cases brought by younger 'populist' judges such as Thierry Jean-Pierre, with strong backing from public opinion as Christophe Fay shows. As Charlie Jeffery and Simon Green argue, German 'Politikverdrossenheit' (being fed up with politics) has been fuelled by the idea of party politicians 'looting the state' in von Arnim's colourful but deadly phrase.[1] Though there have been corruption and conflict-of-interest issues too, much of what is seen as 'looting' consists of surreptitious 'fine-print' allowances and pension entitlements that augment the effective tax-free income of politicians far above their ostensible level, for example in the much-publicized cases of Hesse, Hamburg and Lower Saxony. And rising American public anger at congressional 'rubber bank accounts' and other perks seems to have helped to fuel the 1994 rout of the Democrats from Congress after a forty-year reign.

Nothing much has been found to be rotten in the state of Denmark, it is true, and the same seems to go for the other Scandinavian countries. The public debate on this issue over the Danish EU Commissioner 'double-dipping' by drawing a ministerial pension as well as the generous EU salary, (particularly since the Commissioner elected not to draw the former during her period of office following the debate), as discussed by Jørgen Christensen, would hardly register on a sleazeometer calibrated to the levels of what has been happening in Spain and Greece or alleged to have occurred in Belgium. Moreover, precisely what is being complained about as 'sleaze' certainly varies from case to case. In some cases, sexual as well as financial aspects of sleaze have been salient (as in the UK), while in others only financial questions have been at issue. In some cases, the focus has been more on conflicts of interest in combining private interests with public office, notably in jobs after politics, second jobs combined with politics and acceptance of dubious gifts or payoffs (for example, France, Italy, Japan, Belgium). But in others it has been more on the growth of a patronage 'gravy train' in the public sector, together with semi-concealed perks, allowances and pensions (Germany, USA). Again, in some cases, what is at issue is practices which are fairly clearly illegal (such as kickbacks on public contracts), while in others the practices being characterized as sleaze are more like tax avoidance rather than tax evasion—that is, behaviour such as generous perks, extramarital affairs, political consultancies which is quite legal but attracts (increasing) public disapproval. And as in tax, there is an intermediate category of behaviour (like tax 'avoision') that comes somewhere between the two, such as the grey areas of party financing or patronage.

No ready-made explanation yet exists as to why the sleaze backlash takes different forms in different contexts. But the overall sleaze backlash across many of the OECD member states during the last half-decade suggests that malaise about politics in one form or another has been a widespread phenomenon (going well beyond British tabloid obsessions with politicians' sexual liaisons), and almost seems to have echoes of the Progressive-era reaction against corrupt politics by middle-class reformers at the turn of the century.

Responding to the sleaze backlash: five ways out

The reasons for that backlash are far from self-evident. Scholars are still arguing about the reasons for the rise of the environmental movement from the late 1960s. Was that movement a response to an objectively dirtier or more dangerous environment? Or did it rather reflect a cultural shift involving a new ascendancy of what Douglas and Wildavsky[2] call 'sectarian' beliefs and values, for whom environmental-ism represented a heaven-sent issue, since it enabled them to fix blame on big organizations and governments for the alleged harm they did to 'innocents'? The causes of the 1990s sleaze backlash are similarly debatable (though the debate is even harder to resolve, since sleazeo-metry is still in its earliest infancy in political science).

Was that backlash a cultural shift producing a new 'pollution taboo' for practices which had long been conveniently ignored as 'normal politics'?[3] Or is the backlash a reaction to an increasing pollution of politics and government produced by the growth of career politics, the rising cost of electoral campaigns, the lengthening frontier between the state and the private sector as privatization extends and the 'regulara-tory state' develops? Certainly, it cannot be taken for granted that the sleaze backlash simply reflected a sharp deterioration in standards of conduct by high public officials.

After all, it can be argued that there is little fundamentally new about the patronage power wielded by the British Prime Minister, which may well have been greater in the high noon of empire or public enterprise than it is today;[4] current 'sleaze' issues need to be seen in perspective against some of the British scandals of the earlier twentieth century (such as the 1912–3 Marconi share-buying affair, the sale of peerages under Lloyd George, the Poulson bribery scandals of the 1970s), while Roger Mortimore's discussion of British poll evidence suggests declining public tolerance of politicians' sexual adventures. Likewise, it seems hard to argue that there was much that was basically new about Italian kickback politics in the 1980s or early 1990s, or the close ties between business, politics and the public service in France. Contemporary US politics may well be rather cleaner than in the days of the Teapot Dome oil leases scandal or the corrupt big-city machines of the earlier part of the century.

On the other hand, pressures for new sources of political financing triggered by the increasingly capital-intensive nature of modern electoral politics, as noted by Paul Heywood, may produce new stimuli for sleaze, along with the get-rich-quick atmosphere in which politicians worked in the yuppy years of the 1980s. And the rise of semi-concealed but legal political rewards—the German version of 'sleaze', as noted above, echoed in American concerns about congressional perks—does seem to reflect a pattern of steady growth rather than sudden reaction against previously accepted behaviour. Possibly the answer to the question whether the sleaze backlash reflects a new pollution taboo or a dirtier political environment could be a bit of both—that is, a 'clericalization of the church' taking place just as the cultural mix was shifting towards a polarization of fundamentalism and individualism, and producing an explosive combination?

Whatever the causes of the sleaze backlash may be, it is likely to pose a challenge to politicians and other high public officials. If the backlash proves to be only a short-lived phenomenon, followed by a return to politics-as-normal, the challenge is only to weather the squall. But if the sleaze backlash is more than a passing fad or temporary media preoccupation (as suggested by those who link it to long-term changes such as the end of communism, the rising capital cost of politics, or broader cultural shifts), something other than a temporary battening down of hatches is likely to be called for. In the latter case, asceticization, dishonesty and 'pay for ethics' are three out of the possible strategic responses available to holders of high public office.

The ascetic road involves forswearing a comfortable lifestyle (in reality as well as in appearance), accepting politics and high public service as a moderately-paid 'talking profession' like teaching or social work. Adopting the opposite strategy of dishonesty as the best policy means forswearing a comfortable lifestyle in appearance but not in reality, by covering tracks more carefully or finding even more devious and obscure ways for officials to leave office substantially richer than they entered it.[5] 'Pay for ethics' is reflected in the deal accepted by the US House of Representatives in 1989 when politicians agreed to trade in lucrative but controversial sidelines for a much higher straight salary by agreeing to a cap on outside earnings like speaking fees.

Those three strategies are laid out in the table, which also includes two intermediate possibilities. One is to fast first and feast later—that is, to take politics as a first career, to be followed by something more lucrative later. The other is to feast first and fast later—that is, to acquire money before going into public office. The table identifies three out of the various criteria on which the different strategies can be rated, namely material reward, joint action need, and downside risk of loss of esteem. The material reward level column (2) denotes pay and perks in cash and kind; that is, the level of comfort at which politicians or other high office-holders can live off politics. Material comfort is high for the pay-for-ethics and dishonesty response, low for asceticism and medium for 'first career' approaches to politics (since both of those involve a mixture of feast and fast). The 'joint action need' column (3) denotes the degree of collective action which is needed to make each strategy work. It is high for pay for ethics (because politicians need to develop a common front across party and factional lines for that purpose), medium for the dishonesty policy (because of the joint action required for effective cover-ups) and low for all the others. The downside risk column (6) relates to the differences between columns 4 and 5—that is, the amount of loss of esteem that is at stake in the difference between the best-case outcome (for example, when the voters are trusting and plans work out) and the worst-case outcome (for example, when plans fail and the voters are distrusting or vindictive).

1: Five responses to the Sleaze Backlash

STRATEGY	'Material Reward' Level	Joint Action Need	Best-case Esteem Level (voter trust, plans work)	Worst-case Esteem Level (voter distrust, plans work)	Downside Esteem Risk
(1)	(2)	(3)	(4)	(5)	(6)
Strategy A: ASCETICISM	Low	Low	Very High	Medium (if voters do not believe ascetic stance)	Low
Intermediate Strategy A/B: Politics as Second Career	Medium	Low	Medium	Medium (very low after accidents	Low to medium
Strategy B: DISHONESTY POLICY	High	Medium or high for coverups	High (or very high because of air of self-sacrifice)	Very low (after accidents) otherwise low	High
Intermediate Strategy B/C: Politics as First career	Medium	Low	High	Medium (because less accessible for *ex post* attack)	Low
Strategy C: PAY FOR ETHICS	High	High, to present a common front	Medium	Very low (highly visible target for attack by the resentful)	High

The value placed on these elements, and the preferred trade-off among them, will naturally vary from one high public office-holder to another. For example, politicians clearly vary in the extent to which they are prepared to trade esteem for cash and perks, and (as will be shown later) the dominant strategy depends on those relative values. But a notional 'identikit' politician might be expected to prefer the strategy which combines high material rewards, low joint action requirements and a low downside risk. Unfortunately, no such happy all-purpose option seems to exist. It therefore seems doubtful if any single response is to be expected.

A move towards asceticization of politics (Strategy A in the table 1) might on the face of it seem an unlikely response to the sleaze backlash, considering what is often claimed to be the 'worship of greed' unleashed by the economic liberalism of the 1980s and the much-discussed rise of the career politician, supposedly yearning for the pay and lifestyle of top lawyers or corporate executives rather than the more modest wages of schoolteachers or social workers. Moreover, in the worst case that voters are highly cynical and distrustful, the high personal sacrifice involved in asceticization could be wasted, in the sense that cynical voters might still believe that politicians are secretly banking their ill-gotten millions in numbered Swiss accounts even if they are really practising considerable self-denial (the dilemma faced by Denmark's politicians, according to Jorgen Christensen).

But there are individual politicians in almost every political system who do follow the ascetic path (Jimmy Carter is perhaps the clearest American example). And though such behaviour perhaps runs against the grain of the 'Chicago theory of government' which holds that politicians aim to maximize their personal self-interest in a fairly narrow way, it is quite possible that the asceticization path might be more widely chosen. Indeed, the ascetic way is broadly what politicians seem to follow in the only major group of OECD states relatively unaffected by the sleaze backlash, namely the Scandinavian countries. And even for political systems with a quite different tradition, there are historical precedents for asceticization movements — as in the famous case of the Sanscritization of India and the Christianization of the Roman Empire,[6] meaning that a more general ascetic response is not culturally impossible. At least it seems fallacious to argue that the 'materialization of politics' is an inevitable consequence of the rise of the career politician. Just because a group has careerist aspirations does not mean that those aspirations will necessarily be satisfied. The logic of events could well dictate otherwise. It has happened before. And if the waves of public reaction against sleaze keep rising, asceticization may finally be the only stable solution to the problem of how to live off politics. Whether it is a desirable response is another matter, to be briefly discussed in the final section.

A second possible response to the sleaze backlash is the 'dishonesty policy' (Strategy B) — the smoke-and-mirrors approach of making sleaze appear to go away by covering tracks more carefully. It involves either legal but surreptitious income supplementation by politicians in office through hidden allowances and the like (as in the German version of 'sleaze'), or surreptitious and illegal income supplementation by politicians in office through payoffs and kickbacks (as in the old-regime Italian and Japanese versions). If some politicians turn to asceticism in the face of the sleaze backlash, others may turn to greater deviousness. From a narrowly tactical point of view, the advantage of the dishonesty approach is that if voters are trusting it makes politicians look noble and public-spirited, while if the voters are cynical and disaffected it offers no easily visible target for a vengeful response.

Indeed, a variant of the dishonesty policy could be argued to be very largely what high public officials have actually been doing for at least two decades across many OECD countries, making their incomes steadily harder for outsiders to discover and understand by hiding them behind a facade of allowances, tax breaks or confidential bonuses. The senior civil service is certainly going this way in many of the OECD countries, and such data as are available show a widespread pattern of erosion of visible pay for politicians in the form of straight salaries, often accompanied by rising but less visible allowances.[7] The emphasis has been on in-kind perks (such as limousines, travel, flunkeys) and allowances (such as increasingly generous pensions and office allowances) rather than upfront salary rises. Such a trend may well be tax-efficient (though some critics question whether senior public servants should be paid in ways that undermine the income tax laws which they are expected to uphold). Perhaps more to the point, it is easier to defend than salary rises which inevitably invite comparability disputes in relation to what other deserving groups are awarded. But the more such a trend develops, the harder it becomes to make the clear distinction between public and private life which traditional Weberian ideas of public probity involve.

However, the dishonesty policy, in both its variants, has a high downside risk. Like a nuclear power technology, it requires what safety engineers call 'high-reliability organization' to avoid leakage of politically dangerous material.[8] And like nuclear power, the consequences of an accident are potentially catastrophic even if the probability of its occurence is low. But it seems highly unrealistic to suppose politicians or other high public officials in modern OECD states to be capable of meeting the stringent conditions of high-reliability organization in such matters. The chaotic conditions in which they typically work look in organization terms much more like the structures which predictably produce what safety sociologists call 'normal accidents'.[9] Indeed, the less trusting and deferential citizens at large are towards their masters (as the poll data from Roger Mortimore and some of the other contributors suggests), the less easy it is likely to be for them to conceal the true level and nature of their rewards from intrusive media. Consequently, the accident risks of the dishonesty policy seem very high, in the sense that scandals will in fact continue to break, endangering the overall legitimacy of the political system still further.

Pay for ethics: a triumph of hope over experience?

The pay-for-ethics approach (Strategy C) might seem at first sight the most attractive one in a general public policy sense. Certainly, such a strategy tends to be much advocated by business-minded commissions on top public pay, which typically see it as natural that politicians and high civil servants should enjoy incomes and lifestyles on a par with, or at least not far short of, company executives. And the pay-for-ethics approach fits the idealistic Hegelian 'alimentation' theory that well-paid high officials, freed from the need constantly to worry about their own precarious financial positions, will focus their energies instead on the general good of the state.

The pay for ethics approach can in principle be applied at varying levels of 'ethics', in terms of renunciation of outside interests and acceptance of restrictions on employment after public office. It does not necessarily require an all-or-nothing approach. As noted earlier, a form of pay for ethics was adopted by the US House of Representatives in 1989 and at the time of writing seems likely eventually to be extended to the Senate as well. The 1995 report of the UK Nolan Committee on Standards in Public Life, recommending some restrictions on the jobs which ministers may take immediately after leaving office and a prohibition on MPs doing paid work for lobbying firms might well herald a step in the same direction in the UK.

Nevertheless, before 'pay for ethics' can become a widespread anti-sleaze strategy at more than a token level, some fairly stringent conditions need to be met. To work, this strategy requires that politicians be willing to 'come out', in the sense of abandoning their previous shyness about being seen to enjoy a high standard of living at the expense of the taxpayers. It also requires that voters be willing to respond generously, rewarding rather than punishing politicians for voting themselves large tax-financed salary rises which most of the hard-pressed taxpayers will be denied in an era of relatively flat basic incomes and rising taxes.

These conditions may be met in some cases, and the American House of Representatives experience may be replicated elsewhere. But there are at least two reasons for supposing that those conditions are unlikely to be satisfied everywhere. First, politicians are only likely to adopt pay-for-ethics if they all 'come out' together, meaning that the strategy requires an effective cartel by competing political parties or candidates. But cartels in their nature require major organizing effort and are notoriously unstable. And where parties compete for the votes of a 'Toquevillian' electorate, there is always likely to be a rich electoral reward for parties or candidates who defect from any all-for-one cartel and bid for votes on a platform of opposing their rivals' self-serving careerism. Indeed, the key role of the Greens in exposing cosy cartels over allowances by the major parties in Germany in the 1980s, notably in Hesse, the opposition by several Danish political parties to the 1986 proposal to raise MPs' pay (as discussed by Jørgen Christensen) and the appeal of Ross Perot's hostility to congressional salary levels in his 1992 US presidential candidature, show that the problem is not just a matter of abstract theory.

Second, pay-for-ethics will only have the desired effect if the citizens at large respond to the politicians 'coming out' (in the sense of visibly making money while in high public office) with suitably Hegelian attitudes of trust and respect. But if citizen attitudes are less generous (less Hegelian, more Tocquevillian), high public office-holders who adopt this strategy risk being cast in the role of Marie Antoinette, in the sense of flaunting their opulence paid for by the taxes of the oppressed citizenry, and of provoking an even sharper reaction against the political class. The low esteem for politicians displayed by public opinion polls in many OECD coutries suggests that the Marie Antoinette response is far from unlikely. Australian politicians tested the theory in 1988 by awarding themselves a 36% pay rise. They immediately faced a no-win challenge from the airline pilots' union which demanded a comparable pay rise and grounded the country's civil aviation for six months. Similarly, pay-for-ethics did not save the Democrats from being routed in the 1994 US congressional elections.

Accordingly, any expectation that the pay-for-ethics strategy might become a general response looks like a triumph of hope over experience. If 'low' assumptions are made about the motives of high public office-holders, the pay-for-ethics approach is dominated by the dishonesty policy (Strategy B) in a game theory sense, in so far as dishonesty offers the same (high) level of material rewards at the expense of the same (high) downside esteem risk, but for less joint action in the sense of upfront collective agreements to make the strategy work. And if 'high' assumptions are made about politicians' motives, pay-for-ethics is dominated by the asceticization approach (Strategy A). Unless most high public office-holders are entirely unconcerned with levels of material reward, the dishonesty policy seems a more likely short-term response to the sleaze backlash than either the pay-for-ethics or asceti-cization approach, even though it is likely to be the most self-destructive for the political system in the longer run.

Intermediate strategies

This, however, still leaves the two in-between approaches shown in the table 1 which are half-way-houses between total unworldliness and total dishonesty. One, coming in between full-blown asceticization of politics and the dishonesty policy, is the feast-first-fast-later approach (Strategy A/B). In this approach, people in high public office go about making (or marrying) their money before entering public service rather than during or after it.

Historically, such a pattern is far from unusual. It was common in Britain before the age of career politics in its modern form. It has commonly applied to US presidential and other politics; and it has been dramatically recreated in 'post-revolutionary' Italy by the short-lived prime-ministerial career of the media tycoon Silvio Berlusconi. Like the asceticization of politics, feast-first-fast-later makes low demands on collective action by politicians. But unlike asceticization, this strategy seems to involve a medium level of material reward (because, although income is low during the office-holding period, it avoids the need for a lifetime of monastic self-denial).

In general, the downside esteem risk of this strategy seems low to medium, lying mainly in an 'accident' leading to embarrassing allegations or revelations about an individual's accumulation strategy pursued before high public office. But the risks of such an accident vary with social context, and they will be very high if an egalitarian mood makes public tolerance of misbehaviour much lower for those in high public office than those in private life (as is suggested for the UK by Roger Mortimore). The difficulties faced by Silvio Berlusconi in relation to allegations about the political activities of his companies before he achieved high public office (as described by Hilary Partridge) suggest that the problem is not an abstract one. And the same goes for the problems (in relation to their earlier lives) experienced by many US candidates for high public office during Senate confirmation proceedings. The recent case of Zoe Baird, President Clinton's nominee for US Attorney-General in 1994 who failed to secure Senate confirmation because she had hired an illegal immigrant as a nanny, is a dramatic example of very different standards applied to corporate lawyers and high public officials, creating major risks for those embarking on politics as a second career in a low-trust political environment.

The other in-between strategy, coming between the dishonesty policy and pay-for-ethics is the fast-first-feast-later approach (Strategy B/C), with politicians launching a lucrative second career on the strength of their political contacts and know-how. Such second-career moves may be into the private sector, as with the well-publicized cases of British Cabinet ministers leaving politics for well-paid jobs in the boardrooms of companies that they privatized while in office, or they may be into equally lucrative appointments in the European Union or other international organizations like NATO or WHO. There is a parallel with the characteristic Japanese civil service pattern of 'descent from Heaven' as senior civil servants move out of their departments on retirement to typically much better paid jobs in independent public bodies linked to their departments and later into private business jobs at an even higher salary level. The tendency of politics to become a first career in Australia has been noted[10], and some have noted similar tendencies in some European countries, such as the UK and Gemany.[11] Such a pattern is perhaps facilitated by the tendency in several countries for increasingly generous pension entitlements for politicians, meaning that today's politicians need much shorter periods of service to qualify for an adequate pension, which leaves them well-placed to embark on a second career in business, media or consultancy.

Politicians who have never been engaged in any walk of life other than politics are in principle less vulnerable to skeletons from their earlier lives coming out of the closet than those who opt for politics as a second career (although of course very similar problems may afflict them when they embark upon that second career outside politics). A development of a 'politics as second career' trend can also fit with the logic of a high lifetime earnings strategy in which lean years spent as an apprentice in politics or public service are more than made up for by the fat years afterwards. Like feast-first-fast-later, fast-first-feast-later seems to involve a medium level of material reward (because the good life comes only after an initial period of asceticism) and a low joint action need (because it works mainly through individual action). But the downside esteem risk seems rather lower than the other hybrid because by the time public anger breaks, the victim is out of electoral politics and hence less vulnerable to loss of esteem.

Accordingly, it can be argued that asceticization, dishonesty and pay-for-ethics are not the only possible responses to the sleaze backlash. And if (or more likely when) such strategies fail, first-career politics and second-career politics, or some mixture of the two, constitute alternatives which do not require all politicians to follow a monastic life of poverty and chastity and are less vulnerable to collective action failures than pay-for-ethics (or even the dishonesty policy, where collective cover-ups are needed). But the further development of either first-career or second-career politics (or both) would be a paradoxical outcome in the light of conventional wisdom about a worldwide trend towards greater political professionalization. Though both are compatible with careerism in one sense, neither of these two intermediate strategies is wholly compatible with a shift towards full-blown lifetime career politicians, often held to be the long-term direction of political modernization. On the contrary, politics as first career suggests that politics becomes something that qualifies you for a good job afterwards—an episode in a career rather than a lifetime career in itself. And politics as second career also implies something very different from a lifetime career as a politician; in fact, such a strategy could well mean a return to just the de facto aristocracy which Tocqueville feared. If concerns with sleaze fuel further development of first-career or second-career politics, the implication is that politics would come to be part of a broader range of careers rather than a self-contained lifetime career.

Conclusion

As the contributions to this volume show, what counts as sleaze is by no means uniform, and all of the five possible responses to the sleaze backlash which have been discussed above may find a niche. But if this analysis is correct, it suggests that pay-for-ethics, the apparently most 'wholesome' approach and the one currently favoured in the United States, may not prove to be the all-purpose solution that it might at first appear. Although it is inherently hard to enforce (and thus could be combined with a dishonesty strategy in some circumstances), and although it may well be the first response to surface in the aftermath of political disasters, it seems politically more vulnerable to collective action difficulties and voter vindictiveness than any of the other approaches. Asceticization, dishonesty and the two intermediate strategies appear less vulnerable and hence responses of this kind seem just as likely as pay-for-ethics, if not more so.

However, all of these responses are potentially problematic for democracy. The dishonesty approach has high accident risks, with obvious long-term dangers for the legitimacy of democratic politics. The feast-first-fast-later intermediate strategy is less likely than the dishonesty policy to produce dramatic accidents but still involves a definite risk of slow-onset insidious effects in the form of 'ersatz' aristocratization. Even a widespread asceticization of politics is not necessarily the ideal world that it might seem at first sight. After all, government by sexually neuter ascetics obsessed only by politics and power can scarcely be called a representative democracy in any sense.[12] A political system registering modest readings on the sleazeometer is no doubt better than one with continuously high readings. But it may also be better than one which registers zero.

The politics-as-first-career response has its shortcomings too in the conflict of interest issues which it generates and the likelihood of widespread public cynicism about politics as a staging-post to a more lucrative second career. On the other hand, it also has its positive side in capturing young talent and moving it on before it gets stale. And it avoids the aristocraticization risk in politics-as-first-career, the risk of major system failure and moral deficit in the dishonesty policy, and the risk of unrepresentative government inherent in asceticization. In those circumstances where pay-for-ethics is politically unfeasible and in a world of no free lunches, politics as a first career may be the most acceptable substitute for accommodating what Riddell terms 'honest opportunism'.

1   H. H. von Arnim, 'Is Criticism of the German Political Parties Justified?', *Legislative Studies*, 1994/1.
2   M. Douglas and A. Wildavasky, *Risk & Culture* (California University Press, 1983).
3   J. T. Noonan, *Bribes* (Macmillan, 1984), pp. 598–600.
4   A. Sampson, 'When the Great and Good are Hard to Find', *Independent*, 14 March 1995.
5   V. Cable, 'What Price Integrity Today?', *Independent*, 18 April 1995.
6   M. Douglas, 'The New Wave of Austerity: Effect of Culture on Environmental Issues', lecture to L'Association Descartes (Paris), 1991. See also P. Brown, *The Body and Society: Men, Women and Sexual Renunciation in Early Christianity* (Columbia University Press, 1988) and M. N. Srinivas, 'A Note on Sanscritization and Westernization', *The Far Eastern Quarterly*, 1952/4.
7   C. Hood and B. G. Peters, *Rewards At the Top: A Comparative Study of High Public Office* (Sage, 1994).
8   S. Sagan, *The Limits of Safety* (Princeton University Press, 1993).
9   C. Perrow, *Normal Accidents* (Basic Books, 1984).
10   P. Weller and S. Fraser, 'The Younging of Australian Politics or Politics as a First Career', *Politics*, 1987.
11   P. Riddell, *Honest Opportunism: The Rise of the Career Politician* (Hamish Hamilton, 1993).
12   Lenin has been described in such terms; see L. Lundquist, *The Party and the Masses* (Almqvist and Wiksell International/Transnational Publishers, 1992).

INDEX